Day & Swing Trading for Beginners

Make Winning Trades + Turn Price Swings into Profits Using Simple and Proven Trading Strategies

A.Z Penn

A huge credit to Andrea Kirkby for her contribution in proofreading and editing the book.

TABLE OF CONTENTS

Day Trading for Beginners

Swing Trading for Beginners

Day Trading for Beginners

Make Winning Trades Using Simple and Proven
Trading Strategies in the Financial Markets Today
with Zero Trading Experience Required

A.Z Penn

A.Z Penn

HOW TO GET THE MOST OUT OF THIS BOOK

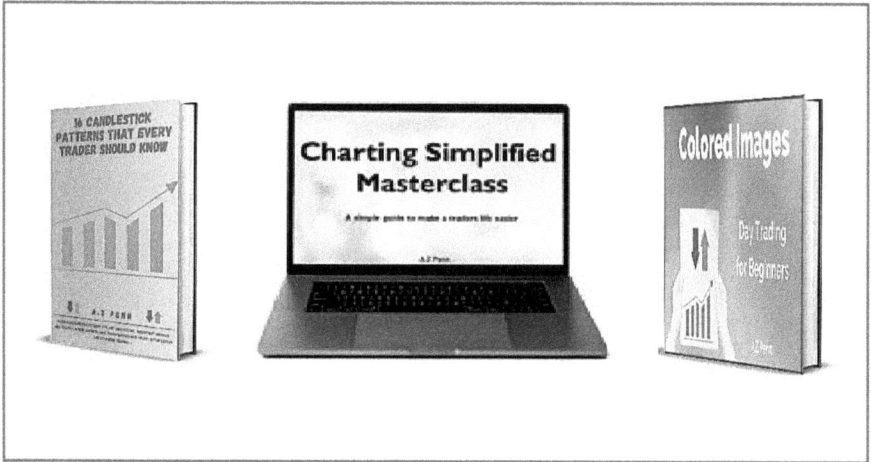

To help you along your trading journey, I've created a free bonus companion masterclass which includes video analysis of real life stock examples to expand on some of the key topics discussed in this book. I also provide additional resources that will help you get the best possible result.

I highly recommend you sign up now to get the most out of this book. You can do that by going to the link or scanning the QR code below:

www.az-penn.com

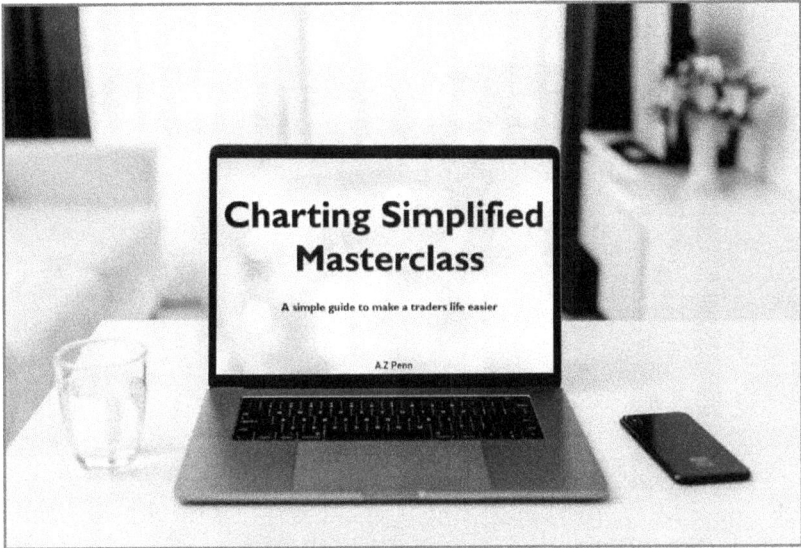

Free bonus #1: Charting Simplified Masterclass ($67 value)

In this 5 part video masterclass you'll be discovering various simple and easy to use strategies on making profitable trades. By showing you real life stock examples of a few charting indicators - you will be able to determine whether a stock is worth trading or not.

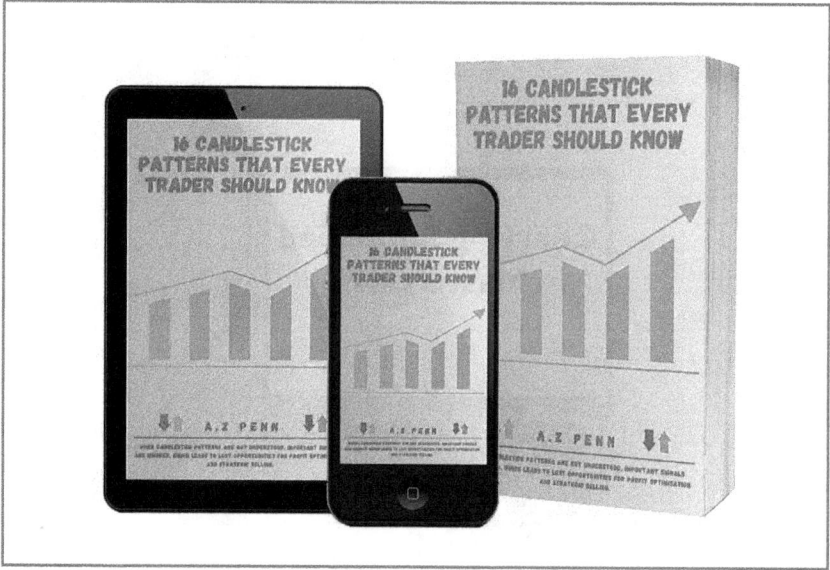

Free bonus #2: 16 Candlestick Patterns that Every Trader Should Know ($17 value)

Stay ahead in the trading game with our essential guide on the patterns that are vital for reading market signals, identifying trend reversals, and making profitable trades. Equip yourself with the knowledge to make informed decisions and maximize your trading returns.

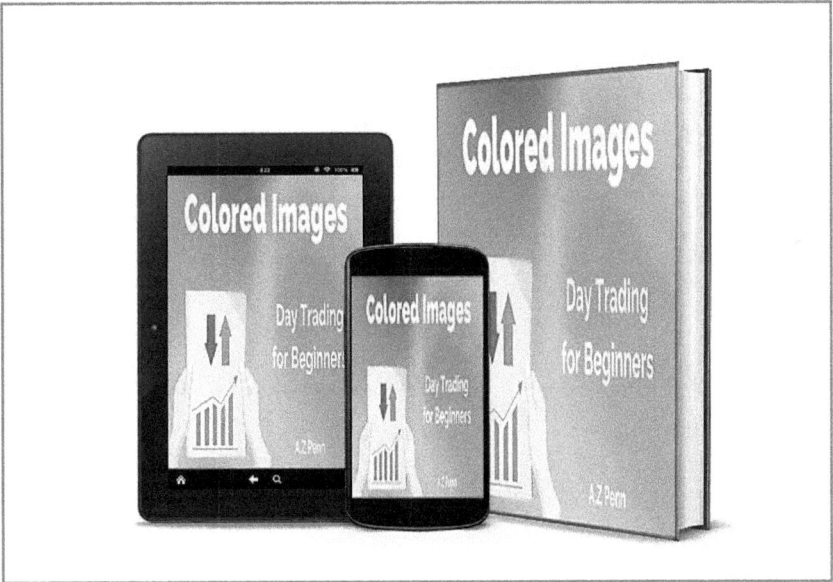

Free bonus #3: Colored Images – Day Trading for Beginners

To keep our books at a reasonable price for you, we print in black & white. But here are all the images in full color.

All of these bonuses are 100% free, with no strings attached. You don't need to provide any personal details except your email address.

To get your bonuses, go to the link or QR code:

www.az-penn.com

SCAN ME

Introduction

Let's give you the bad news first. The shocking fact is that 80% of rookie day traders quit within their first two years. 40% don't even make it to the end of their first quarter. If you're going to succeed in day trading, you're going to need to be an exception to the rule.

Even experienced day traders can sometimes go wrong. At first, you might be a success like Matthew Jay, who had six successful years making good money. But he wanted more - more money, more risk, more excitement. He started making bigger and bigger trades. Eventually, he lost $127,000 before he managed to regain control. You can watch his video on YouTube by searching "How I Lost 127k Day Trading the Stock Market!!"

Day trading is tough and I'm going to show you things the way they are, with no sugar coating. Day trading is not a get rich quick scheme. You might as well say that starting a search engine or making electric cars is a get rich quick scheme. Yes, it worked for Google, and it worked for Tesla… but day trading is hard work if you want to get it right.

Why do so many day traders quit so quickly? Some expected a lot more profit much more quickly, and just ran out of enthusiasm. Some are scared by a run of losing trades. Some are bored; they thought day trading would be fun, but it turns out watching stocks move isn't the most fascinating way for spending a day. Some just lack confidence, and of course, some never really get started, often because they can't see where they need to focus their efforts.

Often, too, they jump into the market without being adequately prepared. They haven't read enough about trading, they haven't set their trading station up properly, they haven't backtested their strategy or 'paper traded' for long enough to sharpen their reactions. So they make easy mistakes, get panicked, have a series of losing trades, and decide trading is too hard for them to hack.

Have you done a few trades and had a poor experience? Or do you want to day trade but you're not quite sure how to get started? There's so much information out there on the internet these days from YouTube content creators and brokerage firms and trading systems, but it's often contradictory and you never know whether you can trust it. If these are your issues, I think this book will help.

Yes, this book will teach you how to read charts, identify potentially profitable situations, and trade them. But more importantly, this book will teach you how to manage your trades as a business; how to identify and focus on the best situations instead of having a scatter-gun approach to the markets; how to manage your risk so that you never bet the bank, and come out ahead more of the time; and how to find the right strategies, which are those that will be most effective for you - not necessarily the same ones that work for me.

In between, you'll learn how markets work, how to choose what assets to trade - though we'll concentrate mainly on stocks - and how to deal with a losing trade (because make no mistake, it will happen).

This book *won't* teach you exactly how to do any particular trade. You will need to develop your own trading system - that's part of the job, and you'll need to refine it as you continue to trade. Imagine you are a chef, you might start off with some very basic recipes, but you'd soon want to develop your own twist on the old favorites or develop your own signature dish. Trading is the same; you can start with tried and tested strategies, but over time, you'll find your favorites, and you'll find little extra touches that will boost your profitability.

To succeed as a day trader, you only need to find three or four types of situations that make you money. You don't need to be able to read every kind of chart and trade every market. When you start, it may take you a while to find out what are the trades that really 'click' for you. Maybe you should try a few different setups while you're still a junior trader. But when you focus on the trading strategies that work best for you, you'll be doing less work for better results, and you can vastly increase your profitability.

So, in this book, I'm not selling my system of trading. I do trade, and I make money at it, though it's not my full-time job. I also invest for the long term, so I know just how different the worlds of the day trader and the investor are; I have to 'change hats' several times a day!

Both as an investor and as a trader, I've made plenty of mistakes on my way to becoming more successful, but I've learned from them. I've also read a lot of different trading books, some of which were really thought-provoking and useful, and others less so. In this book I try to boil down everything I've learned to the essentials, and give you what you need to know to get started. I'll talk you through all the different types of trades you might consider, but most importantly, I'll give you a way to structure your trading business so that you find your optimum style and get the best returns you can.

So, shall we begin?

1

Chapter 1: Is Day Trading Right For You?

The first step on the way to becoming a successful day trader is to understand what exactly day trading involves, and assess whether it's a lifestyle that is going to suit you. Along the way, we might need to address a few myths about day trading - there are quite a lot of those! So, let's look at what day trading actually is, first of all.

What is day trading?

The first thing to understand is that day trading is not the same as investing. In fact, although traders and investors use the same markets, the two ways of making money are as different as night and day. An investor generally looks at buying a financial asset over the medium to long term. They may be interested in getting income from that asset, for instance dividends from a company, or interest payments from a Treasury bond. Investors need to think about the quality of what they're buying; they ask questions like "Is this a good company?" or "Is Germany likely to default on its bonds?"

A trader, on the other hand, is simply aiming to buy an asset now and sell it at a profit. If a trader sees a chance to trade a company that's really on its beam ends, has a lousy product and terrible financials, they will - unless it's likely to go bankrupt in the immediate future. The question is, will it go up? And if there's a good reason that it should, they'll buy it.

As a trader, you don't care about the long-term future of IBM, or the German economy, or what is going to happen to the world shipping markets. You are simply a speculator; you care exclusively about making a profit out of each of your trades.

Day trading is a particular subset of trading, in which you close out all your positions at the end of the day. You do not have any trading positions open overnight. All your trades are executed within a single day, most of them within half an hour or even just a few minutes.

For the day trader, there is no tomorrow. Unlike an investor in a young tech company or a turnaround situation, you don't have the luxury of waiting around till the market recognizes the value that you've already seen in the business. You need to get in and out, fast. You never leave your money at risk overnight.

If you trade in the derivatives markets you may also come across *hedgers*. They will be using the same securities you're trading to hedge their holdings of stocks or commodities. Oil companies may hedge by selling oil ahead to lock in a favorable market price. Electricity companies may buy futures contracts of energy sources to reduce their input costs. Hedgers may be willing to take small losses on the derivatives in order to avoid much worse losses on the actual commodity - and one reason you can walk away with a profit!

Another way of looking at what traders do is to see their job as looking for volatility - prices rising or falling fast - and managing risk. The market will go up and down whether you're there or not. Your business is to jump in and out of market flows, piggy-backing them as long as they're going in the right direction. Sometimes you need to jump in just before a change of direction, so you need to read the whirls and eddies very carefully to see which way the river's flowing.

To do that, you'll need to have real self-discipline. A lot of our images of traders are swashbuckling - George Soros taking a $1bn position against the pound sterling and nearly "breaking the Bank of England" in 1992, Elon Musk putting money into Bitcoin, or The Big Short in which a bunch of traders brought the US mortgage securities market tumbling down.

In fact, these examples are the reverse of what day trading is. Soros and the fund managers who went short on the mortgage market based their actions on fundamental analysis, on detailed research about what was really going on. That's not trading - that's investing!

And no day trader would ever take a billion dollar position. Day traders are more interested in taking a few pennies out of Bath & Body Works when it bounces off a support level, or making a couple of percent out of Omega Healthcare when the market overreacts to its slightly below par results.

Because day trading profits are typically small profits, you need to make sure your losses are even smaller. That's one big reason that you need discipline. You need the discipline to set tight stop losses, and exit a trade the moment it stops working the way it's supposed to. You'll also need a trading strategy that doesn't let you go veering off after distracting great ideas from TikTok or Reddit that will lose you money, and you'll need to stick to it. Self-discipline and a good system are the only things standing between you and panic, greed, fear, and the deep red ink.

The other thing these great stories of 'trading' don't tell you is that as a day trader, you are not looking for that one great transformative trade that will pay off your home loan and let you retire somewhere with sunshine and pina coladas on tap. You will be looking for nine or ten trades a day. Some will lose, some will make a small return, and you are looking to manage your trading so that overall, you're ahead. That's not quite as exciting as it is in the movies, is it?

Myth and reality

The myths about day trading are everywhere. "It's exciting! You can get rich quick!"

"It's easy" - that's another one.

Day trading is not easy. It's not easy for me, and I've been doing it a while. It's even harder when you're getting started.

And you can't get rich quick, if you're using a good risk management system. For the first year or so, you'll be working hard for a relatively small return - though at the same time, you'll be keeping your hard-earned capital safe.

However, as the size of your trading book grows, you will be able to take on bigger trades without any extra risk. As you get more experience in day trading, you will refine your strategies and become more effective at executing them. After 18 months or a couple of years, your trading will start to bring in more and more profit as compounding works in your favor - reinvesting your trading profits in bigger trades.

The difficult thing is keeping yourself motivated until that happens.

Let's look at some more myths.

"Day trading is dangerous! You could lose all your money."

No doubt some people do, but they lose money because they don't trade with discipline. First of all, let me be very clear about this, you don't trade with money you can't afford to lose. You do not trade with money that's intended as downpayment on a home or that you need to pay your home loan or your bills or your medical insurance. You never, ever trade with "scared money." You trade with money that you could afford to lose.

And you always control the risk. In fact, if you always use stop losses properly, and if you always close your positions at the end of the trading day, and if you use a money management system (which I'll tell you about later), you're very unlikely to lose all your money. These are the boring things about trading, and the people who lose all their money skip over the boring bits when they read about how to trade profitably - or they decided to ignore them.

"You are only as big as your last trade." This can be useful to remember if you're getting cocky. But it's not actually true. Your success as a day trader will never be defined by a single trade but by your batting average - your day-to-day average success.

After all, no one sets up a hotel and then says "Success!" after *one* guest stays *one* night. You build a hotel to accommodate a large number of simultaneous guests over a long period of time. In the same way, trading is your business - it's not a single trade. You are only as big as your risk capital - the money in your trading account - and that depends on your win rate, profitability, and risk across all your trades.

"Trading is for alpha males who need to win."

Well first I should tell you some of the best traders I know are female. So that's one part of that myth demolished.

But you don't need a big ego to be a good day trader. You don't need to win every trade. You don't need to bet the bank. No one is watching your performance and no one expects you to put your house or your life on the line. And you know, your friends are considerably probably more interested in talking about the Superbowl, where you went on vacation or how your kids are doing in school than they are about how you cornered the market in silver futures.

Challenges and Rewards

Why day trade? It's actually not a bad lifestyle.

First off, you will be able to achieve financial prosperity. Okay, you could also meet this by being a top surgeon or owning five apartment buildings, or by inventing the app that everyone needs. But you don't need to have any certifications to day trade, the in-price is lower, and you don't need to code (though if you want to automate your trades, it helps).

If you're successful as a day trader, there is no limit to ambition. Even the most successful professionals eventually run up against salary limits. Equally, a top surgeon may well not be able to retire, even though there is good money coming in; as a day trader, you can attain financial freedom much more quickly.

If you have a career as a day trader, it promises you complete independence. You are responsible only to yourself (and perhaps your family). No boss complaining you were in two whole minutes late because your three-year-old is sick. No finance department sending you new targets for next month or complaining you didn't meet last month's targets. You make the rules!

There's no b.s. factor - you don't have to wear a suit or give PowerPoint presentations or learn the latest corporate jargon about low hanging fruit or being world class, or whatever. You don't need to be on-brand and no one is policing your social media profile. You are responsible for your own success, that's your one and only responsibility.

You can structure your trading life, whether it's three hours every morning, Asian markets overnight, or taking Wednesdays off. You can work from home, rent an office, be a digital nomad, or live in a cabin in the Adirondack Mountains or a chateau in France, as long as you have good internet access.

Of course the downside is that if you're your own boss living in a tropical paradise - which you could be - you're going to need the self-discipline to get up and trade the open every day, *before* you head to the pool or the cocktail bar!

The challenge, of course, is making winning trades and containing your losses.

In some ways, day trading is like dieting. Everyone's an expert, but no one gets any thinner. People day trade, but they never get richer. And the reason why is the same in both cases; a lack of self-discipline and the ability to lie to yourself.

If you're paper trading and you miss out on a few losing trades when you're calculating your return rate, you're lying to yourself. If you plan for a crazily high ratio of winning trades, you're lying to yourself. Just like if you're dieting and you say, "But one little Reese's Peanut Butter Cup isn't going to make me fat" … you're lying to yourself.

Another challenge, and I should be very clear about it right now, before you go any further, is boredom. Some people can't keep their attention on anything for more than a few minutes. You'll need to be able to track the market on a computer screen for hours at a time. Blink and you'll miss the best entry point for a great trade.

You will be stuck behind a desk, on your own, watching computer screens, for as long as it takes you to trade. That might be two hours. It might be all day. You will be looking at scanners full of numbers, and trying to make sense out of charts, and it can be mind-numbing.

It can also be the greatest way to earn a living, ever.

Why do most day traders fail?

Why do so many day traders flake out early in their careers? I think that fear has a lot to do with it.

They are afraid, because they are not comfortable with the idea of loss. But if you can't take a loss making trade, even a day that loses money, you will not become a successful trader. The fear will haunt you, and either make you feel anxious all the time (which is no fun at all), or push you into mistakes.

For instance, the fear of making a loss makes many beginner traders hang on to trades that are going wrong. Rather than lose a penny a share, they hang on to their positions and end up losing $2 a share. Other times, traders end up like a rabbit in headlights, looking all around but unable to actually do anything. "Paralysis by analysis" is another symptom of fear; not being quite ready to click the buy button, and looking at those charts again and again instead of entering the trade.

There's also FOMO - fear of missing out. The market starts to move, the trader's not quite ready, and then seeing the stock going up, the trader chases the stock price upwards and ends up buying at a price that's too high to make a good profit. Or second-guessing what would actually be a good trade, by worrying too much about the downside, or getting panicked by the market.

Some traders keep changing their strategy all the time. They're looking for the one "100% winning" strategy, which, by definition, cannot possibly exist. (In fact, you can lose more than half the time and still make money, if you exercise stop losses rigorously and ensure your risk/reward ratio is correct.)

Fear and greed push traders into emotional decision making when they should be using hard numbers and well planned and executed strategies. Some traders really want to get an adrenaline rush out of their trades; that's not conducive to good trading. There's a sort of magical thinking that can take over when things get stressful; your lizard brain is trying to kill and eat the market as if it was a sort of woolly mammoth. Of course, if you're using your human brain to think with, you know that nothing you do can change a losing trade.

The other thing that causes new traders to fail is that they don't run their trading as a business - which is what it is. If you start a business, you need a business plan. You need to define how much money you're risking, what kind of trades you plan to do, and how much profit you seek to make. You also need to test your trading strategies to be sure they work; that's where businesses use surveys, pilot projects, and focus groups, but you'll be using software systems and market prices.

You must have an edge

Every really successful business has an edge. Apple, Adidas, UFC, and Disney have an edge because they have fantastic brands. Amazon has an edge because it's made a huge investment in logistics, so it can deliver faster than virtually any other store. Warren Buffett's edge as an investor was doing his own very detailed and thorough research.

So, what is your edge going to be?

I can't tell you this; you're going to have to work it out yourself. But I can help you with the process of finding it.

Remember that the market is a continual tug-of-war between buyers and sellers, creating a continuous flow of price change. You need to find situations that deliver an advantage; you can recognize them by recognizing patterns that have created conditions for good trades in the past. Then you backtest, running your strategy against the market records for the last several years to see whether it would have worked.

What traders refer to as "edge" is all about getting the odds on your side. You're aiming to be like a casino - casinos pay out to gamblers all the time, but because they stack the odds in their own favour, they very rarely go bust. Like a casino, you won't win all the time, but your edge, or advantage, will play out over time, over a large number of trades.

"Edge" is actually quantifiable. For casinos, it's about 2%. For traders, it needs to be a good deal more, say 10-20% (I'll show you how to calculate it later). In many ways, it's more important than your win/loss ratio. You can lose a lot of trades if your edge is high.

Another thing you'll need to quantify is your risk/reward ratio. If you have a straight heads/tails flip, you're risking one to make one - a dollar lost if it's tails, a dollar won if it's heads. You need to win more than 50% of the time for this to work. But if you risk one to make three, you can lose two-thirds of your trades and still make money. Obviously, to do this you need to quantify both your expected profit and the amount of loss you are willing to take - and to stick to your guns and exit the trade if that loss happens.

You will need to develop your trading strategy and "edge" yourself. You could start with an idea; say, that the market often overreacts to news. Then start to think about how you could turn that idea into a trading strategy. And then backtest, to see if that strategy works, and find out how risky it is and how often you would win with it. Alternatively, you could start with one of the strategies suggested in this book, or you might find one that appeals in a chatroom or in a video.

But the important thing is that whatever this edge might be, you have to win *before* you start trading. You'll need to back-test the strategy, you'll need to have an idea of the possible danger points (some trades can be difficult to exit, others have a lot of false signals), and you'll need the discipline to execute your plan.

Preparation is key. Otherwise you're like an actor arriving on stage without having learned their lines.

What personality do you need to day trade with success?

Day trading isn't for everyone. Let's run through the qualities you'll need to make a successful trader.

First and foremost, you need to be self-disciplined. This is the downside of being responsible for your own success. If you can't manage to get out of bed in the morning, day trading is not for you.

You need to be independent and able to handle solitude. That doesn't mean "not being a people person" but it does mean being able to be on your own all morning without going off your head. If you really need the water cooler chat, or to be working in a team, day trading is not for you. (Although it *is* possible to join a trading team. Traders are social enough, but not generally when they are trading.)

You also need to be able to "turn off." It's important that you can close your trade station, go out bowling in the evening, relax with family at the weekend or go off hiking. If you're worrying about trades and markets all the time, day trading will kill you. If you have an addictive personality, its borderline; you need to prevent yourself from getting fixated on trading.

You need to be able to act fast and be decisive. You'll do research, but most of that is done before the markets open. Once you're trading, you need to be able to take a decision fast when you see a good opportunity open up. (You could, of course, set up an automated trade system for some types of trades. If you're a bit of a geek, that could be a rewarding style of business.)

And you need to be a good loser! Part of the discipline that makes good traders is drawing a line under a failed trade; they close it, make a small and controlled loss, and move on. They don't panic, they don't hold on hoping it will come good "real soon now," they don't feel angry or blame themselves - they just move on to the next trade. If you tick these boxes, you can be a successful day trader.

How much money do you need to begin trading?

Surprisingly, you do not need a lot of money to begin trading. Some brokers now accept just a few hundred bucks as an opening deposit, as do some forex and options platforms. Remember, though, that this needs to be risk capital, defined as money that you can lose without putting yourself in financial distress.

If you want to know whether it's risk capital, there are several ways to do so. One is to think about what would happen if your car needed a new gearbox, or if your home needed emergency repairs. Do you have some funds stashed away? Another is to think: if I took this money and blew it on a vacation, instead of putting it in this trading account, would I feel guilty or stupid?

Similarly, when you're trading, if you feel uncomfortable trading a certain amount, it's probably too much to put in a single trade. This is one time when I do think your gut feeling is worth consulting, and that's very rare in day trading.

There is one disadvantage to starting day trading with less than $25,000 in your account, if you are trading stock. It's the Pattern Day Trading rule. A Pattern Day Trader is defined by US law as someone who executes four or more 'round trip' deals (buying and selling on the same day) within five working days. Pattern Day Traders need to have $25,000 in the account. If you don't have $25,000, you will only be able to do three trades a week. However, these rules do not apply to futures or currency trading (unless it's in your equity brokerage account).

Why do you trade?

There is a simple answer to this. The one and only reason to day trade is: to make money!

Many losing traders get started for other reasons. They're trying to prove something to themselves, or they have a dream of being rich without making any effort.

Day trading, like any other business, is intended to make money. You'd buy a fast food franchise to make money, not because you want free burgers. You'd start a tech consultancy to make money, not to tax-expense your computer. You'd drive a taxi to make money, not because you enjoy driving. And so, you day trade to make money. It's as simple as that. It's a business. Treat it like a business, and it will work. Treat it as a fun hobby and it probably won't.

Just to check your understanding, every chapter in this book will have a short multiple-choice quiz at the end. Don't worry; no one's keeping the score, and you'll probably find that you do pretty well in most chapters. If you don't, all that's telling you is to re-read the chapter, maybe after a couple of days, and see if it makes better sense. The quiz answers are on page 272.

Chapter 1 Quiz

1. Which of these behaviours will lose you the most money?
   a) Drinking too much coffee
   b) Getting up late
   c) Holding a bad trade in the hopes it will get better
   d) Not trading if you don't see a good risk/reward ratio

2. You need to be all of these - except one - to be a great trader. Which is the odd one out?
   a) A math whizz
   b) Self-disciplined
   c) Independent
   d) A good loser

3. Which of these is not an advantage of the day trading lifestyle?
   a) You're only accountable to yourself
   b) You'll get a regular return
   c) You choose your own hours
   d) There's no limit to the money you could make

4. Which of these statements about day trading is true?
   a) It's incredibly dangerous
   b) You can get rich quick
   c) You need a big ego to compete
   d) You will get more profitable the longer you trade

5. What is your edge?
   a) The odds of your winning, on average over all your trades
   b) Otherwise known as 'love handles'
   c) Something you can fall off
   d) The wall between yours and the next cubicle

2

Chapter 2: Introducing the Trading Assets

In this book, I'm going to focus mainly on stocks, which is what I trade, but you may find other assets more conducive to making trading profits. A number of different financial assets can be traded, and they all have their nuances; their markets have their own different ways of doing things, too. You may find some suit you more than others.

First of all, let's define what makes a good day trading asset.

It needs to be liquid - that is, easy to trade. So it needs to trade frequently and in reasonable volume. For instance, around 13 million Coca-Cola shares are traded every day, making it a liquid asset. You should be able to buy and sell shares easily, and at the price shown. On the other hand, Newlake Capital, a real estate trust that's traded over the counter (not on one of the major stock exchanges), only trades an average of 25,000 shares a day, and you might find it difficult to execute a large order in the stock.

It needs to be tradable at low cost, including the spread (the difference between the price you can buy at and the price you can sell at, known as the bid and the ask price). If you have to pay high commissions to trade, that will be a drag on your performance and could even prevent you from making a profit.

The price needs to change on a regular basis so that you can trade; a stock that flatlines doesn't give you any chance to do so. In market speak, what you're looking for is volatility (and that can be calculated and screened for - I'll show you how later on).

Some traders also add the requirement that every stock they trade has to have a fundamental driver - that is, it's being driven upwards by good results, or downwards by a negative trend in the sector.

You may also have some other requirements. For instance, if you want to trade with leverage (the use of borrowed money to invest), you may want to use a broker who will let you open a margin account - which is when the broker lends you cash to purchase securities. You can then trade more stock than you have cash, giving you a potential higher return (but also, of course, increased risk).

If you have relatively small resources, you will need to look for assets that fit your position size (size of trade); for instance, in stocks, where a round lot (100 shares) is affordable. A round lot in Berkshire Hathaway would cost you over $40,000. A round lot in Vici Properties would cost you $2,900 - a big difference.

Stocks

A company stock entitles you to fractional ownership of the company's assets, earnings, and cash flow. It is a limited liability asset - you can only lose your investment, but you can't lose any more than you put in (unless you're trading on margin). Stocks trade in relation to the company's earnings prospects, so economic news, earnings releases, new products, and announcements from competitors or regulators, could all move the share price.

Shares are traded in round lots, that is, 100 shares or multiples of 100 shares. However, this isn't quite the difficulty that it used to be for traders with relatively small resources, since many brokers now offer smaller lots and even trade fractional shares. This is something you will need to check out when you are choosing your broker. Outside the US, some brokers let you trade CFDs (Contracts for Difference), but this is banned for US citizens.

When you're trading, you need to have a feel for the size of trade that can easily be filled in any particular stock. You can get this by looking at the trades that have gone through today (or yesterday, if you're planning to trade the opening). You'll find that some shares are easy to trade in lots of 100, but liquidity is tighter for larger trades, for instance 500 shares or more. This applies particularly to smaller stocks and those with less free float, and those with share prices in excess of $100 or so. Larger lots may be filled as long as volume is moving fast, but there is then always a possibility that getting out might be tricky.

Many brokers now offer commission-free trading. However, commission isn't the only cost of trading in shares. There is a *spread* between the price you can sell at and the price you can buy at, which is the market maker's mark-up. For instance, you can buy IBM for $187 but if you want to sell, you'll only get $186, a $1 spread that equals 0.5% of the share price. On the other hand, Iron Mountain (IRM) has a spread of $68.66 to $69.48. That's less than a dollar, but it adds up to more than 1% of the share price - that's a significant cost if you're aiming to make a 4% or 5% return on each trade.

You'll want to trade on the New York Stock Exchange (NYSE) and Nasdaq. Smaller exchanges and the OTC (Over-The-Counter) market do not have enough liquidity. You might also look at London, Tokyo, Euronext, and Deutsche Boerse in Germany.

You can either go long (buy a stock to make money when the price rises) or go short (sell a stock to make money when the price falls). Going long is easier to get started with; not all traditional brokers are happy to let you short a stock. For most trades, they will work both sides, but be exceptionally careful when you go short, as your liability is theoretically infinite. If you go long, the price can only fall to zero; if you go short, the price could double, treble, or go up ten times, and then you're really in trouble if you didn't execute your stop loss.

Bonds

A bond is, basically, an IOU. Bonds are issued by companies and governments who need capital. The investor who buys the bond is lending the company or government money who promises to pay the investor interest (coupons) for a certain period of time, and to repay the bond on a certain date (maturity). Bond issues can be huge. In 2023, the International Bank for Reconstruction and Development (IBRD) issued a $5 billion sustainability bond, and Pfizer issued a massive $31 billion.

Bonds, unlike shares, don't give any ownership to investors over a company's assets unless the company goes bust. If you buy US Treasury bonds you don't 'own' the US! They tend to trade in line with general economic news, and in inverse correlation to interest rates; that is, if the interest rate goes down, bond prices go up (and vice versa).

Bonds have two kinds of risk; there is interest rate risk, and there is default risk - what happens if an issuer can't, or decides not to pay the coupon, as Russia did in 1998. The default risk can be assessed by looking at the ratings issued by ratings agencies (Fitch, S&P, and Moody's); the best bonds will be given AAA and AA ratings (German government bonds are AAA, French and US bond AA). These ratings indicate the highest creditworthiness and lowest risk of default.

Besides US Treasuries, other tradable government bonds include

• OATS (France)

• Bunds (Germany)

• JGBs (Japan)

• Gilts (UK).

Bonds are not as frequently traded as equity, since large pension funds and insurance companies will sometimes buy a bond at issuance and hold it to maturity, in order to match their liabilities (payment of pensions, or of insurance claims). The interest payments received from the bond are predictable, which means a pension fund can cover its expected pension payments with them and be sure it will not be out of pocket. Apart from Treasuries and Gilts (which are listed on the London Stock Exchange), most other bonds trade over-the-counter, so there is no price quote, and no centralized market. Price volatility is not high, so it is relatively difficult to make a good return from day trading.

ETFs

You may be used to the idea of a mutual fund as a pool of money managed by a professional fund manager to buy into the market. An Exchange Traded Fund (ETF) is a similar pool, usually designed to replicate the performance of a particular market, sector, or commodity. Unlike mutual funds, though, ETFs are traded on the stock exchange, in the same way that shares are traded.

ETFs might replicate the performance of an index like the S&P 500 by buying each share in the index, in proportion to its size as part of the index (its weighting). In other cases, ETFs might use synthetic replication techniques, such as using derivatives to achieve a copy of the index's performance.

Not all ETFs have the same liquidity. Some of the sector ETFs and thematic ETFs, such as green energy, cannabis, and infrastructure ETFs may have quite low traded volumes. The most interesting ETFs for stock market traders will be the big index ETFs which copy the S&P and DJIA, the FTSE 100, Nikkei, CAC-40 in France, and DAX in Germany. The most popular with day traders is the S&P 500.

US-traded ETFs include

• SPY - SPDR 500 Trust, which mirrors the S&P 500

• DIA - Dow Jones Industrial ETF, which mirrors the 30 stocks in the DJIA

• QQQ - Invesco QQQ ETF, which copies the 100 top Nasdaq shares and has a high technology component.

Sector ETFs that might be worth considering include

• XLE - Energy Select SPDR

• SMH - VanEck Semiconductors ETFs.

And for major indexes outside the US:

• FXI - iShares China Large-Cap

• EWJ - iShares MSCI Japan

• FLEE - Franklin FTSE Europe

• SPEU - SPDR Portfolio Europe.

Some ETFs offer a leveraged play on the indexes. For instance, TQQQ offers three times the QQQ's returns (both up *and* down), and QLD offers twice the QQQ. However, if you're going to trade these you need to take on board the high level of risk involved. Personally, I don't like leveraged ETFs much. I'd prefer to take my leverage by using a margin account to trade the straight ETF.

You might also want to look at commodities ETFs like

• USO - United States Oil Fund, and

• GLD - SPDR Gold Trust.

Ensure you know what you're getting, as some ETFs copy the performance of oil shares and gold shares, not the actual commodities.

And finally, a bond ETF that might be worth looking at is TLT, the iShares 20+ Year Treasury Bond ETF.

Before you decide to trade an ETF (or invest in one!), always check the tracking error. Sometimes, the ETF doesn't track the index it's based on very well. If I want to replicate the performance of an index or a commodity, I can do 'physical replication', i.e. I actually buy, let's say, bars of gold bullion and store them, or I can do synthetic replication by, let's say, writing swaps contracts and futures contracts that will deliver the same performance. Which is all good in theory, but very rocket scientist intensive, and if you get it wrong for any reason, you could outperform or underperform the index you are trying to copy. For instance you might have overlooked a currency mismatch, bought futures that were too high risk, had trading costs that were too high...

On the other hand, if you actually own the gold (or shares, or barrels of oil) then your performance will be an exact copy. This is why tracking error is one of the things you really need to look at when analyzing ETFs, because some do a better job than others. For instance, the United States Oil Fund (USO) doesn't always track the price of crude oil accurately because it uses futures contracts rather than tracking the spot price with actual purchases of oil.

Since futures contracts reflect expectations about moves in the price, they can vary widely from the spot price today.

Currency

Foreign exchange represents a massive and highly liquid market that never stops, with trillions of dollars traded every day. It's a bigger market than either the stock market or the bond market - or indeed both of them added together.

What's slightly different about the currency market is that it's traded in currency *pairs*, since each currency is quoted against another. For instance, USDJPY quotes dollars to yen, while 'cable' quotes dollars to pound sterling, a slang for the GBPUSD currency pair. The main currencies suitable for trading are the US dollar, Euro, Yen, Pound Sterling, and Swiss Franc. But you might also find less well-known pairs that are interesting to trade, like Australian dollar to Sterling, Hong Kong Dollar to USD, or the Canuck/Yankee combination of Canadian dollar to USD.

Remember which way round the quote works. The first currency is the base currency, or numerator: it's always worth one. So, in USDGBP, you're trading one dollar, and the second currency is what you get for it. USDGBP is currently trading at 0.79, that is, you get £0.79 for $1.00.

There are spot rates for currencies, but you can also trade currency futures or even currency ETFs. Currency can be traded on margin, at 10:1 or even 50:1 leverage. Price changes in currencies are given in pips - the fourth decimal place. Always be aware of the effect of a single pip movement on your total position size.

If you're trading the spot markets, you need to know that there is no organized exchange; it's a free-for-all of banks, traders, hedge funds, dealers and brokers. You will also need to open a dedicated currency account to trade. In return, you have huge flexibility of trading size - and unlike futures, no expiration dates to worry about.

Commodities

Commodities are basic goods, such as metals, wheat, or oil. Now, obviously, you as a day trader don't want to be buying physical products, so you'll just day trade the futures contracts or perhaps ETFs. A big company *might* want a hedge against one of their major costs rising, and be prepared to take physical delivery of a load of wheat or steel, but traders simply want to make money without having to buy the physical goods.

A futures contract is a promise. If you buy a contract, you are basically saying you *will* buy the goods at the price you pay. Now be careful, because you only want to trade that contract, you don't want to take on the delivery. Futures are a kind of derivative, that is, a financial contract whose value is related to that of an underlying asset (a commodity, stock, or index).

Futures contracts are standardized, and you will most probably start off trading one contract. For instance, corn is traded in contracts representing 5,000 bushels, though it is *priced* in bushels; oil contracts represent 1,000 barrels of oil. Each contract has an expiration date (when you don't want to be left holding the baby); some are monthly, others quarterly. You'll see the expiry date in the description - "December 2024 corn" for instance. Before one contract expires, a new contract will already have started, on what's called rollover day; you'll want to jump ship from trading the nearly expired contract to trading the newly-launched one as soon as the trading volume in the market shifts to the new contract.

Futures prices reflect expectations about the future, so they may be quite different from the spot price (current market price).

Futures have longer trading hours than stocks or bonds. The stock market doesn't trade on weekends, but the S&P e-mini (a stock futures contract) does. You'll need to put up 5-15% of the contract size as your initial margin.

Each type of contract has its own tick size, the minimum price change. For instance, the tick for crude is $0.01 a barrel, so a move for a 1,000-barrel contract can be as small as $10. Smaller tick sizes are to your advantage. Larger tick sizes are to your disadvantage; the $12.50 tick is one of the downsides of the S&P e-mini.

Mini and micro contracts were specially developed to appeal to retail traders like you and me, offering a smaller size than the standard futures contracts. Let's take an example, the Nasdaq 100.

• NDA: contract size = $100 x Nasdaq index points

• ENQ - Nasdaq e-mini: contract size = $20 x Nasdaq index points

• MNQ - micro Nasdaq: contract size = $2 x Nasdaq index points.

Futures have one big advantage. Unlike stocks, they are not subject to the wash-sale rule, which can be an advantage for 'amateur' traders (as defined by the IRS). In a wash sale, a trader sells a security at a loss for tax benefits and then purchases the same or a similar security within 30 days, before or after the transaction. However, futures can be much more volatile and higher risk than stocks, as futures trading is highly leveraged and commodity prices often experience large swings and extreme cyclicality.

Types of derivative

Futures contracts are one type of derivative, but you can also trade options contracts. Unlike futures, options do not oblige the holder to purchase the underlying assets; they give the holder the right (but not the obligation) to buy or sell the underlying asset at a given price (strike price or exercise price), up to a particular date in the future (expiry). If exercising the option won't make you any money, you can simply let it expire. Most options traded are options on shares, or on stock indexes.

'Call' options give you the right to buy a share at the exercise price; 'put' options give you a right to sell.

"One Apple June 160 call" for instance gives you the right to buy 100 Apple shares at $160, up to the end of June. Apple is currently trading $183, so those options are in theory, worth $183 - $160 = $23 a share, times 100 shares = $2,300, *before* the time value is taken into account. This is the intrinsic value (real value) of the option.

Options are a wasting asset - that is, they have a time value, but as they approach the expiry, that value diminishes. You can imagine that if you still held that June 160 call an hour before it expires, but Apple had fallen to $150, then your option wouldn't be worth anything - you could buy the shares at $150 in the market, so why pay $160 with your option?

Traded options are standardized, with strike prices in regular increments; each option covers 100 shares. The length of options may differ; they may be weekly, monthly or longer. You can trade options on SPY and QQQ, for instance; these are large and liquid, just what you want as a day trader.

You may also find warrants and convertible bonds on some stocks. Companies issue warrants, which give the holder the right to subscribe for shares in the company at a given price in the future. They work in a similar way to options, and they're valued using the same methods. Companies also issue convertible bonds, which can be exchanged for stock at a given price. These combine elements of a bond and an option, and are traded on the stock exchange. However, in many cases they may not be liquid enough for you to day trade.

The two important things to realize about derivatives are that they have a limited life span, and that they are leveraged. Both these features represent added risk and you need to be sure you understand them.

For instance, a stock trading at $110 will lose you $10 if it falls to $100. If it goes up to $120 you'll gain $10 per share.

However, an option to buy the same stock that trades at $110 for $100 will be worth $10. But if the stock falls to $100 and you hold the option, not the stock, you will be wiped out - a ten percent loss in the stock equals a one hundred percent loss on the option (give or take the time value).

On the other hand, if the stock goes up to $120, your option will likely double (100% gain), whereas the stock will only make you $10.

Brokers will generally allow new traders rather limited choices. To day trade options, you'll need level 2 access, which offers complete access to the order book, showcasing the detailed buy and sell orders behind a stock's current market prices (level 1 is just for hedging stock). Further levels allow more sophisticated options strategies, and eventually, writing naked options (a much higher level of risk). You should note that trading options falls under the Pattern Day Trader rules which I discussed in chapter 1.

The exchanges on which you can trade derivatives are CBOE, and CBOT, NYMEX and CME (the last three are all part of the same group).

Cryptocurrencies

Cryptocurrencies such as Bitcoin are a relative newcomer to the world of day trading. These virtual currencies are tradable at a fairly low cost. They are also often volatile, giving good trading opportunities. You can day trade cryptocurrencies on eToro brokerage, but you might also use a crypto exchange such as Binance, Coinbase, or Kraken.

Understanding 'the law of one price' and arbitrage

You have probably been told to "Buy low, sell high." That makes trading seem very easy. What's less easy is knowing whether the price you see right now is low or high! In fact, as a trader, you need to recognize that, basically, the market is right, and the market sets the price.

The law of one price says that the *same asset* is worth the *same everywhere*. IBM isn't worth $184 in New York and $100 in London or $299 in Tokyo. It isn't even worth $184 in New York and $185.50 in London. Financial markets nowadays are too closely connected and too transparent for this kind of mispricing to happen on a regular basis.

Arbitrage takes advantage of times when the law of one price, momentarily, isn't working. For instance, if you get the chance to buy an option that's priced at less than its intrinsic value, that's an arbitrage. Or perhaps one pension fund in London decided to sell all of its holdings in Shell. It might take a few seconds for all the traders in New York to realize and do their sums, so there might be an arbitrage between the shares and the ADRs (the form in which foreign shares are traded in the US).

Day traders used to do well out of arbitrage, which is low or even no risk. However, arbitrage lends itself to automation, and that means the high-frequency traders, using algorithmic trading on super-powered computers, are exploiting most of the good opportunities these days. They can trade in and out quicker than you can click the button on a buy order. (They also sometimes create "flash crashes" with sudden huge volatility, something you might take advantage of.)

Pure arbitrage is riskless: you buy and sell at the same time in different markets, or through different securities. But you might also use risk arbitrage which is an investment strategy used during takeover deals, and has greater returns. It still involves offsetting two investments, but those might be, for instance, an acquisition target and the acquirer. In simple words, you profit from the difference between the target stock's market price and the acquirer's valuation of the shares. You sell one and buy the other to exploit the fact that the target has shot up and the company buying it has seen its stock fall. However, risk arbitrage trades usually need time to work out, and are more suited to swing trading (where a position can be taken for two or three days) rather than day trading.

Making your choice of assets

When you are choosing what to trade, it's important to find focus. Starting off day trading currency and stocks and commodities all at the same time is the kind of scatter-gun approach that will make you losses because you're not focused enough. You need to define which market you're going to be in.

You don't want to define it too narrowly, either. Just day trading IBM would mean you'd sit things out most days because you wouldn't see an ideal trade. You might select stocks; you might even trade two markets, for instance, if Asian market hours suit you.

If you have existing knowledge of a particular market, for instance because you are already an investor in stocks, that might mean the stock market is easier for you to trade, compared to commodities or currencies where you'll have to learn everything from scratch. That's how I got started day trading the stock market. If you already know crypto, and have been involved in that market for a while, then that might be a good place to start. But remember, being a day trader is different from being an investor or a trend follower.

Pick markets that are open when you want to trade - particularly if you prefer to trade early mornings or late evenings.

Choose markets that are accessible with your level of capital. Using micro or mini lots to trade currency or S&P futures is the best choice if your funds are limited, for example. If you have over $25,000, day trading stocks is a great choice. And make sure the markets you choose are liquid enough to trade without slippage (i.e. paying higher entry prices and having to sell below the market price to exit the trade).

During the rest of this book I'm going to talk mainly about the stock markets, because those are the markets where I trade the most and have the most knowledge. But the lessons of how to set up a trading system, how to read price formations on charts, and how to spot profitable opportunities, are common to all the different markets mentioned in this chapter.

Chapter 2 Quiz

1. What does it mean when we call an asset liquid?
   a) Well, it's liquid, like hot chocolate or water
   b) It's easily tradable at low cost and at any time
   c) It is tax-efficient
   d) It has to be traded on an official exchange

2. What is an ETF?
   a) An Emerging Trust Fund
   b) An Equivalent That's Fungible
   c) An Exchange Traded Fund
   d) An Easy Transaction Fix

3. Which of these is not a tradable commodity?
   a) Pork bellies
   b) Gold
   c) Pokemon cards
   d) Cocoa

4. What is a derivative?
   a) A share in a company that doesn't pay a dividend
   b) When you copy another trader's idea
   c) A special class of municipal bond
   d) A financial instrument based on an underlying security

5. What is arbitrage?
   a) Taking advantage of different prices for the same asset
   b) A hostile takeover
   c) Trading an asset in a different currency
   d) The French name for a referee

3

Chapter 3: How the Financial Markets Work

Daily life has sanitized the markets most of us use. We go to the supermarket and we pay the sticker price. We fill up with gas and we pay what it says on the pump. And we get along just fine with that.

But that's not how financial markets work. In financial markets, a price is part of a discussion between buyers and sellers. You may see a price on the screen, but it's not like a supermarket sticker price - it could suddenly change, in either direction, in response to news, a big sale of stock, a recommendation by a major investment firm, the way the charts look, or a change in the direction of the market as a whole.

So, let's take a look at how the markets work. While the details may differ between markets, all financial markets work in a similar way, which is more like a load of auctions going on at the same time than like a supermarket.

Stock market basics

Wall Street began not with a skyscraper, but with a tree - a sycamore tree in the street that had been named after the wall that the Dutch built to keep the British out. (That worked well, didn't it?) It was here that traders gathered to buy and sell the first US government bonds. Imagine a sort of securities flea market or bring-and-buy and you wouldn't be far wrong. Then, in 1827, the New York Stock Exchange opened at Wall and Hanover Streets. It's been trading ever since.

And although markets went from the tree to the stock exchange building, and then from the trading floor to electronic order fulfillment, keeping those founding fathers of the stock market in your mind gives you a good feeling for how financial markets work. There are buyers, and there are sellers. Buyers push the price up if they get control of the market, and sellers push the price down when they're in control.

While there are, by definition, as many buyers as sellers because someone has to sell the stock for someone else to be able to buy, one or the other side will generally be making more headway. The buyers are 'bulls' and the sellers are 'bears' (so a 'bear market' is one where the sellers are pushing prices downwards, and a 'bull market' is roaring away upwards). It's a teeter-totter, the stock market, and it doesn't take much to unbalance the seesaw.

In the days when you could just turn up at the tree and shout out what you wanted to buy, it was easy to access the market. But in today's sophisticated markets it's not that easy - there are thousands of investors and traders wanting to do so. Different markets link all these participants together in different ways; although you'll go through a broker, how your broker accesses the market will vary.

NYSE, for instance, has *specialists* - or had; as they are now called Designated Market Makers, or DMMs. Each stock has its own specialist, who runs the auction in that stock (and probably a number of others). They also hold stock so that they can provide liquidity when the market is moving fast, and there is high demand. However, they no longer have 'posts' on the trading floor; orders are handled electronically.

Nasdaq, on the other hand, allows any number of different market makers to make bids and offers on stocks in competition with each other. Goldman Sachs, Citadel Securities, and Credit Suisse, for instance, will all quote their own prices. And there are also ECNs, electronic communications networks that put buyers and sellers in touch with each other.

Efficient market theory

Economists have always been fascinated by how the market works, and came up with the efficient market theory to explain it. This says that the market is efficient; the price of a stock *always* reflects the sum total of knowledge about the stock. The market price is always right.

However, the market has small inefficiencies. For instance, it may overreact to earnings announcements, or one major seller might temporarily depress the price. But in these cases, you need to act fast to take advantage.

As a day trader, you are not really worried about whether the market is 'right' to value Microsoft at $404 a share. What you're looking at is what is going to happen to that share price as a result of supply and demand in today's trading session. What an *investor* wants to know about a stock is the business the company is involved in, its expected earnings and cash flow growth, and the assets it owns (both physical and intellectual). But what a *trader* wants to know about a stock is how it normally trades, in what volumes, with what spread, and whether it tends to trade within a particular price range.

What *both* the trader and the investor need to know, though, is the expected dates of major results, presentations, economic statistics and decisions that affect the stock. You don't want to get caught out by a big earnings surprise, or when the market is flattened by the Fed (Federal Reserve) putting interest rates up.

Risk and return

Day trading is not gambling and you shouldn't play hunches. You should always know exactly the risks you are running, and make sure those risks are stacked in your favor. You should know exactly what return you aim to make with a trade. If you can't quantify it, don't trade.

Risk and return are always related. Generally, an investment that is 'safe' will not have a great return. Stick your money in the bank, and you'll get interest every year - but not a lot of it. On the other hand, start-up companies can deliver impressive returns stacking up to many times the initial invested capital, but the risk is also significant - ten percent will fail in the first year, and another 70 percent won't make it past year five. The key to becoming a good trader is to understand the balance, and to spot opportunities to trade where the potential return is greater than the risk.

What is risk? Risk is the quantifiable likelihood of a negative event. Quantifying bad outcomes is what insurance companies do all the time, as well as risk managers within large enterprises; they use statistics to assess the risk of a house in a given neighborhood being burgled, or a shortage of raw materials, or a power outage at a particular data center. They then adjust the premiums their clients need to pay according to their assessment of the risk.

With a trade, you quantify the risk by deciding on a stop loss price - that is, a price at which you know the trade is not working out, and you will definitely exit. Don't worry, for each trade there's a way to do this, which I'll describe when we get to trading strategies. You also quantify the potential return. So, for instance, I may buy a stock at $20, expecting it to go to $22. That's my profit target. I will sell out if it goes to $19. So I am risking one dollar to get two.

It's no good just looking at the risk, or just looking at the reward - you need to look at both together, and have a reasonable idea of their probability. That is the essence of trading.

Note for paperback readers: You'll be seeing the charts in black and white. It just costs way too much to print them all in color. But you need to see them in color - that's the way you'll be seeing the charts you look at on your computer screen, and if you have three moving averages, for instance, you need to be able to tell which is which.

Therefore, I would recommend you please go to my website:
www.az-penn.com and enter your best email address that I should send the colored images document to.

Volatility

Volatility is day traders' bread and butter. Volatility is the amount that prices vary over time. In very simple language, you want to buy a share that goes up and down a lot, giving you plenty of opportunities to trade; a share with high volatility.

There's a statistical way to find these stocks and that's by using standard deviation. The math may not mean much to you, but if you've seen a Bell curve chart (as shown below), you'll know how it works. For instance, if you charted the height of your male friends, you'd find most of them were in the middle of the chart around 5 feet 9 inches tall; there would be quite a lot at 5'6" and 6'2"; but there would be very few at 5'2" and 6'6". One statistician described a typical Bell curve to me as "looking like a python that swallowed a sombrero."

What standard deviation measures is the difference between each individual statistic and the average. You could apply it to your friends, but when you're trading you apply it to all the prices or returns from a given stock. A volatile stock is one that has a greater variation in returns (i.e. a greater difference from the average) than a less volatile one.

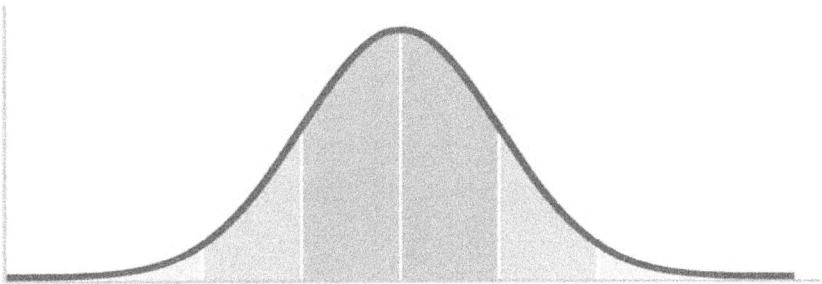

Take this a little further, with stocks, and you might want to see whether, say, Tesla is more or less volatile than the stock market as a whole. To do this you use what's called a beta. The benchmarket is the beta of the market, which is (by definition) one. A beta of more than one means a stock is more volatile than the market - it will go up more in an uptrend, and go down more in a downtrend, than the overall market. Though there's a formula for working out betas, thankfully you don't have to use it as most financial information sites such as Yahoo Finance will give you the figure. For Tesla, it's 2.41 - very significantly higher than the market. A look at Tesla's last five year chart below tells you why!

A high-beta stock is good for trading; the price will move up and down more often. On the other hand, a low-beta stock won't move much at all, and it's difficult (though not impossible) to make money trading stocks that don't go up or down. Take a look at the Walmart share price chart below, and you see a much less jagged outline with fewer big rises and falls. Walmart has a beta of just 0.34.

Opportunity cost

Although this is not as crucial to making money trading as the risk/reward ratio, you need to think about the opportunity cost of your trades. This means thinking about what else you might be doing with your time or money, instead of making a trade.

For instance, your money would make maybe 2.5% annually if you put it into a CD ladder at a bank. If you don't make more than 2.5% with your trading strategy, you are losing out. In fact, because trading puts your money at risk, you need to make several times 2.5% return to compensate for the risk. Or maybe, you'd make $1,000 a month if you applied your spare time to running a dog-walking business, rather than trading. So obviously, you'll need to make more than that trading for it to be a good business for you.

There is a very specific opportunity cost that traders and investors use to work out whether they are doing things right, and this is the *risk-free rate*. If you didn't take any risk at all, what return would you make?

Usually, the risk-free rate is assessed as being the interest rate on three-month US Treasury bills since it has almost no risk of default as they are backed by the US government. According to MarketWatch, it's currently sitting at 5.35%. If you don't make that, forget trading!

That said, if all your winning trades aim to make a couple of percent and you have a reasonable win/loss ratio, you will never make less than the risk-free rate.

The market's day

I didn't know certain things when I started trading, even though I thought my experience as an investor would help. For instance, when does the most stock trading happen in the day?

The opening is almost always the most active time. While futures stay open overnight, volumes of S&P futures reflect the stock market, and volumes overnight are usually low, making the market not ideal for traders. So, if you want the best chance of profit, hitting the New York Open is a must. Unfortunately, if you live on the West Coast, you will have to get up early to do so.

At the open, you will get some excitement from stocks 'gapping' up, as they reflect news overnight or before the open. There is a session of pre-market trading, but I use that for information rather than making trades; it can be very illiquid and is dominated by the big guys. (There's after-hours trading too, but I leave that alone, for the same reasons.)

Usually, there's some good trading volume later in the morning, too. The stock market takes a long lunch, with not much happening. In the afternoon, market makers are generally thinking about what they want their closing positions to look like, and the market will often trade in line with the existing trend - you won't get so many reversals of direction.

If you trade currencies, you'll find that forex trades rotate around the world. The Asian opening session focuses on JPY pairs, and you can trade Aussie or New Zealand dollars, but this isn't a great time to trade Canadian dollars or Swiss Francs, for instance. If you find the right currency pairs for the time slot, you'll have more flexibility in when you trade, as well as probably making better trades.

Market psychology

If you're trading, you're taking on the market. Whichever financial market you're in, it will work the same way. It's a big beast, and you need to know a lot about its typical behavior and reactions, or you risk being gobbled up for its next meal.

The market being made up of buyers and sellers, it reflects the psychology of crowds. You get groupthink, and you get panic reactions. At the extreme, you get the tech boom, the Tulip Boom and Bust of seventeenth-century Amsterdam, the 1929 Wall Street Crash. More often, you get standard market cycles, which can be described as having four stages: accumulation, markup, distribution, and markdown.

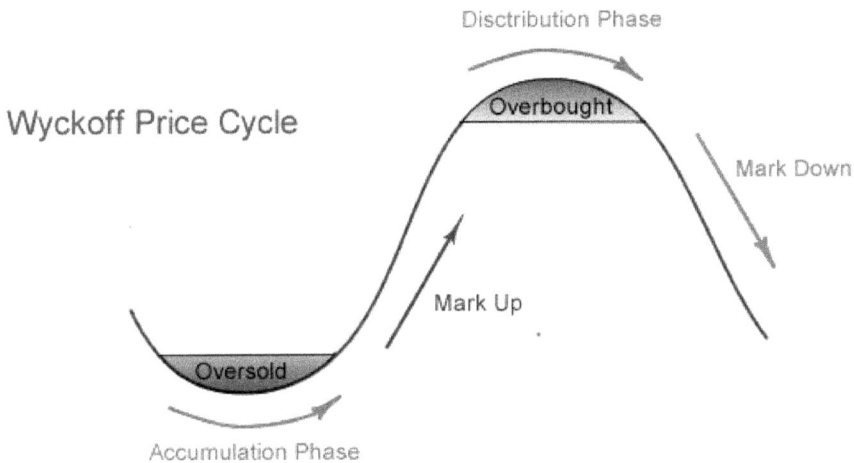

Accumulation happens at the end of a downtrend, and represents a foundation being laid. Buyers begin to accumulate the stock. There is more demand for the stock. The last sellers from the downtrend decide to exit the market. Eventually, all the overhang of stock has been taken up.

The markup phase begins when the overhang has gone; smart money and big institutions drive up demand, and now prices start to rise as well. The volume of stock being traded increases.

The distribution phase sees demand remaining strong, but now, some sellers are taking their profits. This increases the supply of the stock, and the price may start to move sideways rather than up. Eventually, there are too many sellers flooding the market with their stock.

This leads to markdown - demand for the stock wanes. There may be a final sudden spike on very high volume before the price starts to fall. Now, the market is in a downtrend, which will last till the next accumulation phase begins.

Market cycles can last for years. The bull market that began in March 2009 lasted 11 years. But there are cycles within cycles. A bull market will have plenty of what are called corrections, when it trades downwards for a while - these are mini-cycles. Even in a single day, you can see tiny cycles as a stock zooms up, then the sellers come out, and the price stalls and then falls. Or as a stock falls, then the buyers think it's a bargain, and suddenly the price starts to move upwards, fast.

The result of all these mini-cycles is that although markets will typically trade in an uptrend or downtrend, prices don't move smoothly. Instead, they move in zig-zags or steps. In an uptrend, each step will have a higher high, and a higher low; in a downtrend, lower highs and lower lows are the rule (as shown below). It's easy to see on a stock chart; it looks like a slightly wonky staircase.

Within a trend, price movements going with the trend are usually stronger than those going against the trend. Price movements can also be categorized as action or reaction move; a *reaction* is usually limited to two-thirds the size of the existing *action* move, like waves going back down the beach. At the end of strong price movements you usually find a period of consolidation, when the market is balanced between buyers and sellers, with sideways or perhaps choppy price action as neither bulls nor bears win the day.

By the way, parabolic stocks - that is, stocks that are headed almost vertically upward - are terrifically exciting, but you should probably stay clear of them. What goes straight up very often goes straight down again. If you do want to trade really fast-moving stocks, you need to be careful about your setups; buying on a pullback, and using a small position size to get in, then scaling up as you go, with very tight stop losses.

Take a look on the next page at Tesla in late 2021. Bullish candlesticks kept marching up and up. Initially, there's a 45-degree curve during mid-2021, but then the stock price goes straight up. "We have a liftoff!" But if you had bought into that run upwards, you would have needed to be able to exit the stock before it crashed. And parabolic stocks don't often give you a good signal to get out. Buying into the run was a trade that could get flipped very, very quickly!

These stocks offer high reward, which is why we feel our hearts go all a-flutter when we look at the price charts - but they also present a very high risk, so take care.

Chapter 3 Quiz

1. How can a trader best manage risk?
   a) By setting a stop-loss on every trade
   b) By never trading more than their net worth
   c) By only trading NYSE stocks
   d) By not trading on Tuesdays

2. What does a beta tell you?
   a) Whether a company has a stable business
   b) How likely a stock is to go up
   c) The relationship between the stock's price action and the market's
   d) That a stock is not an alpha

3. Which of these would you *not* find in an uptrend?
   a) Higher highs
   b) Higher lows
   c) Higher highs and lows
   d) Lower lows

4. What happens during the accumulation phase?
   a) Companies issue more stock
   b) Governments issue more debt
   c) The overhang of stock that investors want to sell disappears
   d) Nothing

5. What is a parabolic stock?
   a) One that shows a steeper and steeper upwards price curve
   b) One that has a good 'story' to tell
   c) One that has options issued on it
   d) One with a high beta

4

Chapter 4: Tools and Platforms to Get Started

So now you know quite a lot about the different assets you could trade, and how to trade them, and what life could be like as a day trader. But now it's time to look at the practicalities - the nuts and bolts of day trading. You're going to need a broker, a trading platform, an office (even if it's your garage) and some basic infrastructure. Let's talk you through how to choose the right tools to get up and running.

This is a business not a computer game

Think about day trading as a business. It needs a business plan, and it needs some investment in basic business facilities. Building the right infrastructure for your business is important, and it will take you a good deal of work to get it right.

For instance, to make money day trading you need to be well in control of your costs. If your broker charges you too much commission, or can't execute your trades accurately, you won't reach your target profitability.

You also need to have realistic goals. "$5,000 a day real soon now" is not realistic. Don't set a money amount, but work through how many trades you expect to make, what your starting risk capital will be, and what profitability and what win/loss rate you expect.

What brokers to use

Long term investors are often not very choosy about their brokers. They might trade once or twice a month, so they don't worry if the order system is a bit clunky. They are looking to hold the stock for a good while, maybe for years, so they don't care if they always pay a bit of slippage because their broker doesn't get them absolutely the best price in the market, or trade *this very second* but maybe a couple of minutes later. They don't need a broker that can handle order sends order (OSO) and order cancels order (OCO).

Traders, on the other hand, need to be very, very choosy about their brokers. You need to get your orders filled at the right price in seconds, every single time. And you *also* need a broker that has reasonable costs. If you're being charged $25 a trade, you'll never be able to make money, however good your strategy and however high your win rate. If, at the same time, your broker lets you day trade with a tax-exempt account, you are home and dry.

Traders may also be interested in brokers who will give them margin. Many brokers will give you three times leverage or more; so if you have a $25,000 account, you can trade up to $75,000. I'd suggest you don't start to use margin till you have at least a few months' experience of day trading and feel fully confident that you are in control of your downside.

Maybe you're already an investor and you have a broker who meets your needs *as an investor*. Think twice before trying to *trade* on that platform. You may find that your broker has a separate trading platform and different account level that would give you what you need; if so, you will need to move up to that level, which may involve paying subscriptions. It's also best if you can separate your trading account from your investment account - this will help you greatly with tax issues and record keeping.

A few choices that might be interesting are:

• Interactive Brokers, which is inexpensive and also lets you have tax-free trading accounts;

• Charles Schwab's Thinkorswim platform;

• Webull, a cheap platform that might suit the beginner (but doesn't offer backtesting or automation);

• Mondeum, which is a low priced broker-dealer with good order fills, specifically designed for retail traders.

Ideally you need a broker with a good trading platform that can use hotkeys (we'll talk more about it later). You don't need to go through a whole process of loading the stock page, entering your trade manually, pressing a button, confirming the trade, and... whoops, the stock has moved and the trade is no longer attractive! You just have hotkeys to do all that.

A really good broker should offer you direct access to the markets. Direct access routing gives you more control and faster fills, which can add a small margin to your profitability, and means you're not going to see trades fail when the price moves too fast.

Trading platforms

Some brokers have their own platforms, like Interactive Brokers' Trader Workstation, and Charles Schwab, but you can also integrate a specialized trading platform to your broker. In fact, many traders find Trader Workstation too clunky, and spring for a separate platform.

DAS Trader is a good trading platform (as screenshotted below); some brokers will offer it as part of the account setup, while at others you'll have to pay a monthly subscription of $100-200. The ease of placing your orders and the speed and accuracy of execution make it worthwhile.

You might also consider RealTick EMS, TradeStation Securities, eSignal, CyberTrader or MetaStock.

Make sure your trading platform gives access to all the relevant exchanges and ECNs. You also want to spec out:

• the reliability of the platform

• whether 24/7 support is available

• the speed of execution

• a user-friendly interface

• whether you can put all your important tools on a single page

• whether it is user-configurable

• whether you can customize your own charts

• how you are able to track your trading book overall

• how it manages watch lists and stock scanners

• whether it offers program alerts

• whether it offers stock futures access as well as just stocks.

And finally, of course, you need to go through the tariffs with a tooth comb.

It's actually worth taking time to go to a trading conference so you can see the different trading platforms in action, and maybe get to try them out. There is no better way to decide on which system to get than to take it for a test drive. For instance, TradersEXPO, Las Vegas, is in February, both free and paid options (but you have to pay your way there and your hotel of course); Forex Traders Expo and Summit Dubai, in May: London Trader Show in November, from £25 to £129 British Pounds. Many trading gurus also run their own. However, for some shows, the pricing information is not transparent and the detail of the presentations is unclear, so do proper research before attending.

Nasdaq Level 2 and bid/ask

Nasdaq Level 2 is a subscription service that gives you live access to the Nasdaq order book.

Level 1, which you'll see with any broker, just shows the National Best Bid and Best Offer (NBBO). That's the best price you can sell at, and the best price you can buy at. That's good information for an investor, but it won't show you market depth - how many buyers and sellers there are at that price. With Level 2, you can see all the market makers for a given stock, which lets you assess the demand for a stock much more accurately. You'll see the NBBO, but you'll also see the queue behind the NBBO - the 'next best' prices.

You can also see what size buyers and sellers are trading in, so that you can tell the difference between a stock with one market maker willing to meet small orders at a particular price, and a stock with a big sell order stacked up and ready to go.

Level 2 also shows prices from ECNs (electronic communication networks) which can link buyers and sellers automatically. This might help you refine your trade execution. If there is a big seller waiting with a line of stock, and you want to go long, you might want to wait till most of their shares have been bought up. That removes an influence that is keeping the share price down, so you are likely to be getting in at just the right point.

You can also get direct access to the ECNs through Level 2. That's just a couple of milliseconds quicker than going through another route. This is an added refinement that can help get slightly better and faster fills, but it will take you time to learn which are the dominant ECNs for particular stocks.

Buy and sell orders

Don't wait until a potential trade is confirmed to set up your trade. Have an order entry window open for each setup you've identified. If you watch the pre-market, it's a great time to set up your orders for the open. (Most day traders don't trade pre-market or after hours; liquidity is lower then and trades involve more risk.)

Ensure you have entered your limit, the number of shares you are buying, and your preferred trade routing if you're using Level 2 (e.g. ARCA). If you have three or four windows prepared, you are ready to move as soon as one of your watchlist stocks hits the right price.

Hotkeys

If you use Windows, you probably know the emergency reboot command: alt + ctrl + delete. Instead of using a whole load of different commands, one combination of keys works to do the job. Similarly, you might use ctrl + B to make text bold, or ctrl + S to save a file.

The same idea of hotkeys applies in trading. You need to be able to trade fast. Let me talk you through the way I make an order with the broker that I use for my long-term investments.

• I search for the stock

• I select the stock

• I tick 'buy' or 'sell'

• I enter the number of shares I want to buy or sell

• I enter a limit price

• I check 'ok'

• I am then shown the trade and the commission, and asked to confirm the trade

• the trade is sent to the market and I wait a couple of minutes till my order is filled.

You can see the problem. While I'm doing all this, the market is moving, and I could miss the right entry point for my trade. More of a problem, if I have a stop-loss, or a profit target, I've got to go through that all again, and I may miss, particularly if I'm in a 'fast' trade like a momentum trade. I might hit an extra zero by mistake if I'm in a hurry. It's a slow and error-prone system.

That's why traders rely on hotkeys - shortcuts that let you trade quickly. And the best thing about hotkeys is that you can customize them yourself. Useful hotkey commands are:

• sell all my shares in this stock

• cancel all outstanding orders

• buy 100 shares, buy 150 shares

• reverse the position in this stock

• sell half my position - this is useful when you hit your first profit target and want to de-risk your trade

• set a new stop loss at the current price (or 11 cents below it, or whatever).

I should warn you, though; never use a wireless keyboard if you have hotkeys. Always use a keyboard hard-wired into your computer. Wireless keyboards are a liability; they run out of batteries, are slower than wired keyboards (every millisecond can count in day trading), and are susceptible to interference.

And once you've programmed your hotkeys, try them out in simulation first so you get used to them. You need to practice like a concert pianist to get muscle memory for when you really need to trade fast.

Watchlist and scanners

Finding the right trading opportunity is like looking for a needle in a haystack. With 3,300 stocks listed just on Nasdaq, if you just switch on your systems in the morning and start looking, you're probably going to find a good trade just as the market closes at day end. You need to have a watchlist of stocks that you trade, and you also need to have a scanner that will look for stocks that fit a number of criteria that qualify them as good trading potential.

Use the scanner in the morning to find stocks suitable for day trading - stocks that have gapped up or down, with high pre-market volumes, for instance. This will make up your watchlist.

When I am *investing*, I have a watchlist of stocks I'd like to buy but that are a bit too pricey right now. I check it every so often to see if any of those stocks have come down to the level that I want to buy at. But my *trading* watchlist is quite different. It's designed just for a single day's trading, and shows stocks that meet my criteria for "stocks in play" that will give me a good chance of a trade.

Get your watchlist made before market open, if you trade the open. Once you have your watchlist you can start thinking about what kind of trade each stock gives you the best chance at. For instance, if a stock is right at the top of its trading range, you're thinking about a range trade or maybe a breakout, or maybe a false breakout, giving you the chance to trade against it as the stock re-enters the range. If a stock gapped down overnight, a lot of market participants will be panicked into selling; there's a chance it will bounce up strongly once the selling pressure has faded away.

Having a watchlist filters out the noise of the 3,300 stocks all yelling their price tickers at you, and lets you concentrate on a select number of profit-making opportunities. And it helps your discipline, too.

Keep your scanner running during the day to catch new situations, maybe in reaction to news coming in. You might start with scanner recommendations from other traders, but eventually, you'll want to configure your scanner for the type of trades that 'click' with you. Everyone has their own personal favorite trade setups. Here are a couple of ideas:

• scanning for momentum - stocks with a high RSI (described later) plus high 15-minute volume, plus 52-week highs or lows

• scanning for reversals - stocks that are trading close to the outside of the Bollinger band, with very high or very low RSI, and at least four consecutive candlesticks of trend.

Fine-tuning your scanner settings will come with experience. It can be useful to look at your successful trades and see if they all have something in common that doesn't yet feature in your scan. Maybe you could add that, and see if you are getting more relevant ideas from the scanner and fewer flaky ones.

Community of traders

To be a good day trader, you'll need to be okay with solitude, and you'll need to motivate yourself. But that doesn't mean you need to be a complete loner, and in fact it's a great idea to find other traders to chat with.

Many traders are remarkably open to discussing their trades. But being part of the community isn't just about trading ideas. You'll also want to share things like which brokers you've found best, how to set up new hotkeys, everyday frustrations, and even how you relax or what breakfast sets you up best for trading.

You could look for day traders' groups on Meetup - there are two huge meetups in Chicago, for instance. Some major traders run open chat rooms where you can sit in on their trades and hear them explain their strategy. Some trade platforms and brokers have their own trading communities, and these can be worth your time getting to know. Check out whether they are moderated - ideally it's not a complete free-for-all.

Other trader communities such as Warrior Trading, Bear Bull Traders, and OneOption, are paid-for choices, and offer not just the chance to join the community, but also valuable educational materials and research services. Before you join a group, though, check out its reputation; some traders are honest and open, and genuinely interested in training other traders to do well, while others are more interested in selling you their view of the world.

Don't expect other traders to give you your trading system and ideas, though. Do your own thinking and evolve your own edge - and avoid groupthink!

Opening an account and placing an order

Opening an account is quite a paperwork-heavy transaction, particularly for day traders. Your broker or platform needs to know that you're a suitable person to day trade, not a deadbeat, and that you understand the level of risk you're taking on. It also needs to ensure that you're not money-laundering for a Russian oligarch or a drug baron, so it will want to know where your money comes from (e.g. savings, inheritance, bonus payment).

The paperwork is a pain, but you have to get it right. I have a directory on my laptop called 'credentials', and in it I store all the things that I get asked for by banks and brokers - a passport photo, payslip scans, a recent scan of my bank statement, and so on. Then I know how to get my hands on stuff quickly and the necessary paperwork becomes less of a pain.

Once the paperwork goes through you'll need to wire through an initial deposit (or send a check, but why pay the extra postage?). If you are planning to day trade, most stockbrokers will want at least $25,000 in the account, to meet the Pattern Day-Trading Rules. Of course, you don't have to trade all of it. When I started, 90% of the money in my account was long-term investments, and I day traded with the other 10%. Now my day-trading side has grown, I have a separate trading account.

Once the money is in your account, you're ready to trade… or are you? It's best to get well familiar with the system before you go live. Play with it a bit outside market hours and find your way around.

When you place an order, you run **execution risk.** That doesn't mean the firing squad, but what's called 'fat finger', for instance - adding a zero on the end that shouldn't be there. Or buying a stock and a call option instead of a stock and a put option. Or selling instead of buying (an easier mistake to make than it sounds). Or even, selling twice the stock you own because your finger hovered for a moment on the mouse. Practice making trades in real-time till you're super confident that you are not going to make those easy mistakes.

The gear you'll need

First of all you're going to need a good fast computer. This is not the time to install a lite version of Linux Mint on an ancient laptop to speed it up - it's time to get a new computer. You'll also want a second monitor or even a third. You can have your stock scanner on one screen, and your watchlist stock charts ticking away on another, so you can easily see everything you need and never miss the action in those stocks. Your scanner will let you catch any stocks coming into play during the trading session without losing your focus on your prime trading opportunities. It's just too easy to miss a move in a stock you're watching if you're having to tab between windows all the time.

You'll want to ensure you have a second Internet provider, as backup. Of course, this could mean a good mobile provider alongside your broadband provider, rather than a second load of broadband - but try to ensure your two providers are different in case one of them has network outages.

It's also a good idea to have a TV in your office, tuned to a business channel. Don't put it on too loud; you'll soon acquire the ability to tune into any mention of economic news or stocks, so you never miss a major news announcement.

Put some thought into where you put your office. It needs to be a place that keeps you in an alert and positive frame of mind. If you don't enjoy going into your office, you won't get great results. Ideally, you want natural light and plenty of it, but not in your eyes or on your screens - you may need to move things around a bit to get the ideal set-up. You want a chair that gives you good support or a standing desk if you like, and you need a good-sized surface for keeping your legal pad or log book.

Also, you need somewhere away from your keyboard to put your coffee. Don't ask me how I know that!

Day trading is your business: how to structure it

Set your business up like a business. How many trades will you make every day? What are you looking for as a trade setup? That is, what kind of situations are you going to trade? What is your risk-reward ratio? What win rate do you need to be profitable? You should have answers to all these questions as part of your business plan.

You should also know what hours you're working, what markets you will trade, and how you're going to keep records of your transactions. (The tax authorities will want them, but equally, you need to know how you're doing.)

Remember trading is your business. And you trade to make money. But you should focus on setting up and executing your trades efficiently, not on the amount you make. Your business plan may say that on average you'll be making $500 a day, but some days you'll be well up on that figure, other days you might have a losing streak. Don't get up in the morning saying "I want to make $500" or any other number, but "I'll spot at least three good trades and execute them perfectly."

After all, if you run a great restaurant, the aim is to make money. But you don't wake up in the morning and say, "I'll make $1,500 at lunchtime," you wake up and say, "I'll get the freshest fish and meat I can find on the market, and my sous-chefs and I are going to turn it into fantastically zingy Asian fusion food, and we're going to give our customers absolutely the best service." The money, if the business plan is a good one, will come along once you have a name for great food and great service.

Chapter 4 Quiz

1. Which of these do you *not* need from your broker?
    a) Margin
    b) A good trading platform
    c) A cup of tea and a biscuit
    d) Low trading costs

2. What is execution risk?
    a) When your broker might have you shot by the Mafia if you lose money
    b) The risk that a trade might lose money
    c) The risk that you will get your order wrong
    d) The risk that the market will drop while your order is being executed

3. What should your watchlist focus on?
    a) The S&P 500
    b) Stocks with high betas
    c) Stocks in an uptrend
    d) Stocks that suit your preferred kind of trade

4. Which of these do you *not* need to spend money on for your trading business?
    a) A super duper fast computer
    b) A good trading program (unless your broker has a good free one)
    c) Fast internet access
    d) Professional business cards

5. Which of these will your broker probably *not* ask you for when you open an account?
    a) ID
    b) Your bank statement
    c) Your degree certificate or professional qualification
    d) Where you got the funds from

5

Chapter 5: How to Find Stocks to Trade

I've already taken you through how to choose your trading assets. In this chapter, we will look at how to find the right stocks for trading on any given day. You are looking for the stocks that have particular reasons for making strong price moves, which are a good opportunity for you to trade. You'll perhaps end up with some 'regulars' that you enjoy trading and have a good feel for, but they may not always give you the trading opportunities you need.

Stocks in play

Stocks that are likely to see strong trading with good day trade opportunities are "stocks in play." There may be a number of reasons for that; for instance there might have been an earnings announcement, or a takeover in the sector which leads traders to assess the chances of this stock to be taken out.

You can tell a stock in play because it will be having a high volume day. If you see high volumes of trading in the pre-market, you can guess the stock is going to be a trading focus for the day, even if normally it doesn't move. You're looking for a high *relative* volume. For instance, Alphabet (Google) usually trades about 29 million shares a day on average. Your aim is to be trading in the stock on days where it's trading more than that - and you'll spot that if the pre-market seems to be unusually busy.

On a few days at the start of February 2024, Google traded over 50 million shares. The same sales volume occurred in late October 2023, and also late July 2023 and early May 2023.

The shares gapped up in early May and late July, starting an uptrend. In late October, they gapped down, then again in early February (see example on the next page). Financial reports often spark strong price action and high volumes. That's the reason strong price action and high volumes coincided in these cases.

Alphabet Inc (Google) Class A, 1D, NASDAQ O150.22 H152.26 L149.90 C150.67 +0.60 (+0.40%)
Vol 22.149M

TradingView

Fundamental catalysts for price action and trading volume include not just earnings reports and trading statements, but also results and profit warnings from competitors, FDA approval for drugs, large contract wins or losses, mergers, hostile bids, product releases, changes in top management, stock splits or buybacks, demergers and spinoffs. You may also see some stocks linked to commodities markets (e.g. oil stocks when the oil price moves significantly) or to particular countries (e.g. stocks with businesses in Russia) or to particular news (airlines, airports, and hotels during the Covid-19 pandemic).

There is plenty of opportunity around when there is fundamental news causing investors and traders to reassess the stock. Make sure you understand the basic news - 'right, it's a drug stock and its big drug just got approval', 'okay, it's a webstore provider and all its sites have been taken down by Anonymous'. You don't need to do any analysis or get stuck into the detail, but you know what's going on. If nothing *seems* to be happening to cause the price action, then someone else knows a lot more than you do (for instance, that a major investor is selling out), and you don't want to get caught.

Some traders hate stocks which are in the news cycle. They prefer to wait out big announcements for a couple of minutes before trading, or even not to trade stocks with results coming out at all. Me, I think these stocks give you opportunity, but you have to exercise discipline and wait a few minutes while everything shakes down and the price trends show up in the charts. Don't jump in feet first.

I also like to follow TICK and TRIN when I'm trading US markets. (Discount brokers often don't show these quotes, so I get them via my trading system.) These are indexes which show the number of stocks ticking up versus the number of stocks ticking down on NYSE and Nasdaq respectively. They are good temperature takers for the market. If they're headed upwards on a nice easy climb, I am happy with my long positions. If TICK climbs vertically upwards, I'm not happy because it's going to stall. Time to close out my longs, and go short.

On the other hand if both TICK and TRIN are looking poorly, in negative territory, I don't trade on the long side. It's very difficult for a stock to rise against a market that's got no confidence.

Float and market cap

To recap what I already said; you need to trade stocks that have adequate liquidity. But you also need to be sure the market in the stock isn't dominated by high-frequency traders. I look at two things: market capitalization and float.

Market capitalization (or 'market cap' for short) is the total size of the company's share value. It shows up on company data as one of the five or six major data points right at the top, and it represents the number of shares in issue multiplied by the share price. This shows the total size of the pool that day traders are fishing in.

Large-cap stocks are over $10bn market cap, and 'mega caps' are over $200bn. (Alphabet Class C shares have a market cap of $1.88 trillion.) Large-cap stocks have all the liquidity a trader needs, but the problem is that they are also the favorite stocks of high-frequency traders (a type of algorithmic trading). This means you're up against stiff competition from the automatic traders.

In the US, small cap means under $1bn in market cap, with a micro-cap at $50-250m. The smallest of these stocks are likely to be illiquid, making them difficult to trade, but above microcap status, you'll find that some small caps give very good opportunities indeed on the long side (they are still, in my view, not always liquid enough to go short).

Any stock with a market cap between $1bn and $10bn qualifies as a mid-cap. This is a good hunting ground for day trades.

However, as well as market cap, I look for *free float,* that is, the amount of the stock that is available to trade. For float, I'm not looking so much at dollar value as at the number of shares. For instance, a company with a market cap of $10bn but only two shares would not be tradable at all. And a company with a market cap of $10bn and 750 million shares in issue, but where the CEO owned 80% of the company, would also not be very tradable. At the very least, you'd be running the risk that the CEO buying or selling shares would have an undue influence on the share price.

On the other hand, Apple has a market cap of $2,865 billion, and 15.5 billion shares outstanding. Only 6% of those shares are held by insiders (who will probably hang on to their stock), so the vast majority of shares are tradable. Look further and you'll see that just over 50% is held by institutions, who are 'stickier' holders but may quite often adjust their positions in the stock, making lines of stock available to trade.

A good contrast is Value Line (VALU). It has only 9.6 million shares, which is a lot smaller than Apple's 15.5 billion. What's worse is that out of those 9.6 million shares, 91.62% are held by insiders. That means there are very few shares tradable on the market, and this, in turn, leads to poor liquidity, which makes Value Line very difficult to day trade as your trades may be badly executed or not executed at all. Value Line is both a small cap and a low float stock. I wouldn't touch it as a day trader.

Low float stocks that are a bit less extreme than Value Line do offer some good opportunities. They can move very, very fast, but they are tricky to trade; you may not get your order filled. As with small caps, they're only for trading long; shorting them is too risky. If you enter a short trade, you need to be able to exit if the price moves against you, but in low float stocks, you may find that there is not a market for your shares, and you can't exercise your stop loss. (Remember, the potential liability on a short trade is infinite - you can lose *more* than you put in.) The risk/reward ratio for a long position in low float stocks is high, and the best trade is a momentum trade - going with the flow. These can be profitable, but don't make them your main hunting ground.

Another thing you want to look at before you select a share for trading is the Average True Range (ATR). This tells you how much the share usually goes up or down every day. If a stock has an ATR of 25 cents, it's not going to make you much money - trading it would be like trying to train a hippopotamus to win the Kentucky Derby. You'll want to see at least 50 cents for a stock that trades at $50-100 a share, and if you see $1 or more, that's a good target share for day trades.

Pre-market gappers

Stocks that gap up or down in the pre-market - that is, the share price moves up or down in a single big jump, leaving a 'gap' on the chart - are always going to give you interesting trades. Often, they've gapped down because of news, perhaps bad results from a similar company in Europe announced overnight, poor trading from Asian and European markets, or trading news announced during the after-hours the day before. Analyst roundtables or recommendations can also have an impact on stock prices.

A stock screener can quickly find you all the stocks that gapped up or down more than a dollar in the pre-market. Make sure these are stocks that trade in large volume, so that you can trade them easily - over a million shares a day (Alphabet, with 29 million a day, certainly has enough volume going through). Look at the chart above and you can see clear white spaces before the stock gapped up - it's visually quite striking. This tells you there is a situation that might give you a good trading opportunity - but it hasn't created that opportunity yet.

Once you've checked the gappers out, you'll probably find that you can reduce the number of stocks you're going to follow intensively today to just four or five. You might just have two or three. That's fine, because you will get the best trades by really concentrating on just a handful of stocks.

I also like to look for 'follow-through stocks', that is, stocks that had a bull run yesterday and are following it in pre-market trading.

Real time intraday scans

Not all good trading stocks announce themselves in the pre-market. That's why you'll also want to monitor the market in real time. But again, you can't shift the whole haystack to look for your two or three needles; you'll need to have a real-time scanner working for you.

You're looking for shares that fit your other criteria and that have high relative volume today. That tells you there is something going on. In addition, you might look for shares gapping $1 or more during trading. You might want to look for stocks that are up or down more than 3-4%, which tells you there is something happening that's unusual and might give you a trading opportunity.

If you're using a momentum strategy, you'd set up a scanner to look for stocks with high relative volume and high activity in the last five minutes. This is particularly useful if you trade any low-float stocks, as momentum is really the only strategy you can make money out of with these stocks.

You may not need a scanner to get started, and since good scanners will cost you money in the form of a subscription fee, you'll want to be totally committed to trading and have some experience before you put your money down.

By the way, make sure you check for buy-outs and exclude them from your scan results. If, for instance, Warren Buffett decided to take his investment fund Berkshire Hathaway private at $425, it would gap up tomorrow morning from the current $398, but then it would never move again - it would just sit at $425 until it was delisted. (I have no idea whether this is a realistic scenario, but who knows?)

You might also want to check the sector charts. Sometimes, an entire sector, having been neglected for a long time, can become a focus of interest. You may find a lot of stocks in that sector have good trading potential. Commodity charts can show if a stock will benefit or suffer from a sudden change in commodity prices; if the oil price is going up, oil stocks are in play but so are airlines (their fuel costs will jump).

Some stocks have high short interest, and this is worth checking out. NYSE provides monthly short interest reports, which show how many traders have shorted the stock. (Warning: a monthly report is way out of date for a day trader, so don't put too much faith in it.) You may find that a particular analyst report or a particular investor has come out with a detailed argument for shorting the stock - this happened with two real estate investment trusts (REITs) in 2023, Medical Properties Trust (MPW) and Digital Realty (DLR).

Remember, you're not looking to take a view on the fundamental catalyst. It doesn't matter whether the earnings announcement is as good as it looks (analysts will always find something to complain about) because you're not trading on the basis of that announcement. Simply, the earnings release has put the stock into play and created price movement and good volumes of trade; but you will be trading on the basis of the chart patterns and your understanding of the market.

Chapter 5 Quiz

1. What's a good sign of a stock in play?
    a) It beat market expectations for its results
    b) It is trading in high volume
    c) It did not trade pre-market
    d) The company is sponsoring a football team

2. Which of these is not a fundamental catalyst for stock price movement?
    a) Company results
    b) Merger rumours
    c) A big analyst presentation
    d) Someone tweeted about it

3. What are TICK and TRIN?
    a) Two ways of measuring price
    b) Derivatives that track the NYSE and Nasdaq
    c) Stock tickers for Ticketmaster and Trinity Biotech
    d) The TV Hosts of The Great British Bake-Off

4. Why might big stocks not give you great trades?
    a) Their prices never move
    b) Their results are too predictable
    c) There are too many robot traders playing these stocks
    d) They are too difficult to trade

5. How do you trade a stock that's in play?
    a) By taking a view on the fundamentals
    b) By looking at brokers' advice
    c) By analysing the price charts
    d) By just tossing a coin

6

Chapter 6: Technical Analysis Made Simple

Stock cycles - how they help plan your trade

I already talked about how the stock market and other financial markets move in cycles. Stocks become "oversold" or "overbought," that is, the price has fallen so far there are no sellers left, or demand is no longer strong enough to sustain high prices; this results in peaks and troughs. These cycles are a result of crowd psychology, and can occur on a long or short timeframe; a commodities supercycle could take 20-30 years, but within that, there will be numerous much shorter cycles.

Traders use these cyclic patterns to predict what is going to happen to the price of the asset. Remember, markets don't move smoothly, they move in bursts. Imagine stretching an elastic band to shoot it at the wall; it will stretch farther and farther, then when you let go, it will whoosh away really fast. This is the kind of movement you're aiming to harness in your favor.

Technical analysis: picturing price

There are two kinds of analysis, fundamental and technical. Fundamental analysis for oil, for instance, would look at total production, total demand, and new exploration that might bring new oil fields onstream. For a stock, fundamental analysis will look at the underlying business and its management; earnings, dividend payments, news about new products, and so on.

Technical analysis, on the other hand, looks only at the price of a financial asset and the way that price moves. It considers price, time, and sentiment. Technical analysis uses charts to make clear the movement of price and other indicators such as volume.

Investors sometimes use technical analysis to find a good time to buy the shares in which they already have an interest. They use it 'cold' - looking at the pattern up to yesterday's close. They tend to use daily charts and look at a stock over a year or even five years.

But as a trader, you're using the chart 'hot' in real time; you're at the right-hand edge of the screen, looking at the chart unfolding minute by minute (or five minutes by five minutes) and waiting for one of the patterns that you recognize to show up before you initiate a trade.

Charting

Technical analysis involves studying charts of share price, volume, and other indicators to identify frequent patterns. You can expect these patterns to be repeated, as they reflect the psychology of market participants. A simple example: if the lowest a stock has fallen in the last five years is $57, then if it falls back to this level, then a lot of buyers will be tempted to make a prediction that it will not fall below it. They'll buy - and the stock will go up again. Market psychology means that to some extent, these charting patterns exist because people believe in them. If we all stopped believing in them, and all stopped using technical analysis, they wouldn't work anymore. But we believe in them - often subconsciously - and so they work!

Line charts are the most simple charts to use. They show the price on the y-axis and time on the x-axis, running towards the right-hand side. Remember, the right-hand side is where the future lies - that's where the trades are. Take a look at the example below.

By the way, when you see an explanation of a trade in a book or on a website, it's usually the whole chart you're shown, with the order entry halfway along and the way the trade played out all shown on the chart. You really need to cover up the right-hand side of the chart with a piece of paper and work out if you can see the pattern that led up to the decision to enter the trade. That's all you'll have to work on in real life.

OHLC charts give a bit more information; they show the open, high, low, and close for a given time period (a day, five minutes, one minute). Each time period is shown as a bar, with a line on the left showing the open and on the right showing the close. The length of the bar is extra information you didn't have on the line chart; it shows you the range of price during the time period shown (see example below).

Then there are **candlestick charts**, which have the same four components as OHLC, but which many people find visually easier to use. (There will be a section specifically on candlesticks later in this chapter.) A colored and black & white example are shown below.

All of these charts can be plotted for any time frame. The usual charts you'll see in the media are daily, and they're intended for investors, but in trading we'll use much smaller time periods, like 15 minutes, 5 minutes, or just one minute.

But time isn't the only axis we can plot price changes against. **Tick charts** are not based on time; instead, the chart updates either on *every* trade, or on a given number of trades (for some reason, 233, 377 and 610 are popular). Otherwise, they usually look just like candlestick charts - just the candlestick represents a volume of trade rather than a number of minutes.

Range bar charts are also not time-based, but update every time a certain amount of price change has occurred; say, every penny that a stock price changes. The bar can remain open for hours, if the price doesn't change. For instance, you could use six ticks as a basis for charting S&P 500 futures. Every time the price rises or falls six ticks your chart will display a new bar. An example of a range bar chart is below.

The **Renko chart** is just another way to show a range bar chart; it looks like a series of little bricks or tiles as shown below.

A *momentum* range bar chart provides an extra variation that is interesting; it updates when the price breaks *beyond* the range of the previous bar. This gives you, the trader, extra confirmation of the move. (You can easily spot the difference below - the range bars join up at their corners, the momentum bars have a gap between.)

Support and resistance - what they are and how to recognize them

Support and resistance are two of the most basic concepts in technical analysis. Whenever you look at a chart the first thing to do is to identify support and resistance levels. The old way to do it was with a ruler on a paper print-out, but nowadays a lot of trading software will do it for you.

Here, you can see my handouts below, which may be familiar to the readers of the Technical Analysis for Beginners book! See how the share prices just touch the resistance and support lines. A channel has a resistance line at the top and a support level at the bottom - you can make some neat short-term trades inside a well-established channel, but the most profitable trades you'll make are on breakouts - which we'll talk about later in this chapter.

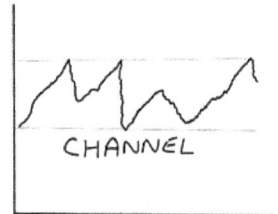

Supply and demand in the market are not price-agnostic. Market participants remember particular key levels, for instance, the price at which an IPO came to market, the lowest low that a stock has fallen to in the last year, or the price at which they bought the stock. That makes particular price levels significant and means that when the price arrives at that point, some of them will decide it's time to trade.

Sometimes, there are also fundamental reasons for a support or resistance line; for instance, a dividend-paying stock might rebound every time it comes to the price at which it yields twice the S&P average, and there might be resistance when it yields one and a half times the average.

Both support and resistance lines run horizontally across the chart. A support line is a floor; the price bounces back whenever it falls down to it. A resistance line is a kind of glass ceiling - the stock price can't get through it. Together, a support line and a resistance line can form a tight range within which the stock trades, and it takes a big push for the stock to break out of the range.

In the chart above, you can see a strong line at 173.40 which is a *resistance line* at the very start of the chart at 18:00, but later works as a support just after 19:00. The next line is at 173.88, and is close to another resistance line at 174.09.

If resistance is broken by a surge in the stock price, the resistance line doesn't disappear - it becomes a new support line. Each trading range is a new 'story' in the price house, so to speak.

The more times a stock tests a support or resistance line, the farther it's likely to go when it eventually breaks through. It's like bouncing up and down on a trampoline before you make a big jump and do a backflip.

Take some time to go on to TradingViews or another good site and use the 'horizontal line' tool to draw support and resistance lines till you feel happy that you're able to spot them.

Money making breakouts and breakdowns

Any time that a stock successfully pushes its way through a support or resistance line is called a breakout, or sometimes a breakdown if it's headed downwards. (Breakdowns are a good choice for short trades.) When a stock that has been in a pullback or a sideways move manages to break through resistance, it will generally move fast to achieve a new high. It will move fastest when there is a high volume behind the move. An example of a breakout, a false breakout and a breakdown are shown below.

BREAKOUT

FAKEOUT
(JUST DIPS BELOW
TRENDLINE)

REAL
BREAK OUT

BREAKDOWN

Take a look at Levi's below. For the whole of March, $19 marked the top of its range. It couldn't break through. Then, on the 27th March, it broke through and raced up to $20, real fast. Turns out there was good earnings news in the pipeline - you can see the stock *gapped up* on the 4th April as earnings estimates were revised upwards.

I also took a look around this morning and the first chart I found that looked like a breakdown was Iron Mountain (see below). There's a downtrend for which I drew the top of the channel, then there are two support levels that formed, and then the stock breaks loose. Now, to be honest, I would have probably wanted to enter this trade a bit early, when it breaks through the $79.56 level just before 17:00. It wouldn't have hurt; as although the price tested that level a couple of times, it didn't break through. However, the real breakdown came at $79.44, half an hour later (just after 17:30) where a temporary support level had been established. I end up with a full dollar profit a share on that short trade which lasted for less than an hour.

There is likely, at some stage, to be a pullback towards the breakdown price. This gives day traders a second chance to go short again. In fact, because you have already had one iteration of the breakdown, entering at this point is a lower risk than entering on the first breakdown.

Shorting a stock is a trading strategy where a trader borrows shares of a stock and sells them on the open market at the current price, aiming to repurchase them later at a lower price. If the stock price *falls*, the trader can buy back the shares at the lower price, return them to the lender, and pocket the difference as profit. However, if the price *rises*, the trader faces potentially unlimited losses.

How to draw trendlines: just join the dots!

Charting can be difficult to get started in. Where an experienced trader sees price-making patterns, you just see them randomly crawling all over the chart. Learning to draw the trendlines will really help you understand the value of charting. Eventually, you won't even need to draw them - you will see them in your mind's eye.

←TREND LINE:
MATCHES ALL THE LOWS

HOW NOT TO
DRAW A TREND LINE

Trendlines aim to take the noise out of price movement. Instead of lots of tiny zig-zags, a trendline lets you see the stock's rate of ascent and descent much more clearly.

If the stock is going up, then it will do so in a number of jumps and pullbacks every time it hits a bottom and jumps again, this is one of the points you need to join fit a ruler to the bottoms - usually a clear line results, though they may not always fit exactly and there will be a few spikes outside. The better the fit, and the more times the price touches the trendline and remains within the trend, the better your trendline is as a prediction tool.

An example of how to draw the trendlines is shown below for Tesla.

Drawing both the top and bottom trendline shows the *channel* within which the stock is trading. When the channel is narrowing, there is likely to be a chance to trade on a breakout. In effect, trendlines act as support and resistance lines, too. When the stock price hits the top trendline, it's likely to pull down again, but if it breaks out, you could see a fast move upwards or downwards in the direction its headed in as you can see in the example below.

Technical indicators

Technical indicators go a little bit further than price charts. They carry out mathematical operations on the price and volume data in order to deliver more insight. For instance, the moving average aims to filter out the noise of the day-to-day price movements and give a clearer view of where the price is actually going. Technical indicators can tell you about momentum - the strength of a price move - and about oversold or overbought markets, where the balance has tipped too far to one side or the other.

The moving average is relatively easy to calculate, though you won't have to; every charting package will offer at least two or three moving averages. It's a simple concept; averaging the stock price across, say, a week or 20 days, so that you see a smoother line rather than the noisy jagged chart of single-day price closes.

The **SMA,** or Simple Moving Average, is the most basic of all these indicators. The 20-day is often very useful, while the 200-day SMA is a longer-run indicator that can show where the stock price is now in relation to its long-term trend. Add a medium-term average, like 50 days, and you have an interesting arsenal of different indicators.

The chart on the next page shows a 9-day simple moving average. There's no great trading idea here, but just take a look at how far the share price ranges from the blue moving average line, and when it follows it closely. One thing I find interesting is that there's nearly always a really large bullish or bearish candlestick when the price breaks through the moving average, which shows there needs to be a real big push for things to change. However, I don't think that has predictive value; you have to be very careful with moving averages as they are a lag indicator, that is, they tend to move *after* the price. You can't use them in isolation; they're most useful in giving you natural trendlines, and when used in combination to pick up changes in the trend.

Tesla, Inc., 2h, NASDAQ O174.14 H174.40 L173.33 C173.88 −0.27 (−0.16%)
Vol 777.262 K
SMA (9, close) 167.71

Rather more advanced, the Exponential Moving Average, or **EMA** gives more weight to the most recent price data, and so it is likely to pick up changes of direction more quickly than the SMA.

A moving average can sometimes form a resistance or support line, which is very useful in confirming other chart patterns. Using 2 MAs together is also very powerful. When the shorter-term MA crosses over the longer-term line, it is often a sign of a powerful price move about to happen. If the short-term average moves higher, you have a 'golden cross', which suggests the price is about to explode upwards. Conversely, if the short-term average moves below the longer-term one, you have a 'death cross' which could signal a collapse in the price.

However, moving averages give a lot of false positives, so you need to keep tight stops if you're using them as a trading strategy, and use other indicators to confirm the signal before you trade.

Looking at the chart below, you get a couple of good golden crosses on 14 November and then again on 29 January (the green line crosses over the blue line), which would give you nice small profits on the remaining uptick. However, the apparent death cross in mid-December (the green line crosses under the blue line) is a lagging indicator, relating to the fact that the share gapped down. If you sold on this signal, you would have ended up in a stagnant or slightly rising share for nearly two weeks before the quick leg down.

If you set up three or more different moving averages you will see a 'ribbon' which is quite interesting. When it tightens up with all the different averages coming closer together that often indicates a change of direction. When all the averages are running at the same angle in the same direction, that shows the trend has a lot of momentum behind it. Again, it's not best used as a signal for a trade, but as a confirmation if another chart pattern suggests a trade, or a sign that you might want to watch the candlestick chart for that stock quite closely today.

VWAP is the volume-weighted average price. This is like a moving average, but it includes the volume traded as well as the price in the equation. Because it includes volume, its relation to the stock price gives you a good feel for the balance of power in the market - whether bulls or bears are in charge. If the stock trades above VWAP, the buyers are winning. If the stock trades below VWAP, the bears are in control.

A lot of traders like VWAP trades. When the price moves towards VWAP, you can treat VWAP as a support or resistance line. In a long trade, you'll enter the trade as soon as you see a confirmation of VWAP, and your stop loss is any close below VWAP.

P.S. In Class 5 of the free bonus #1 companion masterclass, I demonstrate some practical ways of how you can use some of the indicators discussed in this chapter with real life chart examples. I would highly recommend you watch the free masterclass video after you finished reading this entire chapter by visiting: www.az-penn.com.

Momentum indicators

Momentum indicators are useful for judging the likely strength of a price movement.

Bollinger Bands (not named after the champagne, but after their inventor, John Bollinger) uses a moving average as the center, and shows the standard deviation of price movements as a ribbon on either side. That is, you can see both the average, and how much prices have diverged from the average over recent days. Most of the time, the price will move within the bands, and that can give you ideas for range trading - if the share price is close to the bottom of the band, it is likely to go back to the middle of the band, so it could be worth buying.

The width of the bands can also give you useful information. When they get closer together, it's as if they're winding up like a spring - this sets the scene for a big move in the price. If you look at the 'squeeze points' in the chart below (around December 10, and then around January 15) you can see how the biggest 'squeezes' are followed by big price rises that go as far as the top band before reversing.

MACD (often pronounced 'Mack-Dee') is the Moving Average Convergence/Divergence indicator. It shows the relationship between different EMAs, and is usually shown at the bottom of the chart (sometimes on the chart itself) as two lines and a histogram.

Many traders use the 9, 12, and 26 time-period EMAs. In this case, the 'signal' line would be EMA 9, and the MACD line is the difference between the two other moving averages. Meanwhile, the histogram shows the difference between the 9-day average and the MACD line.

If the MACD line crosses the 9-day line, that often indicates the price is about to move in the direction of the cross. Most importantly, though, the histogram is there to be used as a check on the price information. If the price is hitting new highs, but the histogram is diverging, that suggests things could reverse quickly and the price could fall fast.

For instance, in the chart below, you can see how the MACD in the early part of the chart supports the price rises with notable peaks in early November and then again in December, but when the price rises in March, the MACD doesn't support it all, having very limited movement either side of its centre line.

The Relative Strength Index, or **RSI**, is used to show how strong a trend is. It runs from 0 to 100, and often signals reversals if it's at the top and turns lower (or vice versa). RSI divergence from the price action, as with the MACD, suggests a reversal might be on the cards. You won't know for sure till you see the candlestick chart. A useful feature of many charts is that they will show an RSI higher than 70 or below 30 colored in, alerting you to an RSI that is likely to be a good price signal.

In the chart below for AVGO, you can see how the two colored sections of the RSI above 70 accompany sharp price rises in mid-December and late January. If you had bought the stock when the RSI had just got into this zone, you would have benefited from some fast price movement.

You may have spotted an issue with all of these indicators - they are lagging indicators. That's why they're only used to scan for possible trades, or to confirm trades, not to initiate trades.

Oscillators

Oscillators will help you know if a market is overbought or oversold. One oscillator is the **Williams %R,** which looks similar to the RSI: it moves from 1 to 100 and shows the relationship between today's price and recent highs and lows. Below 20, the stock is oversold and could start to rise again, while above 80, it is overbought and is likely to fall.

In the chart below, DLR's price movements and the Williams %R are quite often related, but I don't see anywhere that I would have traded just on the basis of this indicator. However, in October, the stock formed a double bottom pattern, and if I had wanted to buy the stock at the bottom of the second part (right-hand side) of the 'W', I would have checked the Williams %R which showed oversold territory and that would have confirmed my choice of trade.

Stochastics are quite similar, though the math behind them is different. The stochastic oscillator compares the share price today to the share price history over time. The basic concept is that there's a certain average price progression, so if the stock has gone up very fast or down very fast, it has 'stretched the elastic', you might say, and will likely rebound in the short term.

The stochastic oscillator is shown as a figure from 0 to 100. Under 20, the stock is probably oversold, and over 80, it is probably overbought. In this chart above, you can see how Starbucks was going parabolic (a very fast upwards curve) and at the same time the stochastic, at the bottom, crept over the 80% mark showing the stock was overbought. Trading short against the bullish trend might have been a good idea, but I might want to check some other indicators and perhaps have a look at a couple of different charts (a longer term chart for trend/support/resistance lines, or a different time period chart e.g. 1 minute instead of 5 minutes).

Oscillators are really useful if you range-trade. Suppose prices are at the bottom of the range and you want to take a long position to take advantage of an uptick, then if the stochastics show a value of 10, the market is oversold. That makes it a good time to buy into the trade. On the other hand, if the stochastics are still well above 50, that suggests you might want to sit this one out.

Before we move onto candlesticks, I would like to mention some good news. If you have enjoyed the topics of technical analysis, then I have an excellent book on Technical Analysis for Beginners by A.Z Penn which goes into more depth on this great subject. You might want to check it out!

Introduction to candlesticks

Believe it or not, the candlestick chart goes all the way back to seventeenth-century Japan, when rice traders invented a way of tracking the rice price. It's now most traders' charting method of choice, using one, five, or (sometimes) fifteen-minute candlesticks.

The candlestick is a box that is made up of the opening price and closing price for the period. If it closed up, the body is hollow (white); if it closed down on the period, the body is filled in solid (black). Sometimes, you'll see charts using green for upticks and red for downticks.

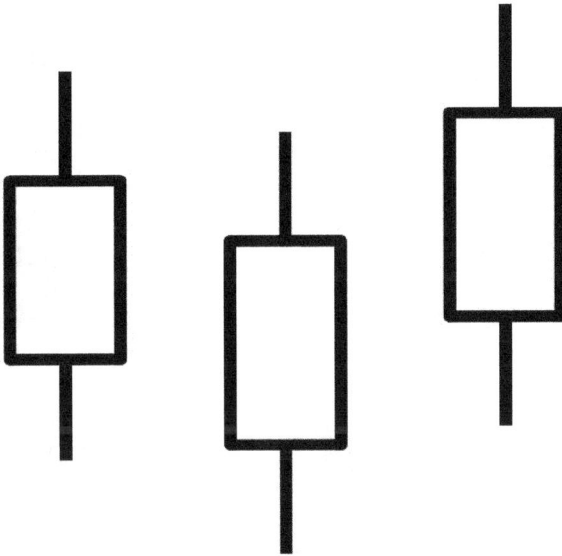

The highest price during the time period, if it is higher than the open/close, is shown as a line drawn sticking up above the box - the 'wick' of the candle. The low price, if it is lower than the open/close, may be shown by a line drawn hanging down below the box (a tail). The wick and tail are also often called 'shadows'.

Bullish and bearish candlesticks

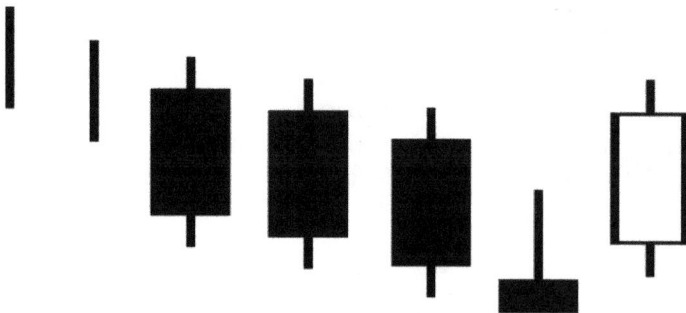

You'll often see a whole load of filled-in candlesticks in a downtrend. Conversely, uptrends often show white candlestick after white candlestick. The filled-in candlesticks show that for the given period, the price closed down; the white candlesticks show that for each given period, the price closed up. This is extra information that the line chart doesn't give you, and it enables you to see whether the buyers or sellers won the battle during that period. A white candlestick shows the buyers were winning - buying pressure sending the price up; a black candlestick shows the sellers were winning - selling pressure sending the price down. So a white (or green) candlestick is inherently bullish and a black (or red) one is naturally bearish. Examples are shown below.

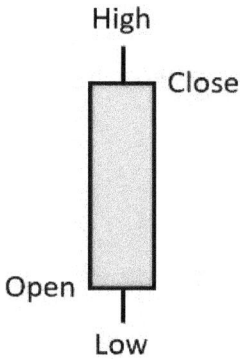

Bullish candlestick   Bearish candlestick

With any bullish or bearish candlestick, the larger the body, the more bullish or bearish it is. A very long 'pole' (or wick or tail) can confirm a reversal, and is often followed by another.

However, remember that when you're reading candlesticks you need to read the whole pattern, not just one candlestick.

Indecision candlesticks

When the market is indecisive, the share price will generally trade with only small variations from a flat line, and the candlesticks will bear this out. There's often a good spattering of both white and black candlesticks, and they will generally have tiny bodies and tiny wicks and tails, showing that the price has gone pretty much nowhere during the time period.

However, there's one candlestick that should make you sit up and take notice: the "spinning top." It has a tiny body, but it has a long wick and a long tail.

Spinning Tops

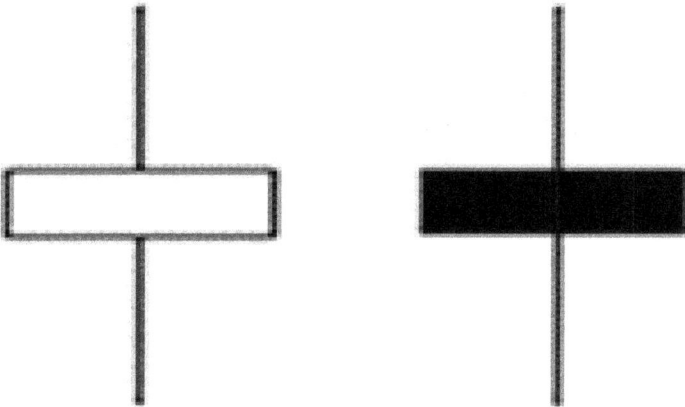

Let me talk you through what's happening in this candlestick. The share price opened, and then the bulls pushed the price up all the way up to the top of the wick, and the bears pushed the price all the way down to the bottom of the tail, but in the end neither of them won and the share price closed almost where it began. So, right now, the market is teetering on the edge, and it could take just a little push to move the price either way. That's why the spinning top is often the first signal that a reversal trend is about to start.

The spinning top will be the same color as the trend that is just about to be reversed. You trade in the *opposite* direction from a spinning top.

A special kind of spinning top is the **doji**. The doji is a spinning top that has almost no body. (In fact, the two spinning tops shown on the previous page are both dojis!) Often, the body is so small it looks like two lines crossing each other. When there is a very long tail on one side or the other, you have a very interesting doji, indeed.

The **hammer doji** looks like a hammer head on a long shank, and often tells you a bearish trend is going to reverse. The hammer doji's handle points downwards, in the direction of the old trend. What happened during the time period shown by a hammer doji is that the participants in the existing trend, the bears, pushed the price a long way in their direction; but by the close of the period, their opponents, the bulls or buyers, had pushed the price back to where it began. In other words, the tug-of-war was won by the bulls after a really hard struggle. That shows they are now in control, and the breakout is coming. An example of the hammer doji is below.

CLOSE

OPEN

LOW

HAMMER ⟶

SIGN OF
UPTREND

There is a very similar doji to the hammer doji that shows the end of an upwards trend. The only difference is that the handle of the hammer points upwards - it's usually called a **shooting star**, on the basis that it's a meteor falling to earth with its tail flaming out behind it. (But if you ask me, it's just a hammer the other way around.)

If you look at the Walmart chart below, just before 16:00, at the top of the last leg of the uptrend, there's a classic little shooting star, which I circled for you!

Candlestick patterns

The most important thing about candlesticks is learning to read patterns. If you don't, you'll make mistakes. For instance, the hammer doji works really well as an indication of the end of a bearish trend. But if you find the hammer at the end of a bullish trend, it won't help you. In fact, a lot of chart readers call it the 'hanging man' when it appears at the end of an uptrend, and see it as a bearish sign. It's the pattern leading up to it, not just the hammer doji, that's important.

HANGING
MAN -
BEARISH

Top and bottom reversals

The nice thing about trading top and bottom reversals is that both your entry and exit points are very clearly defined.

If a stock is falling in the pre-market, it's really difficult to get in on the first trend of the morning - besides, you have no way of knowing how far it will go. But you can watch it for a reversal, and that's a good trade. At some point, you will see an indecision candle (a spinning top or a doji or hammer or shooting star), usually following a couple of very small-bodied candlesticks. This is where a reversal is likely.

To ensure that you don't buy into a continuation of the downtrend, you need to confirm two other indicators. First, the stock should be trading outside or close to the outside of the Bollinger Band, and secondly, its Relative Strength Index is extremely low. Then, your trade is set up, and you just need to wait for the first candle to make a new high. That shows you the doji was right - the trend is changing.

Buy at this point and at this price. Set your stop at the lowest low reached before the reversal. If the price falls, you're out. If the price trades sideways for more than a couple of minutes without reversing the trend, you should also exit. But if the price rises, stick with it and adjust your stop-loss upwards as you go. Your target is the next support level that you can clearly identify on the chart.

Only trade when the trend is strong - at least five, and better, nine or ten candles of trend followed by a doji or indecision candle. If the trend is not a strong one, the reversal (if there is any) won't likely be big enough to make you a profit.

Trend trading based on moving averages

Using moving averages together with candlesticks can give you new trading ideas based on trading with the trend.

For instance, when a rising trend falls back to the moving average line, and then follows it again upwards, you can trade that trend upwards. A 9 EMA is a good moving average trade, but you might find success with other moving averages (20, 50, or 200) - try them all while you are considering the trade.

Buy the trend at any point where the candlesticks *confirm* the moving average as support, and run the trade till a candlestick breaks the support line. Either use trailing stops, or monitor the trend and take some profit out once you have a winning trade, to reduce your risk.

So in the chart below, you can see how the price successfully tests the moving average line around January 20 but pulls away above it again after January 22, and then when a candlestick finally breaks down below the moving average support around February 13, it's time to exit the trade.

This could be a trade that takes some time, even two or three hours. The next trading setup, Bull flag momentum, is a much faster one.

Bull flag momentum

This is a very fast trade; you need to get in, grab the profit, and get yourself out again. So you probably want to wait to trade it till you are fully confident with slower and easier trades.

The chart for the Bull flag looks like a flag on a pole. A couple of big bullish candlesticks represent the 'pole', which is followed by a 'flag' flying out more or less horizontally with small candles. This 'flag' is the consolidation area.

Ideally, you're looking for a preceding upwards movement that was strong, with big bullish candlesticks, followed by much smaller bearish candlesticks. That shows the bulls have the upper hand, even though the stock price is taking a breather.

Buy the first candlestick
to make a new high

You start to buy as soon as the chart starts to show white (or green) candlesticks within the consolidation area. The stop-loss is the bottom *tail* in the consolidation area, that is, the lowest the stock has fallen during consolidation. (This is one reason using candlesticks rather than a line chart is really useful.)

One of the nice things about TradingView is that you can see other traders' ideas arranged under different headings. I checked the site this morning and someone in India had identified a nice bull flag pattern in BSE, the Bombay Stock Exchange index. A very strong move upwards, and a consolidation moving more or less horizontally and with very small candlesticks compared to the run-up. I might take another look at this one!

The trade setup works like this: you're looking at stocks that are headed upwards fast. You then want to see them trading sideways - not reversing the trend, but just flatlining or consolidating. So here in the chart below, BSE is a classic bull trend that ends up consolidating. At this point, you want to see either a horizontal 'flag' or a triangular 'pennant', and you want to draw in the lines that make up this flag (as shown with the red lines in the example on the previous page). Here, the bottom line is horizontal, but the top line is slowing downwards slightly. When you see a bullish candlestick break through your upper trendline, as it does with the very last candlestick here, it's time to execute your trade.

You might even get two bull flags, one after the other that you can make money out of. That's a great play. However, don't get suckered into a third one - it's usually flaky. Bull flag trades typically need to be played within a strong trend, in a small size, and fast.

By the way, if you're still unsure on bullish flag and pennants, I would definitely suggest you watch my free bonus #1 companion masterclass because in Class 3 I demonstrate examples of both patterns with real life charts – which will hopefully help your learning!

Chapter 6 Quiz

1. What makes stock charts work as a means of predicting price movement?
    a) The law of nature
    b) Market psychology
    c) Mathematical calculations
    d) Magic

2. Which of these are breakouts/breakdowns?
    a) The stock moves upwards through a resistance line
    b) The stock moves downwards through a support line
    c) The stock moves upwards through the top line of the trend channel
    d) The stock falls through the moving average line

3. What is a golden cross?
    a) The short term moving average moves up through the long term moving average
    b) The short term moving average crosses the share price
    c) The RSI moves higher than 80
    d) A bullish candlestick

4. In which of these cases would you want to trade on a price signal?
    a) Volume is abnormally low
    b) The RSI is trading in the middle of its range
    c) Volume is high with an RSI at the bottom of its range
    d) The moving averages are both going up

5. What is a doji?
    a) A candlestick with almost no body at all
    b) A bullish candlestick
    c) A bearish candlestick
    d) Somewhere that people study judo

7

Chapter 7: Planning Your Trades and Trading Your Plans

You won't get far writing a novel just sitting in front of a computer screen and a keyboard, waiting for inspiration. The same is true for trading; you can't just sit there and hope a profitable trade will appear, and you'll know what to do. You need to plan what kind of trades you're looking for, how much risk you'll take, and when to close the trade. Not planning properly is one of the most common ways beginner traders ruin their own performance, leading them to drop out of trading, often with significant losses.

Good traders make plans. They know what assets they want to trade, and what kind of trade they are looking for. They're willing to sit things out if they don't see a good trade today. It's the same with horse racing. I once went racing with a friend who was a big gambler. In a six-race card, he didn't bet on the first race. Or the second. Or the third. Or even the fourth. But on the fifth race, he checked the horses in the paddock, smiled, and went to place his bet. He'd chosen the one race which gave an attractive price on a good horse, he explained. He won - and chose not to bet in the remaining race.

What assets are you going to trade *today*? You might choose just one to concentrate on, or a number, but don't spread yourself too widely. Then think about how you're going to trade that asset; how much money you're going to commit to your trades, the level of risk you want to take, what events might have an effect on the market (including any announcements coming out today), the mood of the relevant market, what other traders might be doing.

You can now say whether on the whole you want to be long or short (whether you think the price of the asset is going up or down), whether you want to leverage, and what percentage of your total account size you want to use today. You also want to have a feel for your profit objectives and for how tightly you want to control losses. For instance:

• you might decide you want "risk two to get three"

• you know how many winning trades you have to make to reach your daily profit goal

• you know exactly when you will close out a losing trade (for "risk two to get three" as soon as your position is two ticks down on your buy price, for example).

Closing out your positions

How long does an investor hold an asset? As long as it takes. How long does a day trader hold an asset? No more than a day. Ever. It's in the name!

Day trading significantly reduces your risks. If you close your positions at market close, you have no risk during the hours the market is closed. If there is an earthquake in Japan, a profit warning from a stock in which you hold a position, or some other catastrophic event - you're not at risk. One of my friends swing traded a tech stock he was sure was on the rebound. One of its competitors in Taiwan came out with a profit warning while the US market was closed. It very nearly bankrupted him. If he'd been a day trader, he would have been fine.

It also reduces your costs, if you trade on margin. Overnight borrowing is expensive.

And it's a very good trade discipline. It stops you looking at a losing position and saying, "But maybe if I just hold it till tomorrow, it'll make money."

Don't believe the clichés

The markets are full of clichés. Many of them have some truth, but others are completely misleading. Take them all with a pinch of salt.

"Buy on rumor, sell on news." The grain of truth here is that markets are driven by expectation, so that a rumor will drive the price up in advance of the good news. Then, when the good news arrives, the market has already priced in (discounted) the information, so the price goes into reverse. However, not all rumors are based on fact, so you might be buying into a wild goose chase rather than a trading opportunity.

Also, markets often overreact to new information, so you might find 'wait for news, then exploit the overreaction' a good trading strategy instead.

"Cut your losses and run your profits." Or, as famed Fidelity fund manager Peter Lynch said, "Don't cut your flowers and water your weeds." That's a good motto for long-term investors, but maybe not so much for day traders. Remember, you need to track your value at risk as well as your profit on a position, so if you are ahead, but you now have a big proportion of your total value tied up in a single trade, it can make sense to close or at least reduce the position. With a lot of trades, you will have identified a target price based on the chart pattern; don't get greedy.

As for cutting losses, though - that is 100% right. Use stops and limits to ensure your losing positions don't keep losing you more money.

"The trend is your friend." Yes, some trades work best within a defined trend. But day traders work on a very short term basis. An investor might be interested in a long-term trend like the move to electric vehicles or sector rotation towards growth stocks. Day traders, not so much. The trends they care for are within-the-hour price trends. And sometimes your best available trade will be a reversal.

"The market is always right." Investors often don't believe this. They are looking for a good company they can buy cheaply because the market got it wrong. But as a trader, you should believe the market is always right. It will do what it will do. Your business is not to argue with it, but to jump on its back at the right point - and jump off again quickly if it starts running in the wrong direction.

"Pigs get fat, hogs get slaughtered." Take this one to heart; you should know the difference between aiming at a good profit, and getting greedy. If you start treating stocks like horses in a race and thinking that shouting at your trading screen can make them go up faster, you're leaving day trading for gambling territory - and getting greedy. However, I really love another phrase with pigs in: **"root hog or die"** - get rooting around for good trading opportunities, or you're never going to survive! In other words, *work hard*.

"Never catch a falling knife." If an asset's price is headed straight down, let it go. You run lower risks if you look for some stabilization or slowing down of the price declines before you buy into the trade. (Equally, never chase a stock that's going straight up.)

Setups and trading strategies

You can get all kinds of trading setups out of books or off the internet, but for the best returns you'll want to create your own, and then backtest them before you start trading.

Two basic types of trade that work well are breakouts and reversals. With breakouts, always trade in the direction of the breakout, and put a stop-loss just below the support level (for long trades) or just above resistance (for shorts). Prices may retrace to the support level several times before breaking out definitively, but if they fall below the support level, that's usually a sign that the breakout has failed.

Not to worry! Failed breakouts can also be a great opportunity. If the price looked like breaking out upwards, but the breakout failed, it's often a great time to open a short trade in the expectation that the price will fall fast back into the trading range.

Reversals can make great trading opportunities, but they are a higher risk than with-trend trades. Classic chart patterns like the double top or head and shoulders may show that a reversal is on the cards.

DOUBLE TOP

If you're in an in-trend trade and a reversal starts to occur, it can make sense to reverse your trade. For instance, a price might have broken out of its trading range and you've gone long. If you then see the price coming back to test the new support line a couple of times, it could be making a double top. It's time to close out your long position and maybe think about going short, to take advantage of a likely strong move back below support.

Pullback in a trend

Prices don't move smoothly. In any trend, there will be pullbacks. Even long-term investors know that you can take advantage of pullback to "buy on weakness" and lower the average in-price of your investment.

You're not looking for just any pullback, but for one where the price is coming close to a support level, or to a key price point or a moving average. That's a good time to buy, and wait for the uptick. You also know exactly where to put your stop-loss, and that's just below the support level or key price point.

However, pullbacks could be the start of a reversal. So take a look at the MACD for confirmation, and also take a look at a longer time frame chart to check there's no reversal building up.

Divergences

Divergences between the price action and technical indicators like the MACD or stochastics can signal a reversal. For instance, when a strong price uptrend is not reflected in the MACD, it could mean the bull move is running out of steam and prices could move strongly to the downside - a good time to place a short trade.

Check a divergence with the overall chart patterns before you decide to trade. This isn't a strong indicator on its own, but if it matches a pattern like a breakout or double top, you have confirmation of the trade idea. Examples of a positive and negative divergence are shown below.

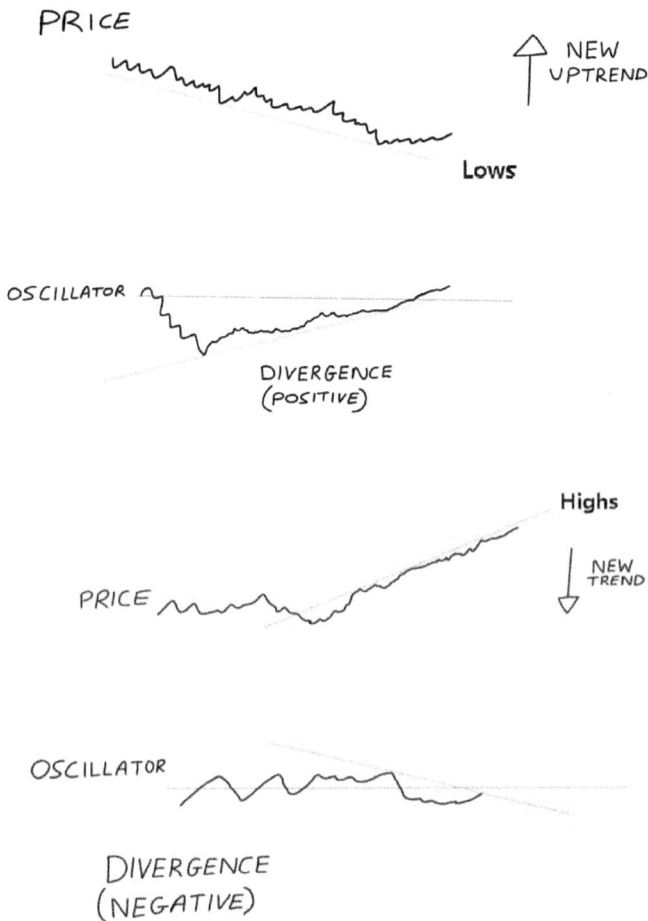

PRICE

NEW UPTREND

Lows

OSCILLATOR

DIVERGENCE
(POSITIVE)

Highs

NEW TREND

PRICE

OSCILLATOR

DIVERGENCE
(NEGATIVE)

Head and shoulders is a chart formation that has two 'shoulders' separated by a higher 'head'. It predicts a trend reversal, from the bullish trend that led up to the 'head', to a new bearish trend. If the right shoulder is weak, in other words, smaller than the left shoulder, that's a good sign there may be fast price action on the way down - the bulls haven't managed to push the price back up far enough.

HEAD & SHOULDERS TOP

To plan the trade, you need to draw the support line, or 'neckline', that connects the two lows. You will then initiate a short position when the price dips below the neckline. The price target is equal to the difference between the lowest low and the highest high in the pattern (same as the distance between the top and the neckline), which becomes your target price fall from the neckline. You can create further targets at 1.5x and 2x the initial target, and take some profits or move your stop loss when the ce hits any of the target lines. This is a great system, because it prevents you closing your trade when there is still profit to be gained, but it limits your risk and with the 2x target as a hard limit, prevents you from getting greedy and following the trade too far.

The head and shoulders can also be inverted, in which case you would trade long, not short.

So, in the chart above, you can see how a head and shoulders pattern was established with a bottom at just over EUR 65 at around 13:30, and the neckline at EUR 65.10. So since that's a ten cents a share difference, I'm looking for roughly 10 cents a share downwards to my first target level, that is, EUR 64.90 (remember, we are shorting this position).

I'll go short as soon as the price breaks through the neckline convincingly, and it does, with a big bearish candlestick to give me confidence, just before 16:00.

On the other hand, I need a stop loss at EUR 65.10 because if the stock goes through that level, it will have destroyed the head-and-shoulders pattern, and all trades are off. Let's just put that stop-loss a couple of ticks higher, though, at EUR 65.12. That means I will only be stopped out if the pattern is decisively broken, and not if the price is just testing that EUR 65.10 resistance line.

That's my basic trade setup. However, I don't have to settle for ten cents a share, as head-and-shoulders formation often gives you a really good strong move that you can take more profit from.

One way to work these out is to look at further ten-cent declines - remember, that was the difference between the base and the neckline. So my next target would be EUR 64.80.

In that example, the stock nicely confirmed the pattern, and I would have exited my trade with a 20-cent-a-share profit, about 16:15.

Pullback setup

This is a low-risk, relatively high-reward trade that is quite easy to spot, so it's a good one for beginners.

A pullback in a rising trend (sometimes called a correction) will usually be followed by continuation of the rising trend. Learn to spot the end of the pullback, and you have a great opportunity to open a winning trade. To get this one right, look at the 20 and 200 moving averages. If the lively 20 picks up speed and starts chasing higher, it's a great indicator of a rising trend starting.

It's also worth noting that reaction moves like pullbacks often end when they touch the 20 MA. This is your hint for a profitable trade. An example of a pullback setup in action is on the next page.

Today, I saw Broadcom (AVGO) in a rising trend, as we see in the chart below. The blue trendline shows how the price was developing. There was then a pullback just *after* 19:00. The moving average didn't help me here, but based on the candlestick action I would have bought around $1324.50 just *before* 19:30. I might have sold out in the small pullback to $1328.64 that you can see just after that nice run of green candlesticks, and that would have made me around $4 a share profit in ten minutes or so.

However, at this point, I took a look at the moving average and saw that it had started moving up more markedly. That gave me the confidence to hang on for more. At $1337 or so (far right side of the chart), I would be out - the stock price has gone parabolic, which is never a good sign. The best profit is one you can take out in ready cash!

Look for the space

When the support and resistance lines are close together, trading is often choppy. But when there is a lot of space between them, the price will often move through the open space for a long time with no pullbacks. So look for the price moving into an open space, buy when it's a few ticks/pennies into the space, and sell five ticks/pennies later, or at least minimize your loss by selling half your position and letting the rest run. Some traders refer to these open spaces as "windows." Look to see how much room the stock has to run until it hits another support or resistance line - you may be lucky enough to hit a really good, long run.

You can also look at four lines on your chart to spot open space; previous open, previous close, previous high and previous low. Wherever the space is widest, that's where you'll get great trades.

However, you'll need to do some backtesting to find the right stop-loss position. You don't want to have a trade stopped out if there's just a little choppiness at the start, but you do want to get stopped out if the price starts heading in completely the wrong direction. You might also backtest whether adding second and third profit targets, with trailing stop-losses, would increase your trading profit significantly.

Let's have a look at two stocks that behaved a little bit differently today. In the chart below, Tesla has lots of resistance/support lines all over the place which are close together. There's a lot of zigzagging going on. This might be quite difficult to trade as you can't see exactly where things are going, but it's not impossible.

On the other hand, Apple, as we see in the chart below, has just **two** main lines of resistance/support, farther apart, and there's relatively little zigzagging going as the price moves from one to the other. So, if you spot the share price breaking through one of the support/resistance lines, you can predict that it will probably go pretty fast towards the next line, "filling in the white space." That's always an indication that you might be able to get some highly profitable trades out of the stock.

Keep looking

Sometimes, you will miss a first chance at a trade. Don't give up! Sometimes, you'll get a second chance. For instance, the price won't break out where your first chance happened, but will retest the support line. That's your second chance. Other times, you'll have a short trade planned and miss it, but if you stay around, you may see the price breaking out upwards, giving you a second chance to trade - though in the opposite direction.

Trade Execution

You could be the world's best reader of candlestick charts, but if you don't manage to place your trades correctly and get them filled by your broker, it won't do you much good. Flawless trade execution is important, and it's much more complex than just saying 'buy' or 'sell.' You need to know about different types of orders, and how to stack up automated series of orders to minimize the amount of work you have to do (and the chance of error).

An investor clicking the 'buy' button is usually making a **market order**. "I want 1,000 shares of IBM and I'll pay the market price, and I'll hold on to them until I change my mind." That's a bit vague for a trader, so you'll want to use orders that bring a bit more control. The risk with a market order is that you'll get your stock, but you may pay ten cents a share more than you were expecting. That could dramatically alter the risk/reward profile of your trade. To control that risk, you'll want to use a limit order.

The place for market orders is if you need to exit a position speedily. Say you went long of IBM at $183, but the stock started to fall rapidly and went through a key support level. You need to be sure you get out of that stock. If it's starting a major downtrend, you do not want to be left in IBM because your trade wasn't filled. In this case, you risk using a market order to close the trade (and ensure that if you have a stop-loss order, it's canceled at the same time).

A **limit order** lets you specify price. "I want 1,000 shares of IBM, but I won't pay above $186 for them." IBM is currently trading at $186.34, so the market will need to dip for your order to be filled. But if it does, and you get your stock, you will have paid exactly what you intended.

It's sometimes smart to use a little offset - that is, to use a limit order just a few cents higher than your intended buy price. For instance, I want to buy a stock at $55, but the stock might go through $55 fast, and my order won't be filled or might only be partially filled. So, instead, I'll use an offset and put in a limit order of $55.40 or $55.60 (avoiding the fifty-cent price, which is likely to be a key level for some traders), which will still get me into the stock around the right price. Most likely, part of my order will be filled at $55 and the rest at the slightly higher price. (Don't use an offset of more than 5% or so, though, or you're going to wreck your trades with slippage.)

A **stop order** also specifies a price - a trigger price for the order. For instance, if you have spotted a potential breakout but don't want to buy until the price has moved up to $186.50, you can say, "I'll buy IBM when it hits $186.50." That's a market stop. You can also make a stop-limit order, which also says, "I'll buy IBM when it hits $186.50 *and at that* price." If you're trading IBM and the market is not racing too fast, you'll probably get filled - but there is no guarantee.

Stop-limit orders are a good way to enter trades, since they partly automate your trade and mean you won't miss it because your attention wandered for a moment or you were occupied with another trade. You also won't enter your trade at far too high a price because the share price roared through the $186.50 level and your order was filled further up the spike.

However, stop-limit orders are not a good way to stop out a trade. Use a stop-market order instead for your stop-loss. Having bought your IBM at $186.50 with a limit order, you want to add a stop order to sell it if the price goes below the support level at $185. This limits the risk on your deal.

Why don't you use a stop-limit order? The answer is quite simple - if things go wrong, the price could move all the way past your stop-limit price without your order being filled. You would then not only have failed to control your downside risk, you would be incurring more and more losses by the second.

Ideally, you should create a 'bracket' when you open the position, with a limit order to close the position at your intended profit level and a stop order to close if the position starts to make a loss.

A **trailing stop** locks in profit, since the stop-loss is automatically adjusted as your trade moves into profit. If I bought IBM at $186.50, with a $185 stop, the stock might go all the way to $190 and then fall back to $184 fast; my stop-loss would be effective, but I would have lost all my profit.

On the other hand, using a trailing stop, once IBM got to, say, $188, my stop-loss would adjust upwards to $187. At $190, the trailing stop loss would adjust to $188.50. So when the price subsequently fell, it would hit the trailing stop-loss, and I'd be out of my trade with a perfectly acceptable profit.

Trailing stops are so useful, I would make availability of trailing stops a criterion in my choice of broker and trading system.

As a day trader, you need to remember to close all your trades at the end of the day. But this, too, can be automated through an order type - **market-on-close**. Any open trade with this order will automatically be closed at the end of the day.

Two other order types that investors don't use, but that traders really need, are OSO and OCO - order-sends-order and order-cancels-order.

• **OSO** puts your stop-loss and target orders in as soon as you open your position. Your opening order 'sends' the stop-loss and target orders as soon as it is filled.

• **OCO** ties up the loose ends. If your stop-loss is activated, it will automatically cancel the target price sale order. If your target price sale order is activated, it will automatically cancel the stop-loss.

If you bracket your trade with target and stop-loss orders in this way, your entire trade has been programmed. You have simplified your job; it's simply to spot the right opportunities and define the levels of acceptable risk and return. All the watching-price-moves-and-yelling-down-telephones stuff has been taken out of the equation, so to speak.

Although you have automated a lot of the thinking and acting, you need to ensure everything goes through as intended and that you don't have any orders left open that should have been closed.

For instance, if your trade hits its target, take the time to verify that your closing trade has been done - otherwise, enter a market order to close (market out) and ensure any stop loss or target price limit orders have been canceled. You might also "market out" if your trade is just sticking a penny or two below your target price.

By the way, always put your stop-losses just the other side of a key level (e.g. a round price, or a support level). You want to stop out just the other side, so that you don't sell out when the key level is being tested, but only when it's been broken. For instance, if you're buying a stock and there is a support level at $125 - a round number - then put your stop loss at $124.70. That way, you will probably be stopped out only when the trade is going against you, not when the price falls back before finally being able to push upwards.

Plan your trade, then trade your plan

A lot of day traders start without any particular plan. They learn a bit about the market, and then they just jump in and start trading. Most of them probably end up in the 90 percent of traders who don't make it.

The best way to ensure you'll make money day trading is to ensure you have a plan. Even if you don't understand exactly why a certain strategy works, if you've backtested it, run a simulation, and found that it produces a profit, stick with it.

You need to create trading rules which will let you quickly scan for trading opportunities, assess and limit your risks, and removes "gut feeling" and emotion from the equation. In other words, you are controlling your trades, rather than the market controlling you.

You should think about setting rules not just for individual trades but for when and in which markets you trade. Rules might include

• "trade the first hour of the NYSE"

• "finish trading by 11 pm"

• "I can quit if I'm ahead by lunchtime"

• "I will quit if I lose more than $150"

• "I will not run more than three trades at a time"

• "I will not trade a stock the day of its results"

• or alternatively, "I will focus on stocks that overreact to their results, on the day of the results, or on the morning after"

• "I will only range trade"

• "I will not trade within the first five minutes after a news release"

• "I will never risk more than 10% of my capital on one trade"

• "I will always check the MACD or stochastics before I trade"

• "I won't trade days with major economic announcements"

• "I will trade only when I can see a risk-reward ratio of two to three."

But don't forget you need to test those rules before you apply them. And then you need to stick to them. You'll need rules for your trading strategies, such as "Always move the stop-loss once you have hit your price target, to minimize your risk."

It's useful to have a rule about your daily targets. How many trades should you be doing a day? When should you stop trading? For instance, you might decide to stop for the day if you have a positive result after three trades, or by lunchtime. Then you can go to the park, play soccer, make sushi rice, cuddle your kids, whatever. This may sound dumb, but it guarantees you have some downtime and it also keeps your mind in a positive attitude. A musician friend of mine practices for an hour, and then waits till he plays a piece really well to put his violin away for the day. It leaves him feeling like a great player, instead of someone who has to do scales and arpeggios and still plays wrong notes.

You might also decide to quit for the day if you're on a losing streak; decide how long that has to be for you to quit, maybe 10 losing trades, or just a dollar amount in losses. That stops you trading in a negative mindset or with the desperation to make back your losses - which can result in taking trades with a poor risk/reward ratio, and losing more. But instead of relaxing, do some thinking. Why didn't your plan work? Did you miss the right entry point and pay too much? Was there a confirmation check that you missed out before making the trades? Is there something wrong with the plan? Or were you just out of sync with the market, which does occasionally happen?

You need to have dynamic rules that can adjust to different market conditions. For instance, if a trading rule says, "Set your price target where you make a 2% profit," that's not a dynamic rule; if it says, "Your price target for trading a head and shoulders should be the same as the distance between the top and the neckline," then it automatically adjusts to the situation and is therefore a dynamic rule. A lot of the rules you hear, like "always take ten ticks out of the market" or "wait for the MACD to go below 20," are not dynamic, and they will prevent you from taking good trades that will make 9 ticks, or where the MACD has been falling but is at 21, not 19.

You also need three key rules that you will never break. These are:

Rule 1 - stick to the trading rules.

Rule 2 - stick to the trading rules.

Rule 3 - stick to the trading rules.

Another rule I have is that I keep a written record of every trade. It's a great help when my mind goes blank halfway through a trade! Some traders just use a yellow legal pad or a notebook; I've printed out a basic log so that I just need to tick some boxes and add some numbers. That cuts down on the amount of writing I have to do but also makes sure I don't forget anything.

You may need to refine your rules from time to time. Don't be too quick to do that - sometimes the market will be just wrong for your system for a while, but if you have a well-tested, working rule, don't change it just because you have a poor streak for a few days. However, if you find that applying your rules has stopped you out of trades that subsequently came good, or that your limit orders are frequently not filled, you might ask yourself what could you do differently. Is your stop-loss too tight, or should you adjust for key levels? Are you being too optimistic or too demanding about your entry prices?

Having rules - trading rules and business rules, and risk and cash management rules - is what distinguishes the successful trader from the rest. You identify the chart patterns you're going to trade. You determine what is an acceptable level of risk and return. You set your rules. You use limit orders and stop-losses to manage your risk. And if you do this, you are going to make money. That's why you are trading, after all.

And if you feel the need for some adrenaline in your life, don't try to get it out of trading. Trading is for making money: climbing walls and paint-gun ranges and fast cars are for adrenaline.

Trading in action

Let's go through a trade. I've been watching a stock and I've seen it make a double bottom, a formation like the first three lines of a 'W'. I expect it to bounce off the bottom and roar upwards. (Here, I'm taking a swing trade rather than a day trade, which took about a month to work out, but the patterns are similar for day trades.)

DOUBLE
BOTTOM

I first need to plan the trade. This means analyzing the chart patterns so that I can analyze expected profit levels and stop loss, and see if the trade fits my requirements for profitability.

So, 1) I'll go to the chart above and draw the support line for the 'W', that is, the line at the *bottom corners* of the W.

Then 2) I then draw the resistance line across the top of the *middle corner* of the W. Working from the patterns on the chart gives me everything that I need to know. My stop-loss will be just below the support line that we drew in the first step, and my initial target price is at the resistance line at $1.65. That would give me 20 cents a share in profit.

At 3) I can also see an interesting resistance/support level around $2, so I draw that in as my next profit target. I could also add another potential profit target at $2.40 based on the next resistance/support level, which you can see in a consolidation at the beginning of the chart, in October. There is a pretty clear gap up from $2 to the $2.40 level, so if the stock is running nicely, it's not likely to stop on the way up to that level.

If I didn't see these important levels quite clearly, I might just take the difference between $1.64 (at the top of the middle of the W) and $1.37 (at the bottom of the right side dip) - that is, my target profit. That's an expected 27 cents profit.

As a rule of thumb, once that profit target has been hit, the two further targets can be set at 1.5x and 2x the profit. That would give me $1.64 + ($0.27 x 1.5) = $2.04, and $1.64 + ($0.27 x 2) = $2.18.

When I hit my initial target, my plan is to sell half my position, then run the rest up to the next level, and I will also adjust the stop-loss to the previous target price, locking in my initial profit.

Now I have to decide how much to trade. That's easy since I personally have a 2% fixed-limit rule on my portfolio balance. That would be $500 on a $25,000 portfolio balance, for instance. And remember, this applies to only my risk on the trade (i.e. the amount I would lose if my stop loss were activated), not to the size of the trade I take.

I can now set up all the orders; a limit buy when the price bounces back off the bottom of the W, confirming the double bottom; a stop-loss; a stop-limit on half the position at the initial target price, and a stop-limit on the whole position at the next target price. All of that is entered, and so if the first order is triggered, my trade will play out automatically.

Step by step to a successful trade

Just to recap on everything you've learned in this chapter, let's go through a successful trade step by step.

First of all, you will have built your watchlist. You will just be watching a few stocks only, not the whole market. You'll have identified shares that offer interesting potential for a trade. So, among other opportunities, I am looking at a share that has been trading in a downwards trend today - Tesla - but the trend is slackening off. Will we see a reversal? In the chart below, at 13:30 (the extreme bottom left-hand side, which you can't see on the chart), the candlesticks are still bearish, but I can check some other indicators.

So at 13:35, while I'm waiting for a signal from the candlestick chart, I check the RSI for confirmation. The RSI is at 20 (the bottom line of the RSI part of the chart), suggesting this stock is oversold. I get a feeling that the bear trend could be running out of steam.

Remember, to succeed at trading, you need to make sure your preparation is perfect. You don't just see an opportunity and jump into it; you need to assess, for a given opportunity, exactly what you need to see in order to make a trade, whether that's increasing volume, the breaking of a resistance line, or a hammer doji, whatever. It's a lot of work, and sometimes the trade you're looking for never happens. But when it does, you'll be ready to go.

Now, here, I'd like to see declining volumes, too. However, in the chart below, when I added trading volumes, I see that they are still high, though not quite as high as 15 minutes ago (13:45 vs 13:30). So, I'll need to see a pretty clear signal from the candlesticks to be ready to trade.

Now, I work out, very quickly, where I need to put my price target and my stop loss. Is there a resistance level that will be retested if the stock starts to rise? I had a look at the earlier trading today which didn't really help, so I switch for a moment to the five-day chart, and there, I do find a level at $171 that looks like a good support/resistance level.

So $171 will be my price target - that's the place at which if the stock is going to fall back again, it will do so. In fact, I'll put my price target just *before* that, so that I will exit before anything nasty happens. If you hang on for every last penny, you're likely to find other traders exiting before you and the price falling before you can get out. As for my stop loss, I'll put that a couple of pennies below the consolidation point, when I see the consolidation in the candlestick, so if the stock heads downwards again, I'll be stopped out of the trade with only a small loss. But I won't know that till the actual trade is ready to go.

I also know the amount I can risk on this trade ($500, remember?). I have already got everything ready to go. I'm bracketing my buy order with two other orders, a stop-loss and a sell-limit order, so that all I need to do is hit the button when the price hits my target; which makes my job much simpler.

As I watch, by about 14:30, I see a spinning top appear. However, it's followed by a large bearish candlestick as the bears have one last go at driving the price down. Next comes a big bullish candlestick, and it's followed by another spinning top. I don't have what I really want, which is a hammer doji.

However, if I can get in at $168.50 at 14:00, put a stop loss at $167.50, and run the trade to $171, I'm risking $1 to win $2.50, which is a reasonable return. The RSI, together with the chart pattern, tells me I have a good chance of a reversal even though the hammer I wanted as conclusive evidence didn't appear. I place my trade.

The stock runs to $170.20 before encountering trouble about 14:30. If I get out after I see that big bearish candlestick, I will exit at $169 or so, so I've only made a 50-cent profit. But the stock rises to $170.90 at about 14:40 before the uptrend is definitively broken by a series of red-bodied indecision dojis.

No signal is faultless. The stock retraced nearly all its gains and didn't reach the $171 I expected. However, this was a *successful* trade. It was properly planned, executed, and under control. It didn't, as it turns out, make me much money, but I controlled the trade and didn't court undue risk by hanging on to the stock in hope.

Even if I had lost money, it would have been a successful trade because I am still solvent, still trading, and confident that my trading plan will work for me over the long haul.

In fact, as I'm still watching that previous chart, Tesla decides to give me a second bite at the cherry. By 14:30, the bear run is nearly over, as shown by a number of indecision dojis, and there are two bullish candlesticks, the second of which breaks out of the consolidation range. If I buy at $169.50, after that second green candlestick at around 14:35, I actually do get that run up to $171 that I was looking for, just before 14:45.

A final warning

Remember to always have a backup! So if your computer freezes, have a smartphone, or a broker you can phone. If you have a power outage, have a laptop with a fully charged battery and access to a mobile network while your wifi's not working.

You may even want to have two brokerage accounts... just in case.

P.S. Before we go onto Risk Management, if you are finding this book useful so far - I would really appreciate if you could spare 60 seconds and write a brief review on Amazon on how this book is helping you. It would mean the world to me to hear your feedback!

Chapter 7 Quiz

1. When should a day trader hold a stock overnight?
   a) When the position is losing money but it might turn around
   b) When the position is making money and will make even more tomorrow
   c) When the company has results tomorrow
   d) Never

2. Which of these gives you a good second chance if you missed the trade first time round?
   a) Bad results push the stock price back to its earlier price
   b) The stock retests the support line after an earlier move
   c) The RSI moves into overbought territory
   d) The price move falters on low volume

3. Which of these orders should you not use?
   a) Market-on-close
   b) OSO
   c) OCO
   d) Market order

4. Which of these is a good trading rule?
   a) I will take the afternoon off every Thursday
   b) I will never trade S&P 500 stocks
   c) I will always stick to the trading rules
   d) I will always make 2% profit on a trade

5. Which of these should you always have for a stock trade?
   a) A price target
   b) A stop loss
   c) A written record
   d) A good reason

8

Chapter 8: Managing Your Money and Your Positions

While making a successful trade is one of the things you need to be able to do, making a business out of day trading isn't just about trading. It's also about managing your account properly, in particular, managing risk. Failure to manage risk and to manage losses is one of the main reasons that beginner day traders drop out.

Risk and account management

You will lose some trades. By definition, you will make some losing trades. If you have a win rate of 93% (and that's really exceptional; you won't), you will still lose 7% of your trades. It's your job to ensure those trades do not lose big.

Look at the worrying arithmetic of loss: if you lose half your money, you will need to *double* your money to get back to where you were before. A 50% loss needs a 100% return to make it back. The odds are stacked against you whenever you make a big loss. (Which, incidentally, is why I am somewhat hesitant about trading leveraged ETFs.)

So, the first part of risk management is finding trades with a risk/reward ratio that will make you money. A lot of traders like to "risk two to make three." a 2:1 win/lose ratio.

If you buy 100 shares at $53 with a price target of $55, your risk if you just went long of the shares with no stop-loss would be $5,300 to make $200. That's a trade that is stacked against you. However, if you have a stop-loss at $52.20, your total risk has been limited to $0.80 a share, or $80 in total. You're risking $80 to win $200, which is a reasonable risk/reward level.

Of course, you'll need to make sure that you have correctly identified your profit target." I think it will go up" is not a reason to trade. "I think it will go up *till it hits the next resistance level at $55*" is a quantified and valid reason to trade.

Trades come along every day. Don't get FOMO and don't think you will never get another trade if you miss this one.

Trade management and position sizing

Your trading plan should include a clear statement of the maximum dollar risk you are prepared to accept. Say it's 2% of your portfolio; work out what that is first thing in the morning based on your total cash value. You might want to round it down or write it on a post-it note on your computer so you can remember it easily.

Let's see how many 100%-loss trades would be needed to wipe you out. If you risk 100% of your portfolio, that's easy: just one. If you risk 10% of your portfolio, that's ten. At a 5% position size, it would take 20 losing trades to wipe you out, and at 2%, 50 losing trades in a row. That's why it's a good idea to keep your position size low and never, ever bet the bank.

When you're looking at a trade, you need to estimate your risk per share, that is, the difference between your entry point and the stop loss price. Now, divide your total dollar risk by the risk per share, and you know how many shares you can buy. If I have a total cash value of $25,000, 2% of that is $500. So, looking at the trade I already mentioned, where my risk per share is $0.80, I said I was going to trade 100 shares. But in fact, with a $500 risk maximum, I can trade $500 / 0.80 = 625 shares.

I hate to tell you this, but you need to be able to do this calculation on the fly every time you are setting up a trade. I keep an old-fashioned electronic calculator so that I can do this without taking up real estate on my screens. A friend I know has a ready reckoner for various sizes of stop loss. Other traders do it by mental math. Work out how you're going to do it, and stick to your position sizes - this is what will stop you getting bankrupted by your bad trades.

Managing your money and positions is at the heart of becoming a successful trader in the long term. Every trader will strike a slightly different balance, but you need to be quite clear about the way you will manage your trades.

At the extremes;

• take too much risk, and you could end up bankrupt;

• take too little risk, and you won't make enough money to keep going as a trader.

Somewhere between these two extremes, you should be able to find your sweet spot.

First, find your **expectancy** - the return you expect to make. You'll need to test your trading system to do this, and you are looking for three figures;

• the percentage of winning to losing trades,

• the average percentage loss on losing trades, and

• the average percentage profit on winning trades.

You can then work out your average expected return on every trade. The math is simple: *(your percentage of losing trades x average loss) + (your percentage of winning trades x average profit)*. For example, let's say it comes out at 0.6%, then you'd expect to make 0.6% on every trade you make, on average, over time.

You can also work out your **probability of ruin.** That's a more scientific way of working out how bad a run of a few bad trades can be. Or rather, how bad does it need to be for you to be out of the game for good?

Take your advantage - the difference between your percentage of winning and losing trades. For instance, if you win 55% of the time and lose 45% of the time, your advantage is 10% (55% - 45%).

Then, work out the size of each position in terms of your total account value. Maybe you say you'll never risk more than 10% of your total - and you'll make 10 trades a day at that size. (Why 10? Because the math is easier to do, it's that simple. You might want to do 12 trades a day, or 20...)

Now work out the formula:

(1 - your advantage) / (1 + your advantage), to the power of your position size *divided by* your initial capital.

Yes, it's complicated. In fact, there are quite good tables that will show you the risk of ruin for given combinations of edge and position size.

Win rate	Probability of X consecutive losing trades within a 100 trade sequence									
	1	2	3	4	5	6	7	8	9	10
5%	100%	100%	100%	100%	100%	100%	100%	100%	100%	100%
10%	100%	100%	100%	100%	100%	100%	100%	100%	100%	100%
15%	100%	100%	100%	100%	100%	100%	100%	100%	100%	100%
20%	100%	100%	100%	100%	100%	100%	100%	100%	100%	100%
25%	100%	100%	100%	100%	100%	100%	100%	100%	100%	99%
30%	100%	100%	100%	100%	100%	100%	100%	100%	98%	93%
35%	100%	100%	100%	100%	100%	100%	99%	95%	85%	71%
40%	100%	100%	100%	100%	100%	99%	93%	79%	61%	42%
45%	100%	100%	100%	100%	99%	93%	76%	54%	35%	21%
50%	100%	100%	100%	100%	95%	78%	52%	31%	16%	9%
55%	100%	100%	100%	98%	83%	55%	30%	14%	7%	3%
60%	100%	100%	100%	92%	63%	32%	14%	6%	2%	1%
65%	100%	100%	99%	77%	40%	16%	6%	2%	1%	0%
70%	100%	100%	93%	55%	21%	7%	2%	1%	0%	0%
75%	100%	100%	79%	32%	9%	2%	1%	0%	0%	0%
80%	100%	98%	54%	14%	3%	1%	0%	0%	0%	0%
85%	100%	89%	28%	5%	1%	0%	0%	0%	0%	0%
90%	100%	63%	9%	1%	0%	0%	0%	0%	0%	0%
95%	99%	22%	1%	0%	0%	0%	0%	0%	0%	0%

Have a look at the table above to start your journey. To use the table, you need to know your win rate. Say you have a win rate of 70%, you would run down the left hand 'win rate' column till you get to the row marked 70%. Then, you can read across what is your probability of having a certain number of losing trades in a 100-trade sequence. With this 70% win rate, you actually have 0% chance of having 9 or 10 consecutive losing trades, and only a very small chance (2% and 1%) of 7 or 8 losing trades in a row. However, you would have a 100% chance of having 1 or 2 losing trades in a row though.

Or you can look at risk of ruin for your combination of stake size, win rate and return on your trades. This is a great dose of realism if you are prone to the error of believing that super-profitable trades will let you break even with a poor win rate. And many traders deceive themselves into believing that the next trade will be super profitable!

For instance, at a 10% stake size, the table on the next two pages shows that even with a really high rate of return on winning trades, if your *win ratio* is as low as 15%, you *will* be ruined if you risk a 10% stake size on each trade. (Certainty of ruin has all been highlighted in red. Just track across from 'win ratio 15%' and you will see every single box in the row shows 100% probability of loss.)

If you have a win rate of more than 70%, you do not have any chance at all of being ruined (the winning combinations are in green, indicating a 0% chance).

I suggest you view the table as traffic lights - red = stop trading, and green = carry on!

Win Ratio %	Profit is 1x your stake	Profit is 2x your stake	Profits is 3x your stake	Profit is 4x your stake	Profit is 5x your stake
Win Ratio 10%	100	100	100	100	100
Win Ratio 15%	100	100	100	100	100
Win Ratio 20%	100	100	100	100	46.6
Win Ratio 25%	100	100	100	30.5	16.3
Win Ratio 30%	100	100	27.7	10.2	6.1
Win Ratio 35%	100	60.9	8.2	3.53	2.33
Win Ratio 40%	100	14.2	2.5	1.24	0.888
Win Ratio 45%	100	3.41	0.761	0.426	0.329
Win Ratio 50%	100	0.813	0.226	0.141	0.116
Win Ratio 55%	13.4	0.187	0.0635	0.0438	0

Win Ratio 60%	1.73	0.0401	0	0	0
Win Ratio 65%	0.205	0	0	0	0
Win Ratio 70%	0	0	0	0	0
Win Ratio 75%	0	0	0	0	0
Win Ratio 80%	0	0	0	0	0
Win Ratio 85%	0	0	0	0	0
Win Ratio 90%	0	0	0	0	0

You'll also find a number of risk of ruin calculators on the internet. Those can be really helpful if you are not a math wizard. However, I'm going to take a look at the math to see how it works out. The math for a single trade if you have a 20% advantage, for instance, is: (1 - 0.2 / 1 + 0.2) = (0.8 / 1.2) = 66.67, or rounded to **67%**. (Because your position size is your entire capital, the fraction is 1, so that part of the equation makes no difference.)

On the next page, anyway, is a basic table where you can read off your risk of ruin quite easily. Find your **edge** in the first column downwards, then read across the top row to find your **stake size** as a percentage of your portfolio.

	100 %	50 %	33 %	25 %	20 %	16 %	14 %	12.5 %	11 %	10 %
2%	96	92	89	85	82	79	76	73	70	67
4%	92	85	79	73	67	62	57	53	49	45
6%	89	79	70	62	55	49	43	38	34	30
8%	85	73	62	53	45	38	33	28	24	20
10%	82	67	55	45	37	30	25	20	16	13
12%	79	62	49	38	30	24	18	15	11	9
14%	75	57	43	32	24	18	14	10	8	6
16%	72	52	38	27	20	14	10	8	5	4
18%	69	48	34	23	16	11	8	5	4	3
20%	67	44	30	20	13	9	6	4	3	2

If you risk your whole account on each trade, even with an advantage of 20% (60% win - 40% loss = *20%*), you still have a **67%** probability of ruin.

If you only risk 10% of your account on each trade, even if you have just a 2% advantage (51% - 49% = 2%, meaning that you win 51% of the time), you will have a **67%** probability of ruin than the trader with a 20% edge who risks it all, every time. Have a look at the table on the previous page and see for yourself!

This model assumes that you will lose 100% on all your losing trades, so it is actually a vast overestimate of your chances of bankruptcy. If you use stop losses systematically you should have much lower losses.

This model also assumes that you will put the same amount into every trade you make. In fact, money management should help you do better than the model suggests, and achieve higher returns than your expectancy indicates. A money management system aims to diversify your capital through a number of different trades, rather than betting the bank, and also aims to modify that amount proportionally to the level of volatility in your trading strategy. A good trading software or brokerage will give you an automatic money management calculator, so you don't have to do the math yourself.

Different types of money management system

There are various ways of managing your money. Some are simple, some are complicated, and some are downright dangerous. I have found fixed percentage works fine for me - it's easy to calculate and limits my exposure so that a few bad trades won't do me too much harm.

Fixed ten percent: this was adopted by WD Gann, writer of Wall Street Stock Selector and other texts on the market. It's a simple system, easy to calculate and use. You could use 5% or 2%, if you wanted. Personally, I think 2% is enough! With ten percent, you could lose quite a lot if you have a poor run of trades. However, critics of this system say that it's not very flexible, and it doesn't reflect market conditions.

Fixed-fractional: each trade is limited to a percentage of your account, adjusted for the risk of the trade (what you think you may lose). I dislike this because it lends itself to judgmental fix-ups - that is, you are at risk of infusing emotion into your trades. "I really need to win, so this has to be a low-risk trade, right?" No. Wrong!

The Martingale: doubling down. This money management technique comes to us from the world of the casino, where it improves the winnings from even-odds games like roulette. You start the day with a set amount. If you win, you trade again with the same amount. If you lose, you double the trade. But the problem with this is that it only takes a few losing trades to lose your entire bankroll. I absolutely do not recommend it for day traders. Also, while a casino might give you free drinks and food if you spend enough, the financial markets definitely won't.

The **Optimal-F** system developed by Ralph Vince takes a more sophisticated approach to past performance. It aims to increase your exposure in line with your edge in the market and the risk taken on each trade, as shown in your trading history. In other words, if you win 68% of the time, it will let you take more risk than if you only win 59% of your trades. However, it's a complex system to use - and of course, it won't work until you have a trading history to factor into the system. Most traders regard it as too theoretical for practical use.

The Kelly Criterion, or "edge divided by odds," aims to optimize your position size for your particular combination of winning trades percentage and advantage. However, it can be too aggressive - many traders use *half* the suggested Kelly amount, rather than the whole amount. Remember, too, that even the best traders have the occasional below-par day, in which case the Kelly system could lead to you losing more than with a fixed percentage system.

Protecting profits fixed-ratio system: this is used for trading options and futures, and it tries to balance your desire for exposure to the market with the desire to protect existing profits. The rather complicated formula was developed by options trader Ryan Jones, and it ratchets up the amount you should trade according to the amount of profit you have made *divided* by the amount you need to trade a second contract or lot of stock. This isn't worth it for beginners, but if you become a successful trader you might want to take a look at it to improve the efficiency of your use of capital.

Monte Carlo simulation. This advanced technique works by entering your risk and return requirements, and your account value, and running a software program which will tell you your optimal size of position. Where it scores over other ways of deciding the size of your stakes is that it adjusts to conditions in the market in a dynamic way. If you want to use the Monte Carlo simulation, you'll need to ensure you have access to the simulation package, either through your broker or with stand-alone software. It is *impossible* to calculate manually.

You will also need to think about what to do with your trading profits. If you are day trading as your full-time job, evidently you'll be using at least part of your profits as income to live on. But you might also decide to keep profits in your account, so that you can gradually increase the amount you trade. If you maintain your edge and your trading patterns, you'll then be able to increase your profits, too.

Another possibility is to skim off some trading profits from time to time, and put them into longer term assets. You might choose to keep a good slug of your money in low risk investments such as CD ladders, or to invest in stocks for long term capital growth. The return on these assets won't be as exciting as the return on your trading portfolio, but it should be more predictable, and take much less work. You can even set up an automatic plan with your brokerage firm to automatically move a percentage of your trading funds into another account every month or every quarter.

The principle of compounding

If you keep increasing the amount you trade in line with the increase in your cash available, the principle of compounding will come into play. Every time you increase your position size, if you keep the same win ratio and edge, you will increase your profits; and they will go back into your trading account where you can use them to make even more money.

However, there's one technique that seems superficially a bit like compounding, but is very dangerous. That's pyramiding - borrowing against your unrealized profits during the day. It can work, increasing your exposure in a rising market, but it increases your risk. If you use too much leverage and the market turns against you the whole house of cards can come tumbling down. Ensure, if you do use pyramiding - and it's a perfectly valid technique - that you have enough left to stay in the market even if your trades collapsed.

Managing the risks of day trading

Don't forget that besides the risks of day trading, you also run generic business risks and personal risks.

A major business risk is not having enough cash set aside to cover your taxes. It is a really good idea to set up a separate cash account and feed it as you go with your estimated tax on your profits. That way, you should always have enough, and if you've over-estimated, you can pay yourself a bonus.

You also need to ensure that you can keep control of your cash flow. This will need attention outside of trading hours. You will have subscriptions to pay, internet charges and office rent. Keep track of your expenses with a decent budgeting program.

There are also personal risks. It's very easy to get pulled into a negative spiral, getting addicted to the next trade (careful, you're not a gambler), or getting worried and anxious about the market. When your job takes over the rest of your life, 24/7, you need to worry. Being a good trader, you'll need to manage your emotions. Sometimes, the only way to do it is to lock the office up for the day and go to the park, or take a good long walk.

Sometimes, you can end up just feeling paralyzed, literally unable to hit your hotkeys. You can get overwhelmed. Learn to recognize that feeling, and don't trade while you're feeling that way. It usually means you've pushed outside your comfort zone by trying something new or scaling up your position size, so get back to basics, scale down your trades, and get your calm back before you re-enter the market. You need to be calm, you need to be focused, and you need to be in control of yourself.

Because you can't, ever, control the market.

Risk and fear in trading

Don't trade to make money; trade to *trade well*. Don't focus on the money, but on the perfect setup and execution of your trades. If you do this, and you have a good trading strategy, the money will look after itself.

When you begin trading, start small. When I began to drive, my father drove me to a block way out of town in an industrial area, on a Saturday, and got me to just drive around the block. In first gear. It took half an hour. Then we did it in second gear. Then we did it the next Saturday. There was no other traffic to bug me, so all I had to do was concentrate on starting, stopping, and making smooth gear changes. (Letting me drive an automatic would have been way too easy for my Dad. Manual stick shift was obligatory.) By the time I got on the road and had to look out for other traffic, I was pretty confident about the job of driving, and I could switch my attention to navigating multiple lanes safely.

So start with small trades. Start with just one trade at a time and just one strategy. Get used to that strategy. Get used to the speed of the market. Focus on a single time frame, too - don't chop and change between two-minute trades and longer-term trades. Sharpen your reflexes. Stay calm and focused. When you're ready, you can take on two trades at the same time, or use a new strategy. If you bite off more than you can chew, just clear your mind, and go back to what you were doing before.

Risk management

Some people will tell you "day trading is risky." (Remember that risk is something that needs to be quantified? So there is no such thing as "risky.")

In fact, every day trader decides their own preferred level of risk. You are the one who decides the risk-reward ratio for your trades. You are the one who decides how much value you will risk in each trade - two percent, or ten percent, say, of your total trading book. (I really do not advise 100%. You may not last very long as a trader with that strategy.) You also reduce your risk by not leaving any positions open overnight. You are only at risk when your positions are open.

If you simply buy 100 MSFT at $420, that's a $42,000 trade you are risking. However, if you put a stop loss at $415, you have limited your risk to $5 a share, or $500 in total ($5 x 100 shares). If you're expecting at least $7.50 in profit if the trade wins, that's $750 profit. You are risking $5 to get $7.50, or in other words "risking two to get three," which is a reasonably conservative measure of risk.

Chapter 8 Quiz

1. Which of these statements is true?
   a) You will lose some of your trades
   b) You will only lose trades if you take too much risk
   c) You must win more than 50% of your trades to make money
   d) You must have a 5:1 risk/reward ratio to make money

2. If you lose half your money on a trade, and reinvest what's left, how much do you need to make to get back to where you were before?
   a) You need to make 10%
   b) You need to make 50%
   c) You need to triple your money
   d) You need to double your money

3. If you buy 500 shares in Agglomerated Widgets for $10, with a stop loss of $9, your total risk is:
   a) $500
   b) $5,000
   c) $2,500
   d) Zero

4. What is the probability of ruin?
   a) Sixty percent
   b) The likelihood that a number of bad trades could bankrupt you
   c) Unlimited
   d) Another way of describing credit default

5. Which of these is not a money management system?
   a) Monte Carlo Simulation
   b) Kelly Criterion
   c) Martingale
   d) Vegas Twist

9

Chapter 9: Determining Your Profit and Your Profit Potential

Before you trade - testing your system

Even before you trade, you want to work out what profit your trading system *would have made* if you'd been using it for a while. You have identified the assets you want to trade, and the strategies you want to use. Now is the time to back-test them.

Even if you are using a system that someone else has created, it's important to backtest it. It might have worked ten years ago but isn't so good now, because markets have changed. For instance, there are more automatic trades going through - that has reduced the profitability of some types of trades. It might not work at all! Or it might work, but you need to assure yourself of that fact, and try to understand why and how the system works so that you know, when you get more experience, how you might refine it.

Even before back-testing, you can run a quick viability test. Look at yesterday's chart and see how many trades the system signaled. You might then look back a couple of weeks. Five or six trades is pretty reasonable. If it's only signaling one trade a day, it's not going to make you a living (at least, not on its own); and if it signals hundreds, you'll be run off your feet and probably end up making expensive mistakes.

You also need to check out the level of risk - that is, the difference between the entry price and the stop-loss, compared to the potential profit. Some traders' systems look great until you consider the risks they're running. If the system generates the right number of trades *and* it runs acceptable risks, then it's time to backtest it.

Backtesting uses software to run your strategy against historical price records for the assets you want to trade. You will have to be quite specific about your trading rules: "When I kind of think there's a bit of upwards momentum" *won't* work. "When a stock price in a downtrend reverses to move up by more than 0.5% with volume more than the normal level" *will* work and is the kind of strategy the computer can run for backtesting. Equally, "range trading big caps" is not quite specific enough; "buying AAPL when it hits a resistance level" is a better formulated strategy.

You may want to see what happens if you add more leverage, or make more but smaller trades. You may find that your strategy works with some stocks but not others: for instance, Tesla trades very differently from Microsoft, as it's more news-driven and volatile, so a range-trading strategy that works for Microsoft might not work for Tesla.

If your strategy doesn't work when you back-test it, think about why. You might need to refine the strategy; adding trading volume as well as price movement sometimes reduces the number of losing trades. You might add a tighter stop loss. Think about the idea behind your strategy; does the backtesting result mean that the idea is wrong, or have you missed out an important element of selection for your trades?

Most backtesting software can run an optimization program. This can suggest the best position size, holding period, and amount of leverage for your trading strategy. But be careful not to overcomplicate your strategy. Over-optimization is when you add so many variables that you're turning away profitable trades - it fits the historic data terrifically well, but what you've done is model a strategy that fits that data, rather than a strategy that will work in future as well. It's always difficult to know when you've moved from refining your strategy to over-optimization, but good traders and data analysts get a feel for it.

Remember to backtest your strategy to see how it does in different markets. A strategy that worked well in 2000 as the tech market boomed might not have worked in 2007 as the financial crisis hit. A strategy that works in range-bound markets may not work so well in more volatile markets. Consider periods of economic growth versus recession, high versus low inflation; does the strategy work for both?

Once you've backtested, it's time to start simulation - trading on paper, or 'ghost trading'. Use your strategy, but just write down your trades rather than actually doing them. Some brokers, like eToro and Interactive Brokers, provide simulation packages online, which cuts a lot of the paperwork out and feels more like real trading. Simulation will show you whether your ideas will work out, except for one small weakness; they can't show whether you would have been able to fill your orders. If you're trading small positions in mega cap stocks, probably this won't matter, but in some other markets it could mean your simulation will show better results than you'll get in reality.

Don't hurry this process. It could take you months to find the right strategy and refine it so that it works well. But this investment of time will pay dividends later. Skimp it, and you could get suboptimal returns, which is a nice way of saying you could lose a lot of money quite fast.

Tracking your trades

The simplest way of tracking your trades is simply to use a spreadsheet that shows the asset, date and time traded, price, quantity, and commission, together with the risk taken, and the same data for the close-out, with a final column showing your profit or loss and percentage return on the risk. Also, add a column with W or L for win or loss. This makes tracking your win/loss ratio easier. However, this can be cumbersome for frequent traders, so you might consider purpose made software such as Tradezella or TraderSync.

You also need to daily track your win/loss ratio and your trading profit as a percentage of your trading capital. This is your daily business dashboard. You can also convert your daily profit into "salary"; that is, trading profit divided by the hours you worked. (If it ends up less than $7.25, you're working for less than minimum wage at the moment. How do you feel about that?)

As well as just tracking the numbers, you need to track the qualitative side of your trades. Why did you make each trade? How did you feel about it - confident, or worried? Do you think you closed out too quickly, or not quickly enough? Were you following your system, or a hunch, or trading on news? Even if you're busy trading, scribble something down on a sheet of paper and look back at it at the end of the day before writing up your diary. Trade journaling software makes this part of the process easier.

Calculating overall performance

In an ideal world, you'd start with $25,000 say on January 1st, and you'd trade with that $25,000 all the way through to December 31st without taking any money out, or adding any extra capital, and calculating your annual performance would be real easy.

In fact, you're likely to have taken a bit out of the trading fund as downpayment on a new car, or added a bit when your tax refund came through. That complicates matters. And you also want to know not just how much profit you made, but how much risk you needed to take on to get there (that is, your volatility). So, there are quite a few ways to work out your return.

CAGR, or compound annual growth rate is a time-weighted average, calculated by taking your trading profit as a percentage of the average of your beginning of year capital (B) and end of year capital (E). The formula is $(E - B) \times ([E + B] / 2)$. This is your trading return; you need to ensure it covers your office and other costs!

So, for instance, if you trade for a year on $100,000 starting capital and your trading capital is $125,000 at the end of the year, you'll want to calculate your trading return *($125,000 - $100,000)* = ***$25,000*** as a percentage of *([$100,000 + $125,000] / 2)* = ***$112,500.***

So your CAGR is *$25,000 / $112,500 = 22.2%.*

Using your starting capital of $100,000 would have given you a return of *25%*, which is unrealistically high. That is $25,000 / $100,000 = 25%.

However, if you pay yourself a salary out of your account, that diminishes your trading pool. Or if you add capital once you feel more confident, that increases your trading pool. You'll need to find a way of making allowances for additions and withdrawals, or your performance won't be accurately shown. There are various ways of doing this.

The **Simple Dietz method** is the simplest way to do it. You simply adjust the beginning and ending amounts for cash inflows and outflows. The trading profit is shown *less* deposits and *plus* withdrawals, while your trading capital is shown *plus* deposits and *minus* withdrawals. It's really easy to calculate. However, it isn't particularly accurate, because it doesn't allow for the timing of cash flows.

So suppose you have the same figures as the CAGR example before, except that you took out $1,000 for a downpayment on a new car, and added $5,000 out of savings later on. Your trading profit is now shown as $25,000 *less* $5,000 deposit and *plus* $1,000 withdrawals = *$21,000*.

You calculate this on your starting capital adjusted for changes. That is, $100,000, adjusted for *half* the inflows and outflows. Assuming, it happened half way through the year - though of course that might not be true!

In other words, *less* $1,000 withdrawn and *plus* $5,000 added gives us $4,000 net, and we take half of this which is *$2,000* to add to the starting capital of $100,000, giving us *$102,000* total capital.

The rate of return is *$21,000 / $102,000 = 20.5%*.

The **Modified Dietz Method** is more complicated and aims to solve the problem of just assuming that all your withdrawals and additions happen halfway through the year. Each cash flow event is multiplied by a time factor, so that your starting capital is adjusted by:

$$[(T - t) / T] \times (CF \times t)$$

Where T is the total time period (e.g. 12 months) and t is the time of the cash flow (e.g. 6, for June, 10 for October and so on). If, from this, you have got the idea that Modified Dietz is somewhat clunky to use, you would be right. However, Wikipedia conveniently supplies an Excel VBA file that you can use to automate the calculation.

To get an even more accurate idea you could use a **time-weighted rate of return.** You divide the year into different periods, with a new period beginning every time you increase or decrease your trading capital. You then calculate the CAGR for each individual time period, then those returns are multiplied to arrive at the CAGR for the year as a whole. It gives you a much more accurate idea of your profitability, but the math is complex. Fortunately, you can use apps and websites like **https://www.rateofreturnexpert.com/time-weighted-return-calculator** to do it for you automatically.

Another way of calculating returns is the **dollar-weighted rate of return**, but while it works for investors, it's not really useful for traders because it can't deal with large negative values. In the nature of things, traders quite often do have a negative return for a day, a week, or possibly a month or two - rarely, but occasionally even for a year.

What risk did you run to get this return?

You might think $100,000 is a lot of money. But if I asked you to play Russian roulette with a gun with five chambers loaded and one empty, you might think it's not a lot of money compared to the risk of losing your life. In trading, things are less extreme, but that's a vivid example of why you can't get useful information from looking at returns without considering the risks that you took on in order to get those returns.

The win/loss percentage is one way of assessing whether your risk level is appropriate. A stable percentage of winning trades is a good sign; a handful of big wins making up for long losing streaks is not. It's a good idea to use standard deviation to check on your performance. This will show how much your monthly or daily performance varies from your average. Almost all trading software will now do this automatically for you, but the steps are quite simple if you use a spreadsheet;

• find your *average* return over the period, let's say 10%,

• subtract the *average* from each daily return (so if you made 25% today, that would be *25% - 10% = 15%*. If you made 5% today, that would be *5% - 10% = minus 5%*, for instance),

• square the *differences* you found (this will cancel out and get rid of all the negative numbers, e.g. -5 x -5 = 25),

• add these numbers to get the *sum of the squares*,

• and finally, calculate the *square root* ($\sqrt{\ }$) of the sum of the squares, to get the *standard deviation*.

The sum of the squares will be higher, the more diverse your returns. If every day, day in, day out, you made a 10% return, then your difference every day would be zero and the squares would be zero, and the sum of the squares would be zero, and the standard deviation would be zero. This is, of course, never actually going to happen. If you are taking 11% some days and 9% others, your difference to your average 10% will only be 1, and 1 squared is 1, and the square root of one is one... However, more likely your differences on both sides will be more significant, and the larger they are, the larger your standard deviation.

A high standard deviation, that is, very widely varying daily or monthly performances, suggests you are taking on a relatively large amount of risk. A low standard deviation usually correlates to a less risky trading strategy. In fact, it's useful to know the standard deviation of a strategy you've backtested, because even if it works out, it might have a higher level of risk than you feel comfortable with.

This may sound quite theoretical, so let's just consider a very simple history of *five days* of trading by two traders. Both Albert and Barbara have an *average* return of 10%, but their day-to-day experience is a bit different.

Albert is incredibly steady, scoring daily returns of 10%, 12%, 8%, 9% and 11%.

Barbara has good and bad days - 20% up, 20% down, 25% up, 10% down, and finally pulling the iron out of the fire with an amazing 35% up return on the fifth day.

Remember, we are calculating the difference to their average return of 10%. So calculating the differences for Albert; 0 on day 1, when he makes exactly his average return of 10%; then +2 when he makes 12%, -2 when he makes 8%, -1 when he makes 9% and +1 when he makes 11%.

What about Barbara? When she makes 20%, take 10 from 20 and you get a difference of +10. The next day, she's *down* 20%, though, the difference between 10 and -20 is -30. Day after she's *up* 25%, take 10 from 25 and you get a difference of +15. Then she's *down* 10% the next day, so that's 10 and -10 which is a -20 difference. And finally, after the amazing fifth day, she's *up* 35%, so take the difference between 10 and 35, and you get +25.

Now, to get the squares, just multiply each number by itself (that is, each *difference* by itself) and then add them all together. This is where there's a really huge difference.

Albert: $(0x0 + 2x2 + 2x2 + 1x1 + 1x1) = (0 + 4 + 4 + 1 + 1) =$ **10**

Barbara: $(10x10 + 30x30 + 15x15 + 20x20 + 25x25) = (100 + 900 + 225 + 400 + 625) =$ **2250**

Albert gets a total of 10. Barbara gets a total of 2250!

The *square root* of 10 is 3.16, and that is the *standard deviation* of Albert's performance.

On the other hand, Barbara has a standard deviation of 47.43 (square root of 2250). You can probably have a guess at their different styles of trading from those figures.

Investors usually compare their performance with a relevant benchmark, such as the S&P 500. They want to know that they are getting returns that compare well with the market. However, there is no central benchmark of trading performance. You might look at how EToro's top traders are doing as EToro has a 'copy trader' program which lets you copy their trades. However, they are swing traders and investors for the most part, not day traders.

Having a winning market mentality

All good athletes will tell you that to get top performance, they need to use their heads as well as their muscles. Golfers will visualize their swing before they take it; marathon runners do less running in the last week before the race, but spend a lot of time thinking through the race, dividing it into smaller sections and setting their goals for those.

Traders are just the same. To trade really well, you don't just need stock quotes and scanners and screens and charts and a methodology, you need to have your head in the right place. You need to be cool enough that if there isn't a good trade you can see anywhere, you say, "Okay, it's not a good time to trade." A bad trader, on the other hand, will lower their expectations and take a trade that has a very poor risk/reward ratio just to feel that they've done *something*. Have the discipline to wait till the good trades appear.

Don't get careless. You may think it's crazy, but I still talk myself through my trades, or more accurately, mumble myself through my trades. It means that I have to have a proper game plan, with entry and exit points, stop-loss, and a quantified risk ratio. It also makes it much, much more difficult to lie to myself about the trade. (Bad traders do that a lot.)

I *never* calculate what I'm making on a trade, except when I calculate the risk/reward ratio right at the start. I might make $20 and I might make $200, but my focus is on getting the trade right and protecting my downside. Treat the market as if it's a horse and you're a horse whisperer - be patient and let it come to you. If you start thinking about the money, and cheering the share price on, you're getting emotionally involved - and you're going to start lying to yourself.

Don't beat yourself up if you make a losing trade or a mistake. Think it through rationally - is there something you could and should have done differently? Did you protect the downside? - and then just let it go and move on to the next trade.

Keep yourself grounded, and you'll be a much better trader. No greed, no fear, no brain fog or panic - if that's you, you're already ahead of 90% of other traders.

Chapter 9 Quiz

1. How do you know your strategy will work?
   a) It was recommended by a well-known, successful trader
   b) You backtested it thoroughly
   c) All the times you have seen this pattern, the trade was successful
   d) You can't

2. When should you not trade?
   a) When you are feeling panicky
   b) When you can't see a trade that fits your strategy
   c) When you are feeling angry about a losing trade
   d) When you are hung over

3. What does the standard deviation of your returns tell you?
   a) How much money you are making on each trade
   b) How much overall return you are making
   c) How much risk you are taking to make your return
   d) The average beta of the stocks you traded

4. Why might 'paper trading' or simulation not produce accurate results?
   a) Because your emotions aren't fully engaged
   b) Because it doesn't allow for currency exchange
   c) Because the software is unreliable
   d) Because your orders might not have been able to be filled in real life

5. Which of these is not a way of calculating your return over time?
   a) The Modified Dietz
   b) The Bourne Ultimatum
   c) Dollar weighted rate of return
   d) CAGR

10

Chapter 10: Good Traders Make Good Losses

Is there such a thing as 'good' losses? Yes, there is - a good loss is one that stops you from making a bigger loss. In other words, it's a loss that you defined before you made the trade, and that you controlled successfully.

A 'good' loss is also one that you learn from. You might learn that you're doing the right thing, that you entered and stopped the trade correctly and it was simply one of the times the odds weren't on your side. Or you might learn that you need to check confirmation, that a certain trade is becoming less profitable, or that you were too optimistic going into the trade.

In order to learn from your losses, you need to write down every time you win *or* lose a trade, what happened; why you entered the trade; what happened; what you will do next time. Write it down. Don't just think about it, write it down. That stops you forgetting what you've learned.

You're also going to write your trades down so that you can cut those bad trading emotions - over-confidence (when you win) and fear and panic (when you lose). Once the trade is written down, you've written it *out* of your mind. You can turn the page - quite literally.

What could you do differently next time? Sometimes, nothing. You entered a trade, everything was correct, unexpected news flipped the stock price and you got stopped out correctly with a small loss. You just need to accept that sometimes things don't work out.

Sometimes, the price goes through your stop-loss order and you can't manage to exit the stock at your stop-loss price. In this case, you really need to go for what you can get - even if it's a lower price. Otherwise, you're like the guy who, when his taxi driver drove off a cliff, asked, "At least stop the meter, can't you?"

Sometimes, you recognize that you got greedy. You hung on for a bit more after the stock hit your profit target, and then it fell back again. You get out, if you're lucky, with a small profit - more likely, after it's passed through your buy price and hit your stop-loss. So next time, the one thing you'll do that's different is that you will sell, or sell part of your position, or set a trailing stop-loss, when you hit the price target. Any of these actions would prevent you getting greedy and forgetting the basic reason why you're in the trade.

Another sign of greediness is buying into stocks that are going up real fast. That's particularly the case if they're being bid up by being tipped on a finance TV show or by chatroom or social media interest. It's always good to see a strong upward trend, but stocks that are going too fast, where the trendline is beginning to look more like a space rocket than a Boeing 747 taking off, are riding for a fall. What would you do differently next time?

Maybe, in this case, you bought on emotion, without taking the time to analyze the chart and set a target price and stop loss. Maybe you bottled out of taking your stop-loss, only to see the stock plunge even further. So next time, you quiet your emotions long enough to do proper analysis, and if you've got things wrong, you take your medicine and activate your stop-loss.

Did you get careless? Placing a market order and getting filled at a price that was too high to make a profit? Did you get distracted by a delivery or something on TV, and then the market went against you? Your losses are telling you that you need to smarten up your act. You need to concentrate more, and if you want to wander off and watch daytime TV, then at least close your positions first. Or maybe you worked out the position size wrong and took too much risk. Maybe you bought 1000 shares when you meant 100. It's been done before.

Good losses are small losses

How do you keep losses small? By risk management. By taking the right size of position and giving your trade a tight stop loss. By discipline. And by not taking it personally.

Be good at being wrong!

Trading is not like running in a race, when you have to come first or you lose. It's like playing baseball. You might hit a home run, you might get to first base. You might get one of your team home who is already on third base. The more you hit, the more your team scores. You just have to keep hitting. And there's no strike out in trading!

However, I will suggest that you might want to take time out if you have three losing trades in a row, or if you lose more than $1,500 (or whatever number makes sense in terms of your particular account value). Do this *mechanically* and make it into a trading rule, because so often we say to ourselves, "I am not angry! I am not emotional!" when actually, we're just a fiery little ball of rage after a couple of trades went bad. If you invoke the time out rule, you won't be able to lie to yourself, and you won't be able to lose any more money trying to make back what you've already lost.

Remind yourself that good traders can and do lose trades. If you ask successful traders their win/loss ratio, they'll often tell you, and it often will be quite moderate, like 60-70%. That means they're losing a third of the time or more. How can they be successful with that win rate? Because their profits make significantly more money than their losses lose.

This is why you need to learn to love a 'good' loss; one executed neatly and in line with your original trading plan, and that minimizes your risk level and the negative impact of a run of bad trades. Never, ever, double down. That's a viable plan for investors who can buy a stock when it's down and wait two or three years; maybe they're even getting paid good dividends while they wait. It is not a viable plan for traders - it increases your risk.

A loss taken is a risk avoided. I know the proverb is "Never *catch* a falling knife," but trying to hold on to a falling knife is equally painful.

And to finish this chapter, let's read a boxing quote which resonates with this chapter beautifully.

"Even the greatest all lost and came back. That's just part of it." Deontay Wilder after his loss to Tyson Fury in the world heavyweight championship bout.

<u>Chapter 10 Quiz</u>

1. What is a 'good' loss?
    a) One that is less than 2% of your portfolio
    b) One that you stop lossed out correctly
    c) One that doesn't bankrupt you
    d) One that is less than 10% of the risk taken

2. Which of these might lead to your losing money on a trade?
    a) Greed
    b) Over-confidence
    c) Carelessness
    d) Fear

3. How can you keep losses small?
    a) Manage your money correctly
    b) Use leverage
    c) Use stop losses with discipline
    d) Only trade small cap stocks

4. What can you learn from your losses?
    a) Whether you tend to be too optimistic
    b) Whether a certain type of trade is becoming less productive
    c) Whether you get distracted too often
    d) Whether Goldman Sachs is making money

5. Which of these is something you'd want to record about a losing trade?
    a) The price you bought at
    b) How you felt at the time
    c) Whether in retrospect you made an obvious mistake (e.g. not looking for confirmation before trading)
    d) What the market was doing at the time

11

Chapter 11: Strategies that Work

A strategy for getting started

Some people jump into trading. But it may be best, at first, to ease into trading, gently.

If, for the first couple of days, you just focus on watching a single stock, you can learn a lot about the market in a very concentrated way. You might just spend half an hour a day, till you are able to stay focused for that length of time, and then increase it - don't risk being zoned out because you're trying to concentrate for too long. Catch the open, stick around for half an hour, and you will start learning fast. Trading is a bit like meditation, it takes practice to keep your mind in the right place for more than a couple of minutes!

Track how your stock opens, whether there's a breakout or a reversal. Track the trading volumes. Extend your time till you can watch that stock all day, from the open to the close; what happens as the market comes up to the close and traders need to settle their positions?

Check how the stock trades against its sector index or against the market. Check how it trades against another leading stock in its sector, for instance Realty Income against WJ Carey, Apple against Microsoft, KO against PEP. (If you don't know that last pair of tickers, look them up.)

And at the same time as you're watching the stock on the screens, you want to be flicking between different time period charts, looking to see how it's been behaving over the last month, three months, the last year. Ascertain the trendlines and important support and resistance levels.

Write down, or voice record, everything you notice. The aim isn't to sit there passively, it's to get into the rhythm of the market and learn to spot signals that the share price is going to behave in a particular way. Once you're ready, just *think* about doing that first trade. Think through the set-up, or even better, talk yourself through it aloud; your target price, your stop-loss level, your total risk, and what will be the confirmation that you need to trade, for instance, a doji or a five-minute close above the resistance level.

And then you can trade if you want to, on paper or for real. No hurry. Because you have used this trade to talk through the process, without necessarily having to trade, you'll keep calm; no pressure. This is the way you want to feel every time you trade. Observe how the trade plays out, but don't get hung up on it. It's just one trade. I have done thousands.

Separately from this exercise, remember to do your practice on the keyboard. Practice those hotkeys and practice setting up orders. That will also help to de-stress real trading and ensure your fingers are as fast as your mind. Let's now look at a few tried and tested strategies for day trading successfully.

ABCD

This really is as easy as ABC!

The ABCD setup consists of four reversal points, making the chart pattern look like a slanted W or a bolt of lightning. It can work for long or short trades. I'll describe it for long trades since if you're starting out in day trading, your broker may not let you short a stock.

You're looking for a stock that has hit a significant high at A. Scanning for stocks hitting new highs will give you your basic watch list here.

You then watch as the stock falls to B.

It then bounces up to C, but not quite all the way back to A. This is where it meets resistance and falls again to D, which is a bit lower than B.

At D, you're looking to buy for another reversal.

An example is shown on the next page, but the perfect ABCD conforms to a number of criteria.

• It starts with a significant swing high or low (A to B).

• The countertrend (B to C) only partially retraces the first leg of the pattern. It's always the shortest leg in the pattern.

• The resumed trend leg (C to D) should be the same length as the first leg (A to B). This symmetry is important.

• In a downtrend, point C must be below point A (and in an uptrend point C must be above point A) - if the price falls all the way back to point A, you don't have an ABCD pattern.

• And finally, point D must be a new price high or low compared to B.

You then buy at D, looking for a bullish reversal. Look for confirmation from breached resistance levels, a bullish formation in the candlestick chart (e.g. a hammer doji).

Your stop loss should be set just below D, and your price target is C. Sometimes, with a strong overall bullish trend, the price may continue up, so lighten your position at C by taking out your initial investment, but run the rest of the position until you see a bearish signal or the price breaks to the downside of the bullish trendline.

The nice thing about ABCD is it can happen twice in the same stock on the same day. The second pattern will probably be a bit smaller, and on lower volume, but you can still make money out of it.

Gap and Go

To play Gap and Go, you need to scan for stocks that have gapped up strongly in pre-market trading. This strategy works really well on stocks in the $10-20 price range and that have relatively limited float. You need to see volume, and you need to check out that there's a fundamental reason behind the move, like an earnings release. The higher the volume and the faster the price movement, the better the opportunity.

SCWorx Corp., 5, NASDAQ O3.06 H3.07 L3.04 C3.04 -0.02 (-0.65%)
Vol 3.722 K

Look how SCWorx Corp traded after gapping up, with very high volumes. Although it saw a pullback half way through the run, you would not have missed the boat even if you had bought in late, at $3. The stock ran all the way to $4 before it ran out of steam.

Get your orders ready, because timing is everything with this strategy. The first one-minute candlestick sets your price range. You'll need your charting frequency set at one minute for this trade and yes, you'd be right that I forgot that when I plugged in this chart. The top is your entry price, and the bottom is your stop. And in you jump!

If you miss your first chance at Gap and Go, wait for a pullback - to give you a second chance. If you're not an experienced trader, it will be a more relaxed trade than trying to hit the market open. Look at the pullback to just below $3 - if you had missed the first chance to buy in, this still gives you the entry to the Gap & Go trade.

There is also a slightly later third chance. You *might* have traded from those two green candlesticks just after 16:30, marking the end of a consolidation period, and running from $3.10 to $3.50 or so. But this is not such a great trade and I probably wouldn't have taken it, particularly because there was very little trading volume behind it.

Fallen angel

This is a variant on Gap and Go, and is another trade for market open. The fallen angel stock makes a new high in early trading, but then sells off quickly, on high volume (the trading volume is important for this trade).

Watch the stock. It might carry on downwards, in which case, leave it well alone. But if it consolidates, and holds a support level (such as the low of the pre-market, the 5-day moving average), keep watching until you get confirmation. Confirmation for your trade is high volume again combined with a new one-minute high. If you get the high but without the volume, don't bother with the trade.

Like Gap and Go, this strategy works for low-float stocks but probably won't work for big caps. There are too many high-frequency trading programs involved with the big caps and their computer algorithms will get there before you do. And even with low-float stocks, it is a trade that you should only use once you have some experience, because the drops can be quite fast, as well as the run-ups.

VWAP Trading

Institutional traders who are working for the big banks are often judged by the relationship of their trades to VWAP - the volume weighted average price. Since they have to trade very large blocks of stock, they often have to do so gradually. VWAP, being adjusted for volume, is a better benchmark for them than the unadjusted price index, in which a small trade might have been done for a better price. So the big institutional traders always look to buy or sell close to the VWAP - and that's interesting information for day traders, because it sets up a pattern that can be used to predict price actions.

If a stock tests the VWAP, then one of two situations is likely to happen.

1. Nothing much, because there is no big institution wanting to buy or sell in high volume.

2. A breakout, because a big trader is buying, or breakdown, because they have a line of stock they want to get rid of.

Obviously, you want to get situation 2, but the fact that the alternative is 'nothing much' limits your downside if the trade doesn't work out.

Suppose a stock moves up in early trading, then falls back, with good volume, I'm going to watch the VWAP. If the chart confirms that the stock has found support from the VWAP, then I will go long. A confirmation means it has to have touched the VWAP and bounced off it *twice*. You're looking for candlesticks standing with their tails on the VWAP. If nothing much happens, I can get out. If I get a breakout, I'm ahead.

Alternatively, VWAP might tell you to go short. If a stock has fallen, then moves up, but just hits the VWAP, finding resistance, going short will keep you in the continued downward trend.

So, in the chart below, you can see the stock flattens out at the top, and then suddenly falls very fast. It then seems to consolidate and even moves upwards a little, but it still doesn't manage to break through the VWAP (the red line) to the upside - in fact, it doesn't even get close. When it begins to fall again, as you can see from the line downwards of red candlesticks, you can go short for the continuation of the downturn.

Trade the TRIN

You can run a stock chart with the TICK or TRIN indicator shown at the bottom of the chart. These indexes track rises against declines in stocks traded on NYSE and Nasdaq, respectively. Remember, the 'trading indicator' represents advances *divided* by declines, relative to advance volumes *divided* by decline volumes. If it's less than 1, the buyers are winning, and if it's above 1, the sellers are winning. Extreme levels are often an indication of a reversal. So, by putting your individual stock against the TRIN, you get a feeling of how it is performing compared to the market.

Alternatively, if your charting package doesn't let you do this, then just run the TRIN in a separate window.

The best trade is quite tricky to explain but easy to execute. First, you look for an extreme high in the TRIN, which often (though not always) indicates a fall in prices is likely. This then has to be confirmed by a pronounced fall in the stock price. Third, you look at the Bollinger Bands for your stock. If the stock price tests the lower edge of the bands *but it doesn't go through the band,* but instead it starts to rise again, go long on the stock at this point with a stop loss very slightly below the band.

Run this trade with large stocks like Apple and Amazon. It doesn't really work with smaller caps. In fact, it's one of the few trades that really does work with the big gorilla stocks.

Why does it work? Because you have identified a market in which advances are outnumbering declines, a bullish market, and an uptrend. With the fall in price you have identified a pullback within that uptrend. When the pullback doesn't break through the Bollinger Bands, you've found a good probability that the uptrend will continue.

ORB - Opening Range Breakout

Before the open, search for stocks that gapped up or down yesterday. This will bring out some investors who look at the movement and want to take a profit. For instance, a stock that was *up* 15% yesterday on good results might see plenty of holders wanting to sell at the open.

Wait out the first five minutes, and then pull up the five-minute candlestick. It may well be a very long 'pole' if the stock has traded up or down hard. Now, you simply wait for a candlestick to break out of the range represented by the *body* (not the wick or tail) of that candlestick. If it breaks downwards, enter a short trade; if it breaks upwards, buy the shares. Your profit target is the next key level, but you should also exit the trade if there is a new 5-minute low.

Alternatively, keep a watch on the opening trend, if it's all in bearish candlesticks, and wait till you see the first bullish candlestick.

Doing your R&D

It's important that you keep refining your techniques. Markets change, and you may find that trades become less profitable over time, or that there's less liquidity in the markets you've been trading. Keep monitoring your results, and keep checking how you are doing.

You should also make time every month to do something to advance your knowledge. Buy a new book on advanced trading techniques, find some good YouTube videos to watch (there are some very bad ones out there, so be careful to get recommendations), or do some intensive work on charting techniques and technical indicators.

You can also analyze your previous trades to see what characterizes your best and worst trades, and where you make the most money. For instance, you may find that you're getting the best results from trading a particular type of setup, or during the first hour of trading. You might even find that all your afternoon trades are losing you money, or that you're making almost nothing on your bull flag trades but a whole load of money on head and shoulders patterns. A small fine-tuning can bring in a whole lot more profit.

You may also find that certain strategies play out best at different times of day. Gap-and-Go and Opening Range Breakout of course have to be played at the open, but trading with the trend tends to work better in the afternoon, for instance.

Chapter 11 Quiz

1. Why do you need to practise your keyboard skills?
   a) To enter trades accurately
   b) To enter trades quickly
   c) To de-stress the process of order placement
   d) So you can get a typist job if it all goes wrong

2. Which of these is not a trading strategy?
   a) Gap & Go
   b) Wash & Go
   c) VWAP trading
   d) Fallen angel

3. Which of these isn't something you need to track continuously?
   a) Support and resistance lines
   b) How a stock opens
   c) Trading volumes
   d) The interest rate

4. Gap & Go is a strategy that works
   a) At the market open
   b) At the market close
   c) Only when a company has results that day
   d) Only when a company had results yesterday

5. ORB stands for:
   a) One-off Reversal Breakout
   b) Opening Range Breakout
   c) Official Record of Bankruptcy
   d) Objective Range of Beta

12

Chapter 12: Top Tips for Each Aspect of Day Trading

The top rookie mistakes

1. Starting day trading without a defined and backtested trading strategy. That's gambling, and it's likely to fail.

2. Not writing a business plan and having detailed goals. Trading is a business and it needs to be treated as one.

3. Not having risk management systems such stop losses and daily close-outs, or not being disciplined enough to stick to them.

4. Betting the bank (and other poor cash management habits).

5. Trading too much. Make too many trades for too little profit, and you're making money for your broker, not for you.

6. Getting emotionally involved. The stock doesn't know that you own it, and a currency will not reward your loyalty or patriotism.

7. Letting trading take over your life. This will eventually wear you out.

8. Chasing the stock. Aim to buy when the stock is taking a rest, not when the share price is racing away.

The best ways to reduce your risk

1. Using and wherever possible automating tight stop losses.

2. Skim off the top of a position when the trade has reached your first price target.

3. Use a trailing stop loss, or increase your stop loss once your trade breaks even.

4. Limit the size of risk to 2% of your total risk capital.

5. Ensure all your positions are closed overnight.

6. Not trading when you are ill, tired, or have made a number of losing trades in succession.

Why day trading might not be right for you

1. You prefer to analyze companies to invest in and invest in them long term. If you really enjoy doing this, you probably will be bored day trading.

2. Self-discipline isn't your strong suit.

3. You enjoy gambling. If so, gamble with your pocket money, in a casino or at a racetrack. It's more fun and if you only gamble with cash, what you take with you is all you can lose.

4. You can't imagine spending all day on your own in front of computer screens. Day trading is not a good life for you if you want to see people or be in the great outdoors all day.

5. You're a very emotional person who uses gut feeling and instinct a lot of the time. That won't work in day trading.

6. You are good at putting things off until another day.

7. You want to get rich quick.

The top accessories that will make your trading station a pleasure to use

1. A really ergonomic chair that gives you proper support and is fully adjustable.

2. An adjustable standing desk so that you can stretch when you need to.

3. Excellent LED desk lamps with flexible or articulated arms.

4. Plenty of yellow legal pads for taking notes or jotting down ideas.

5. A good pen holder or mug so you don't spend half your day looking to see where you put your pen.

6. A basket or tray for collecting up all the things that clutter your desk - pens, erasers, staplers, sticky notes, and so on.

7. A coffee corner with a French press, aeropress or Espresso machine, that isn't anywhere it can spill onto your desk.

Chapter 12 Quiz

1. Which is these is a top rookie mistake?
   a) Not having risk management systems
   b) Not having a comfortable chair
   c) Using only one trading strategy
   d) Making relatively small profits

2. Which of these will not reduce your risk?
   a) Using tight stop losses
   b) Limiting your position size
   c) Closing all your positions at lunchtime
   d) Closing all your positions overnight

3. Which of these do you not need on your trading desk?
   a) Good adjustable lamps
   b) Lots of notepads
   c) A tray to keep the desk tidy
   d) A cat

4. Day trading is not right for you if:
   a) You are a loner
   b) You are a math whizz
   c) You are a gambler
   d) You are a procrastinator

5. How much trading is too much?
   a) Three trades a day
   b) Ten trades a day
   c) When your total returns are below 20%
   d) When your broker makes more money than you do

I would just like to mention before we go onto the final chapter on Incorporating Your Day Trading Business, if you are finding this book useful so far – it would mean everything to me if you could spare just a few seconds and write a brief review on Amazon on how this book is helping you so far.

13

Chapter 13: Incorporating Your Day Trading Business

Note: this chapter is written for US-based traders. While the basic principles will be similar in all jurisdictions, if you're based in the UK, Europe, Asia or Canada, or if you're a digital nomad, the details will be different. Ensure you know what rules apply where you are.

Regulation and what it means for you

Regulation can be a difficulty for day traders. For instance, American citizens living in Europe may find it difficult to open trading or even investing accounts, since the regulations applying to them are different from those applying to other nationalities.

I already mentioned the Pattern Day Trading rules, which means if you're trading stocks, you'll need $25,000 in your account. US investors are also barred from trading Contracts For Difference, which is a way UK and European investors can trade the price movement of a stock without actually buying the stock.

But you also need to take care to stay on the right side of tax regulations.

Taxes for day traders

We all hate paying taxes (though tax pays for a lot of things we regard as civilized life, such as education, healthcare, and decent roads). What's particularly annoying, though, is when you pay more tax than you needed to because you failed to plan ahead, or didn't check the tax treatment of a transaction before you made it. And tax law as it applies to day trading is complicated. It can be different depending on the type of asset you trade, for instance.

US tax law divides short term capital gains (on assets held for less than a year, which let's face it, means all your positions if you're a day trader) from long term capital gains (on assets which you have held for a year or more). However, there are a few interesting wrinkles for day traders as this can depend on what kind of assets you are trading!

In the US, regulated futures contracts, non-equity options, and foreign currency trades are taxed 60% as long-term capital gains and 40% as short-term capital gains (the 60/40 rule). This is great for day traders, as 60% of your profits on these assets are taxed at the lower long-term rate. By contrast, if you day trade *shares*, you'll pay the higher short-term rate on all your profits. Because Uncle Sam says so.

Tax is tricky as both long term and short term capital gains tax have different rates, but it's easy to give an example if we make some basic assumptions. Let's suppose, then, that our fortunate, wealthy traders pay tax at the highest rate because they make so much money, Mr 'Shares' Trader pays short term capital gains tax at his highest marginal rate of income tax, which is 37%.

But Miss 'Futures' Trader pays this 37% rate on only 40% of her gains. On the remaining 60%, she pays only 20% tax. So she pays a blended rate of just 26.8% compared to Mr Shares Trader's 37%. That's a huge saving.

Mr Shares Trader	100 taxed at 37%	**37.0**
Ms Futures Trader	40 taxed at 37% 60 taxed at 20% long term rate	14.8 + 12.0 **= 26.8**

However, trading the spot market in currencies doesn't automatically benefit from the 60/40 rule. You'll probably want to work with an accountant, as there are two choices; to report trading profits as short-term capital gains (Section 988), or to treat your spot trades as if they were futures contracts (Section 1256). However, you'll need to make a once and for all choice; it won't be easy to change it later. You'll need to think not just about your trading business, but about your other tax affairs; for instance, whether a certain treatment would put you into a higher tax category.

Stocks

For the IRS to tax your day trading in stocks as 'trading' then you will need to tick a number of boxes. You need to trade regularly and continuously, your activity needs to be 'substantial', and you will be profiting from intra-day price moves, not price appreciation over the long term or dividend income. You need to fulfill *all* of these requirements, not just one or two.

• What does 'substantial' mean? If you're not trading around 1,500 trades a year, it's unlikely the IRS will think you're a professional trader.

• What does 'regular' and 'continuous' mean? If you're not trading most days in the year; if you are part-time as a trader, and have a day job, the IRS is unlikely to consider you a 'trader' for tax purposes.

• The IRS says that, "If the nature of your trading activities doesn't qualify as a business, you're considered an investor and not a trader."

• And finally, the IRS probably won't even consider giving you professional status in your first year of trading.

If you do qualify as a trader, you'll find there are significant advantages. You can take a number of deductions that investors can't; you'll be able to set many of your business costs against tax. As an investor, you would be very limited in your ability to do so.

You need to be careful, if you have an investment portfolio as well as a trading book, to separate the two. Your long-term investments will be treated one way and your trading business another (if you have 'trader' status). It might be best to use two different brokers, and keep two separate sets of accounts, so that it's absolutely clear not just to you, but also to the IRS if they ever want to audit you.

Given the complexity of tax regulations for traders, it may be well worth your while employing a tax adviser. Talking to other reputable traders can help you find an adviser who understands this particular business; accountants may also have their own experts, or work with specialist tax advisers. It's important to recognize that not every professional will understand the specific needs of day traders; a CPA (Certified Public Accountant) will know how to do tax and keep accounts, but may not understand day trading. Enrolled agents, on the other hand, specialize in tax preparation, but won't be able to help you with bookkeeping or advice on financing your business.

You might also, at some point, need a tax attorney. Generally, though, you'll only want to call on one if you are involved in litigation or a dispute with the IRS.

The wash-sale rule

The wash-sale rule is a real annoyance for non-professional day traders. It's intended to stop investors selling shares to make a tax loss, then buying them back the day after, but unfortunately, most day traders also get caught in the net.

The wash-sale rule says that if you have both a loss *and* profit for a particular stock in the same 61-day period (30 days before and 30 days after the sale), you cannot deduct the loss from your taxes. Instead, the loss is added to the cost basis of the stock, that is, to the price that the IRS says you bought the stock at. *Eventually*, the result will be similar, but it means if you're trading, say, Apple every single day, you'll not be able to write off your losses as you go. They'll just be added to the cost base of your next trade. This may make your trading profit for tax purposes larger than you would have expected as you will be carrying your losses over.

It's also important that you keep meticulous records, because you'll need to account for all your trades in a stock together if you trade it several times, or trade it regularly throughout the year.

The wash-sale rule also covers 'substantially similar' securities. That includes options on the stock, so you can't avoid the wash-sale rule by trading the stock and then trading the option. However, futures contracts are not covered by the wash sale rule.

If you qualify as a trader according to the IRS rules, you can elect to be 'marked-to-market', which has a number of advantages for you as you will see soon.

Mark-to-market

This is a form of accounting that only qualified 'traders' according to the IRS rules can use. You'll need professional assistance to fill in Form 3115, and you also need to submit the form with your prior year's tax return.

With mark-to-market, you do not have to track individual gains and losses. Instead, you pretend that you bought your *entire portfolio* at the start of the year and sold it at the end of the year, and the resulting profit is treated as income instead of capital gain. Because of this being treated as income on the entire portfolio, the wash sale rule no longer applies - you can buy and sell the same individual stock all day long, every day of the year.

Costs you can deduct

If you are day trading as a business, you can deduct a number of business costs. Legal and accounting fees can be expensed, and if you end up needing clerical help you can also expense that. Office expenses can also be deducted from your tax, though if you have a home office you can only expense its upkeep if it is used *exclusively* for your business. You can also write off a certain amount against computers and other equipment.

Any *advice* on trading can be expensed. This includes subscriptions to newsletters and research services, subscriptions to chatrooms, books bought for your education, advisory services, and trade coaching. However, you can't deduct the cost of attending seminars, conferences or training courses. Uncle Sam doesn't want you taking a holiday in Hawaii at his expense, even if there happens to be a trader conference going on.

If you incur interest because you're trading on margin, and your broker charges you, then you can expense it. However, you *can't* deduct commissions as a cost. They still reduce your tax, but what you need to do is to add the commissions to the cost of the shares when you are working out your capital gain on a trade. The same is true for transfer taxes, should you pay any.

Using an IRA

You might consider sheltering your trading portfolio inside an Individual Retirement Account (IRA). You'll pay no taxes on any capital gains within the IRA. However, there are a number of limits. You can contribute only $5,000 a year to the account, though if you have a 401k from an employer you have left, you can roll that into the IRA.

However, your broker may limit your trading options. And you won't be able to withdraw any money till you are 59 1/2, unless you pay a 10 percent tax penalty. It's also worth thinking about how you will support yourself in retirement if you do manage to make losses in your IRA. If I was going to use my IRA I think I'd want to have a few years' successful trading behind me. Otherwise, use your IRA for long term investments and day trade a regular trading account.

Chapter 13 Quiz

1. How much do you need in your account according to Pattern Day Trading rules?
    a) $2,500
    b) $250,000
    c) $25,000
    d) $500

2. Which of these assets does not benefit from the 60/40 tax rule?
    a) Foreign currency trades
    b) Stock trades
    c) Regulated futures contracts
    d) Non-equity options contracts

3. Which of these is not a tax-deductible cost for a trading business?
    a) Subscription to a newsletter
    b) Accounting fees
    c) A trading seminar
    d) Books about trading and market

4. When does the wash-sale rule apply?
    a) If you make both a profit and a loss in the same stock in a 61 day period
    b) If you hold a stock for less than a year
    c) If you buy a stock and sell it within 30 days
    d) If you buy a stock and sell it the same day

5. Which of these doesn't count as R&D for a day trader?
    a) Reading this book
    b) Back-testing a trading strategy
    c) Watching a YouTube video on day trading
    d) Changing broker

Leave a 1-Click Review!

I would be incredible thankful if you could take just 60 seconds to write a brief review on Amazon, even if it's just a few sentences!

Customer reviews

⭐⭐⭐⭐⭐ 5 out of 5

4 global ratings

5 star		100%
4 star		0%
3 star		0%
2 star		0%
1 star		0%

˅ How are ratings calculated?

Amazon.com readers
http://www.amazon.com/review/
create-review?&asin=B0FWQB4DZZ

Amazon.co.uk readers
http://www.amazon.co.uk/review/
create-review?&asin=B0FWQB4DZZ

Conclusion

Now that you've read this book, I'd like to tell you that you're ready to trade; but that would be a lie. You are ready to take the next steps towards successful day trading, though; defining, back-testing and paper-trading your chosen trading strategy.

This means that by the time you actually put your money into a trade, you can be confident that you have a trading strategy that will make you money. Very, very few day traders start with that confidence. They cut corners, or trade on gut feel rather than solid strategies.

In this book, you've learned the basics about how markets work. The practicalities of trading, and the different kinds of financial assets that you might decide to trade have been briefly covered, together with the advantages and disadvantages of each market.

You've learned to identify some basic market patterns that have a high probability of working out in particular ways, giving you the opportunity to make trades with a known risk/reward ratio. You've learned how to put your orders through, and in particular, how to create a package of orders that can automate your trade.

You've read about the basics of technical analysis, including candlestick charts, and you've also read up on some strategies for day trading that you can start to employ. This is only an introduction to the basics; there's still a lot more you can learn, whether you decide to follow podcasts or YouTube traders, buy specialized books on technical analysis and particular trades, or find a mentor in the trading community.

I've also shown you how to limit your risks. Risk management is the bit of day trading that isn't fun and doesn't get talked about a lot, but it's absolutely crucial to making money reliably in the long term. Money management, tight stop-losses, and not betting the bank are the only way you can stay in the game without risking a run of loss-making trades forcing you to quit.

You've also looked at issues about human emotions such as fear and greed, panic, and even boredom in relation to trading. You also have a shopping list for your trading business, including software, hardware, and a few creature comforts.

I hope you now have a good idea of whether day trading is for you, and what the biggest challenges will be for you personally. Even if you've decided that day trading probably isn't a great career for you and you'd prefer to focus on another way to make money, at least I've managed to save you a huge amount of work and the possibility of losing your risk capital.

If you've decided day trading is what you want to do, then don't forget to choose your strategy, backtest it, practice trading in simulation, and get yourself well prepared before you actually make that first trade. You will be surprised, if you do your preparation properly, how easy and stress-free day trading can be.

On the other hand, of course, you could just rush off and put all your money into a fast-rising stock you heard about on TikTok. But I don't recommend it.

May all your trades be good ones!

HOW TO GET THE MOST OUT OF THIS BOOK

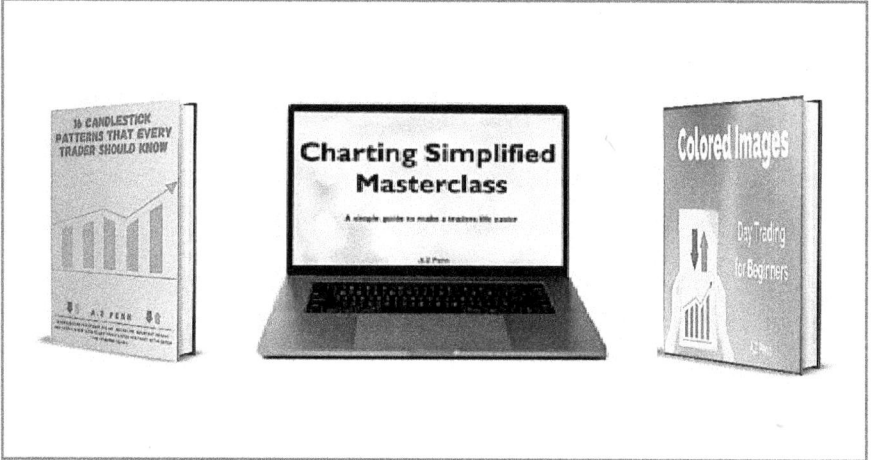

To help you along your trading journey, I've created a free bonus companion masterclass which includes video analysis of real life stock examples to expand on some of the key topics discussed in this book. I also provide additional resources that will help you get the best possible result.

I highly recommend you sign up now to get the most out of this book. You can do that by going to the link or scanning the QR code below:

www.az-penn.com

Free bonus #1: Charting Simplified Masterclass ($67 value)

In this 5 part video masterclass you'll be discovering various simple and easy to use strategies on making profitable trades. By showing you real life stock examples of a few charting indicators - you will be able to determine whether a stock is worth trading or not.

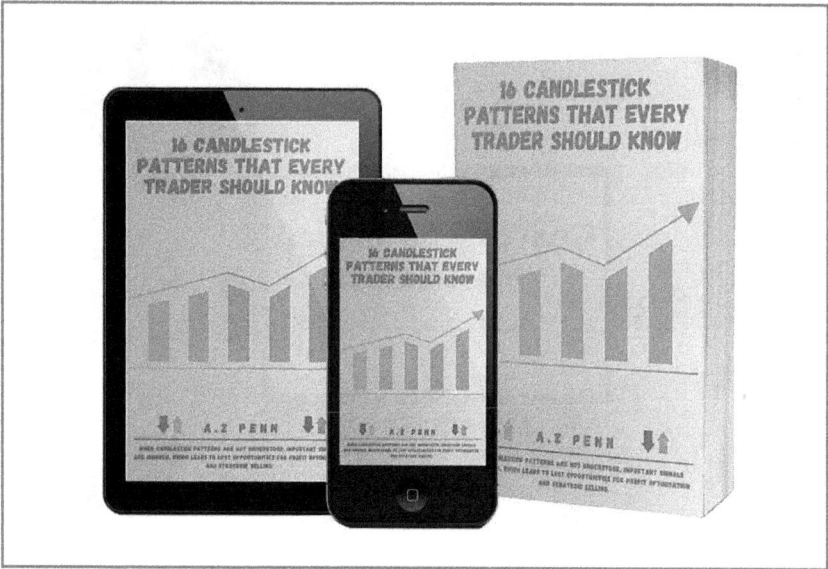

Free bonus #2: 16 Candlestick Patterns that Every Trader Should Know ($17 value)

Stay ahead in the trading game with our essential guide on the patterns that are vital for reading market signals, identifying trend reversals, and making profitable trades. Equip yourself with the knowledge to make informed decisions and maximize your trading returns.

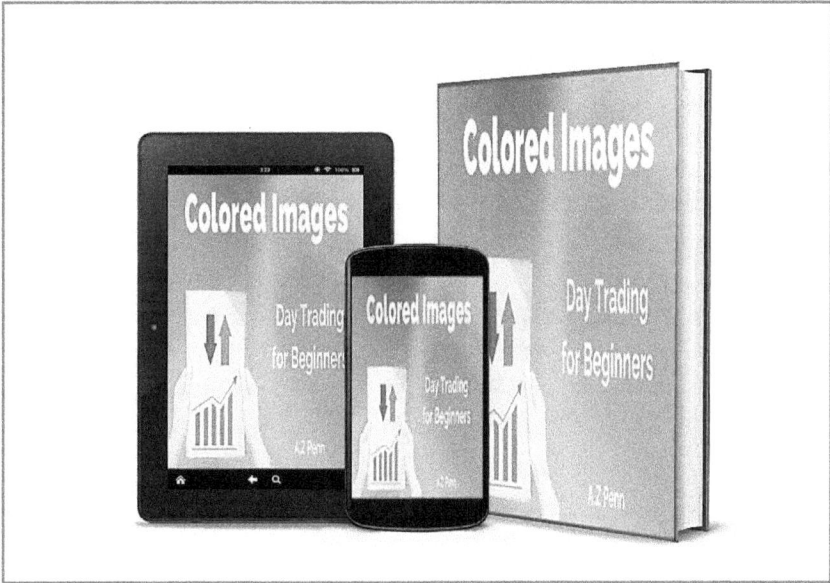

Free bonus #3: Colored Images – Day Trading for Beginners

To keep our books at a reasonable price for you, we print in black & white. But here are all the images in full color.

All of these bonuses are 100% free, with no strings attached. You don't need to provide any personal details except your email address.

To get your bonuses, go to the link or QR code:

www.az-penn.com

Glossary

Arbitrage - exploiting a difference in price for the same asset between two different markets. It's risk-free, but no longer very profitable for retail traders.

Ask price - the price at which you will be able to buy shares (the market maker 'asks' for this amount of money).

Basis Point - one hundredth of a percentage point: 0.01%.

Bear - someone who believes an asset's price is going down, and is selling the asset.

Bull - someone who believes an asset's price is going up, and is buying the asset.

Bull/Bear market - a rising and optimistic market / a falling, pessimistic market.

Bid price - the price at which you will be able to sell your shares.

Breakdown - share price movement down through a support level.

Breakout - share price movement up through a resistance level.

Call option - an option giving you the ability to buy shares at a particular date and price.

Channel - the space between the top and bottom trendlines.

Derivative - a security based on an underlying asset whose price movement is reflected in the derivative.

Divergence - when a technical indicator such as MACD or RSI does not move in line with the price of an asset.

Double bottom - a chart pattern of two successive and equal lows, suggesting a rebound could occur.

Double top - the reverse of a double bottom.

ECN (e.g. ARCA, Bloomberg, Instinet) - an Electronic Communications Network which links buyers and sellers directly.

EMA - Exponentially smoothed Moving Average, which gives more weight to the most recent price movements.

ETF - Exchange Traded Fund: a stock-exchange traded security that reflects the returns of a share index, commodity or other financial asset.

Expiration date - the date on which a futures contract expires.

Fill - the price at which your buy or sell order is executed.

Float - the amount of shares that actually trades, excluding shares held by insiders.

Futures contract - an agreement to buy or sell a standardized quantity of a commodity or currency at a specified future date.

Gap - a price move that is sudden enough to leave a 'gap' in the price chart.

Head and shoulders - a chart formation showing three consecutive highs, of which the second is the highest. Usually foreshadows a reversal of a bull trend and a fall in the share price.

Hedge - a strategy used to limit losses on a financial or real asset by using an opposing derivative or other trade, for instance, limiting the losses on a holding of shares by buying a put option which will make an offsetting profit if the share price goes down.

In-the-money - a call option (option to buy) is in the money when the strike price is less than the current share price.

Leverage - multiplying the return on an asset by using debt (buying on margin), or by using a leveraged derivative such as an option.

Limit order - an order that states the maximum price at which you will buy or the minimum price at which you will sell.

Liquidity - the ease with which an asset can be bought or sold. For instance, your home is not a liquid asset; shares in IBM are. Different shares and other securities have differing liquidity.

Long - to be long is to own an asset. A long position means you have bought the asset.

MA - moving average: an average of a number of time periods' prices.

Margin - the amount by which a broker will allow your trades to exceed the cash in your account. Effectively, you are borrowing from your broker.

Margin call - if the value of your assets falls below a specified amount, and you are trading on margin, a broker can ask you to deposit further funds to support your position. This is a margin call.

Market capitalization - the number of shares outstanding in a company multiplied by its share price.

Market maker - a broker/dealer who makes a market in a stock, offering both to buy and sell the stock from market participants.

Market order - an order to buy or sell an asset at the best price your dealer can get.

Momentum - the speed of price change. Momentum trading aims to 'go with the flow,' purchasing assets that are moving in an uptrend.

Odd lot - a lot of less than 100 shares.

Offer - the price at which you can buy a share: also known as the ask price.

Pip - in currency trading, the smallest amount that a currency can move: the fourth (last) decimal point.

Point - the minimum movement in the price of futures.

Put option - an option giving you the right to sell a share at a given price.

Rally - when having hit a low point, a share price begins to go back up.

Resistance - a price level which acts as a ceiling, creating an obstacle to further increases in price. Once passed, it becomes a support.

Retracement - after a strong run, a share will often retrace part of that move before continuing the trend.

Reversal pattern - chart patterns that predict a given trend will likely reverse. These include double and triple tops, head and shoulders, hammer and shooting star candlesticks.

Risk/reward ratio - measuring your potential loss against the potential profit of a given trade.

Round lot - 100 shares or a multiple of 100 shares.

Short - to sell an asset without having bought it, aiming to buy it at a lower price thus making a profit.

Short Sale Restriction - short sales at the bid price may be restricted if a share's price has fallen 10% or more during the current or previous trading session.

Spread - the difference between the bid and ask price - the prices at which you can sell or buy the shares.

Stock index futures - futures contracts taken out on a stock index such as the S&P 500.

Stop-loss - the price at which your trading strategy dictates you will close a loss-making trade.

Strike price - the price at which you can exercise an option to buy or sell the underlying shares.

Support - a significant price level which acts as a 'floor' to the price.

Swing trading - short-term trading in which market positions are not closed overnight.

Technical Analysis - analyzing share price charts in order to predict the likely course of prices.

Thin market - a market that has a low volume of trade.

Tick - a minimum movement of the share price upwards or downwards.

TICK index - subtracts the number of NYSE stocks currently ticking down from those ticking up - a good indicator of market sentiment.

Ticker symbol - the sequence of letters that identifies a security, e.g. AAPL for Apple, T for AT&T, or GRRR for Gorilla Technology Group.

Trailing stop - a stop loss that is ratcheted upwards as the share price rises, in order to protect profits.

Trend - a price pattern that shows a strong tendency in one direction.

Trendline - a line drawn linking the lowest lows or highest highs of a price chart, in order to show the trend.

TRIN - the Nasdaq equivalent of the TICK index.

VWAP - Volume Weighted Average Price, a moving average that is adjusted for the volume of trade.

Volatility - the amount by which an asset's price fluctuates around the average price.

Volume - trading volume, the number of shares bought and sold during a given time period.

Reference

Ardt, W. (2020). Risk and Money Management for Day and Swing Trading. Torero Traders School.

Aziz, A. (2016). How to Day Trade For a Living. Createspace.

Aziz, A. (2018). Advanced Techniques in Day Trading. Createspace.

Aziz, A & Baehr, M. (2020). Mastering Trading Psychology. Peak Capital Trading.

Cameron, R. (2015). How to Day Trade. AuthorHouse.

Holland, A. (2024). Day Trading Options: Strategies and Techniques for Profiting from Short Term Options Trading. Self-published.

Logue, A. C. (2014). Day Trading for Dummies. John Wiley & Sons.

Noonan, T. (2019). Day Trading QuickStart Guide. ClydeBank Finance.

Quinn, W & Turner, J. D. (2020). Boom and Bust: A Global History of Financial Bubbles. Cambridge University Press.

Tandler, J. (2012). The Mental Edge in Trading: Adapt Your Personality Traits and Control Your Emotions to Make Smarter Investments. McGraw Hill.

Turner, T. (2008). A Beginner's Guide to Day Trading Online. Simon & Schuster.

Quiz Answers

Chapter 1:
1. C
2. A
3. B
4. D
5. A

Chapter 6:
1. B
2. A, B, C
3. A
4. C
5. A

Chapter 11:
1. A, B, C
2. B
3. D
4. A
5. B

Chapter 2:
1. B
2. C
3. C
4. D
5. A

Chapter 7:
1. D
2. B
3. D
4. C
5. A, B, C, D

Chapter 12:
1. A
2. C
3. D
4. C, D
5. D

Chapter 3:
1. A
2. C
3. D
4. C
5. A

Chapter 8:
1. A
2. D
3. A
4. B
5. D

Chapter 13:
1. C
2. B
3. C
4. A
5. D

Chapter 4:
1. C
2. C
3. D
4. D
5. C

Chapter 9:
1. B
2. A, B, C, D
3. C
4. D
5. B

Chapter 5:
1. B
2. D
3. B
4. C
5. C

Chapter 10:
1. B
2. A, B, C, D
3. A, C
4. A, B, C
5. A, B, C, D

Swing Trading
for Beginners

Turn Price Swings into Profits Using Simple
Trading Strategies in the Financial Markets Today
with Zero Trading Experience Required

A.Z Penn

HOW TO GET THE MOST OUT OF THIS BOOK

To help you along your trading journey, I've created a free bonus companion masterclass which includes video analysis of real life stock examples to expand on some of the key topics discussed in this book. I also provide additional resources that will help you get the best possible result.

I highly recommend you sign up now to get the most out of this book. You can do that by going to the link or scanning the QR code below:

www.az-penn.com

SCAN ME

Free bonus #1: Charting Simplified Masterclass ($67 value)

In this 5 part video masterclass you'll be discovering various simple and easy to use strategies on making profitable trades. By showing you real life stock examples of a few charting indicators - you will be able to determine whether a stock is worth trading or not.

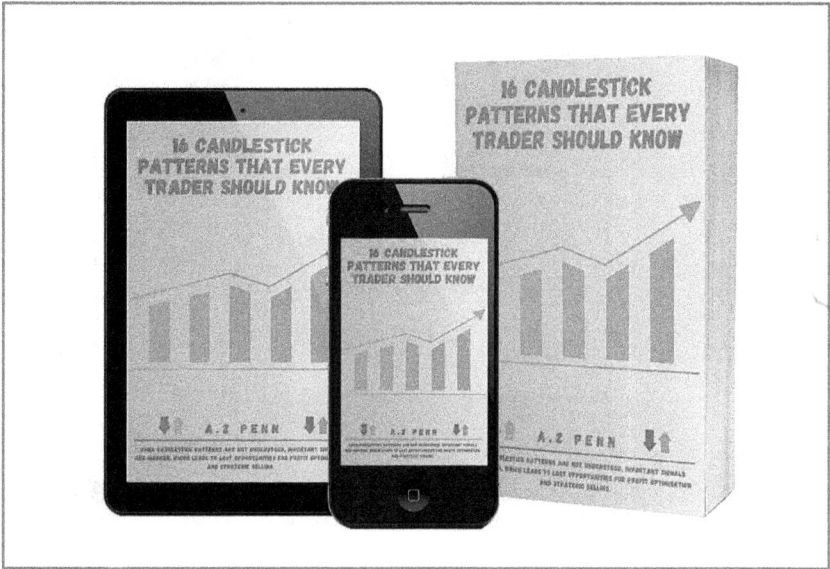

Free bonus #2: 16 Candlestick Patterns that Every Trader Should Know ($17 value)

Stay ahead in the trading game with our essential guide on the patterns that are vital for reading market signals, identifying trend reversals, and making profitable trades. Equip yourself with the knowledge to make informed decisions and maximize your trading returns.

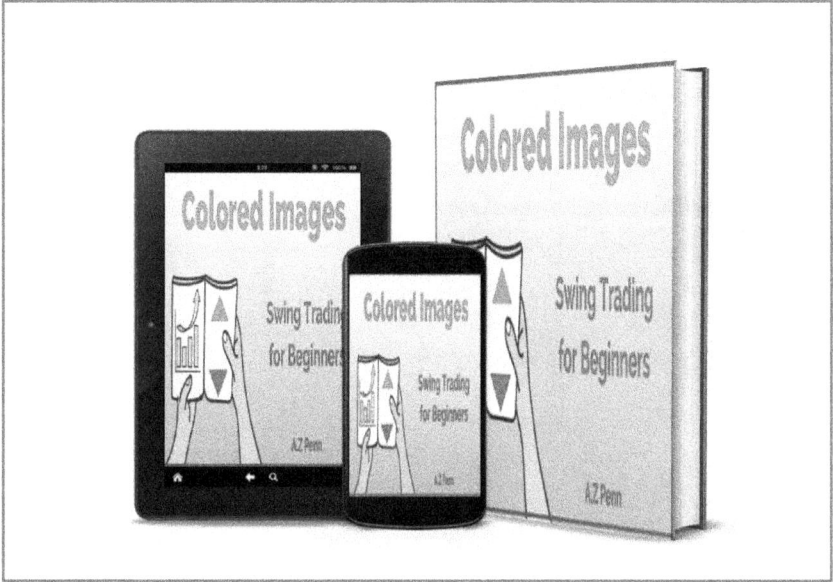

Free bonus #3: Colored Images – Swing Trading for Beginners

To keep our books at a reasonable price for you, we print in black & white. But here are all the images in full color.

All of these bonuses are 100% free, with no strings attached. You don't need to provide any personal details except your email address.

To get your bonuses, go to the link or QR code:

www.az-penn.com

Introduction

Last month, I only made one trade.

I'd found a stock that had produced good results a week before and where the charts suggested it could easily move up fast if it broke through a historic resistance level. I expected it to move strongly up and make me a few dollars a share.

It did. And then it kept going.

I kept checking that the stock still looked good. And it did. And it kept going.

Then, after a couple of weeks, it started slowing down, and I cashed out. I'd expected to make a couple of thousand bucks tops; instead, I'd made a whopping $11,800!

That was a great swing trade. I spotted the trend, jumped on for the ride, and got out before the stock stalled.

I guarantee you'd love to be able to trade like that! The good news is, you can - and I'll show you how to get started in this book.

Of course, not all trades are as good as that. I still lose quite often, but I lose small and win bigger, and sometimes - like last month - win very big. I have a nice income stream from trading, I don't run big risks, and I have plenty of time to enjoy myself outside of the stock market.

It took me a while to get here, as I learned from my mistakes - some were very bad, and I lost a lot of money. That's one reason I've written this book: to allow other traders to learn from my mistakes instead of their own (which will likely be a lot more expensive).

When you get started in swing trading, it can be hard to find your way. There's a lot of information out there, but not all of it is good, and some is contradictory. Many people want to sell you a system, software, or training, but do you want to pay hundreds of dollars or commit to a monthly subscription before you even open a brokerage account? And when you read about multi-millionaire traders like George Soros, and you only have a few thousand to put into an account, you probably feel overwhelmed and doubt you will ever make it.

You may make a few trades that go wrong and feel like giving up. You may make a few trades that succeed, then get overconfident and have a crushing loss with your next one. You may have fantasized about getting rich quickly and found that after three or four months of hard work, you've made a few hundred bucks; would you be better off mowing lawns on the weekend for pocket money?

The good news is that swing trading isn't rocket science. You don't need to be incredibly talented or have a finance degree to succeed. You need some good basic information, plenty of self-discipline, and a well-thought-through process for selecting and trading stocks and managing risk - plus a business plan and a little patience. Whether your business plan is to go full time within three years or just to add a bit of oomph to your retirement plan, that's fine; that's one of the great things about swing trading, that you can make it fit your lifestyle and ambitions.

So, in this book, I will use everything I've learned over my swing trading career to help you get started. I'll explain what swing trading is and what it isn't; I'll run through ways of organizing your life as a swing trader, including using automated orders to make your life easier; I'll talk about risk management, which is crucial to success because it will stop you from losing back all the profit you've made.

I'll also show you some of the basic trade setups that are profitable and talk a bit about understanding the stock market and individual stocks and sectors. You don't need to be a chartered financial analyst to be able to get some useful information out of a company's annual and quarterly reports, so I'll give you a breakdown of what to look for and how to use what you find out.

There's a glossary and references at the end of the book, so you can look up anything you need. And there's a quiz at the end of every chapter to help you check your learning - and for a bit of fun!

Finally, by the time you finish this book, you won't just be ready to trade - you'll have a systematic approach to swing trading, which will help you maximize your returns, minimize your risks, and improve your win rate over time. I wish I'd had that when I started trading; it would have saved me a lot of money, but even more importantly, it would have saved me a lot of soul-searching and frustration.

This book will be full of real-life examples of how to swing trade. Believe it, whatever discouragements or setbacks you experience, I've been through it already. I can show you how to keep going; how to motivate yourself, how to keep a level head, and how to keep learning and improving.

Just keep going is important. 90% of traders (day traders and swing traders) fail within a year, and I guarantee that while some of them lose all their money, others just lose their mojo. It's not so much that they don't have what it takes, more that they get discouraged and let things slide. If you want to be part of the 10% who are still trading at the end of a year and who keep trading and keep getting better at it, then I'm going to show you how to do it. Let's get started right now!

1

Chapter 1: What is Swing Trading?

We all understand "Trading," but what exactly is swing trading? How is it different from day trading? And how does it work? That's what I'll be talking about in this chapter because the level of activity and risk is different from day trading and long-term position trading.

Swing trading aims to use the 'swings' in the share price to make profits. If you look at a share price chart - any share price chart, just go on Google or Yahoo Finance and pull up a one-year or six-month chart - you'll see that share prices don't move in nice smooth lines; they tend to 'swing' up and down, a bit like waves in the sea. As you know, if you're walking along the foreshore, every so often, a big wave will come along, and you need to jump out of the way or get your feet wet. That's the kind of wave swing traders are waiting for.

Swing traders are looking for situations where it could take a few days or weeks to collect their profit. That's different from day trading, where you trade during the day and close your positions overnight. In swing trading, you don't need to sit at a trading screen all day, so it's suitable for part-time individuals with day jobs or even kids. But it also means your position is at risk overnight and pre-market. For instance, if a company makes an announcement before the market is open, you could see your shares rocket upwards or fall downwards. That's why risk management is crucial for swing traders.

Day traders might make four, five or even ten trades a day. Swing traders would regard that as hyperactive. Day traders can easily lose a lot of their profit in trading costs such as commission and spread, while swing traders are less likely to see their trades losing money because they didn't allow for trading costs.

A day trader using a zero commission broker and trading only the mega-capitalisation stocks will manage to keep costs low, but they will be losing a certain amount on the spread every trade. The spread is the difference between the buy (ask), and sell (bid) prices and the spread cost is built into that price.

Day traders' requirements for high reliability from their trading platforms and real-time prices and charting means they often have significantly higher IT and platform costs than swing traders, who can use broker-provided platforms like Thinkorswim for free.

But swing traders aren't long-term investors, either. While they are willing to wait a few weeks to exit a trade, they just want to ride the swing if it's going right. They don't want to 'buy and hold'. They aren't interested in the long term. Basically, they want to be in the share only as long as it's moving up strongly, and not sit around while it zigzags. And they're not position traders, who will take a position onto the trading books for several months or more while they wait for action. They need a catalyst in the short term, something that will make the shares move.

Most swing traders will sell a position if, after a week or two, the share price hasn't moved rather than wait it out, as locking capital up in a trade that's not working out doesn't make sense when it could be used buying into a better prospect. On the other hand, a buy-and-hold investor bases their investment on the intrinsic value of the share - what they think it is really worth - and will be willing to wait a good long time for the market to recognize that value and then have the share price go up.

Buy-and-hold investors typically turn over less than a quarter of their portfolio every year. Swing traders are likely to have traded in and out of all their active positions over the course of a month or so.

Position traders are sort of a hybrid between swing traders and investors. They often take a position based on a fundamental idea, such as that political unrest and high government debt is likely to make a currency weaken, or that lower interest rates will make real estate much more attractive, and they are ready to wait a few months for the market to move in their favor.

One of the results of this different time perspective is that the kind of price charts you're looking at will be different. Day traders will be looking at one-minute or five-minute price charts. Swing traders concentrate more on daily and weekly charts. Intra-day movements (actions within one day) just don't interest them; the daily open and close prices are all they are concerned with.

However, day traders and swing traders have one important similarity. Both of them use technical analysis - that is, share price charts, stock screeners, or scanners to find prospective trades.

Another result of the different time perspective is that your time management will be different. Day traders need to spend time in front of their screens; all market day, if they're full-time. It's possible for them to trade in another market in a different time zone around their day job, but that's a bit of a challenge.

With swing trading, you're more likely to have a daily schedule of looking at the market after the close, finding your setups, and entering conditional orders such as stop limits (setting the highest and lowest price you are willing to accept for a stock). Then, you can close down your screens and get on with playing with your kids, having a romantic dinner with your significant other, or hanging out with your buddies.

Day trading and swing trading demand slightly different abilities. A day trader has to be able to make really fast decisions. That also means a day trader needs a special trading software to execute orders fast - there's no time to spare, as even microseconds count. A swing trader, on the other hand, has time to check and double-check the trade before entering any orders. You'll still need the courage to put your money on the line, but you don't need the ultra-fast reactions of a kung fu fighter that a day trader requires.

Unlike the buy-and-hold investor, though, you can't afford to let your portfolio run itself. Many investors only run a monthly check on their portfolios, but as a swing trader, you'll need to be much more active than that! Daily check-in is vital. If you want to take a holiday, close down all the positions in your trading book first.

One big difference between day traders and swing traders is that day traders are more tightly regulated. Although, full-time day traders have access to tax advantages, which a swing trader would not have.

Anyone who makes more than four-day trades in five business days and who day trades for more than 6% of their total activity in that account is appointed as a 'pattern day trader.' They are required to hold at least $25,000 in their margin account and can't day trade if the balance dips below that amount. Brokers will automatically identify pattern day traders, so there is no way around the issue. The whole regulation is intended to stop people with small resources from getting in over their heads, for instance, someone with just $10,000 in the bank risking huge amounts on margin - though you might think it's a rather harsh way of doing so.

On the other hand, those who are accepted as being a professional trader in securities (basically, full-time day traders) can not only set the costs of their trading business against their profits to reduce tax liability, but they can also use the 'mark-to-market' election on their trading gains. That lets them use the year-end price for all their holdings as if they had sold all the positions at the end of the year so that if they have unrealized losses ('paper losses' - stocks that are losing money, but are still being held in the portfolio) at year-end, they are able to set those against their profits for the year. They are also able to deduct all trading losses rather than being limited to $3,000 (this is the limit allowed by the IRS for investors).

Day traders typically ignore the fundamental analysis of the stocks they trade, that is, the underlying business of the company that issued the shares. Day traders simply aren't interested in a stock for long enough to worry about whether the company's next earnings release will be good or disappointing, or whether management will increase the dividend this year. Swing traders, conversely, can benefit from an informed view of the fundamental analysis, though they won't spend the hours poring over the 10-K or other SEC filings that buy-and-hold investors do. Instead, they're likely to use sites like Zacks, Morningstar, or Yahoo Finance to get a broad overall view of the fundamental analysis of the stock they are interested in.

Because if you're swing trading you are leaving capital locked up overnight, you'll want to check the fundamentals (fundamental analysis) in order to exclude companies that have financial issues. If a company has to refinance a debt, or needs to issue shares to support the balance sheet, that will affect the share price, and it's likely to be announced while the market is closed, so there won't be anything you can do about it. Many swing traders, therefore, exclude companies with weak finances from trading consideration.

Swing traders usually trade in line with the overall trend, so it's useful to know if a company is experiencing fast growth. That gives a solid foundation for 'long' trades (i.e. buying the shares in expectation of further price increases). But for a swing trader, this is just a foundation - for a buy-and-hold investor, it's the be-all and end-all, whether they're buying for the dividend income or long-term capital growth.

Note for paperback readers: You'll be seeing the charts in black and white. It just costs way too much to print them all in color. But you need to see them in color - that's the way you'll be seeing the charts you look at on your computer screen, and if you have three moving averages, for instance, you need to be able to tell which is which.

Therefore, I would recommend you please go to my website: www.az-penn.com and enter your best email address that I should send the colored images document to.

How does swing trading work?

Swing traders aim to identify the 'swings' in a share price between swing lows and swing highs, capitalizing on the difference in movement by gaining profits. For instance, in the case of Innovative Industrial Properties (IIPR), a long uptrend through most of 2024 ran the stock up from $92 to $136. That would have made a long-term buy-and-hold investor $44 a share profit had they bought in at the lower $92 mark.

However, a swing trader who read the swings within that trend correctly could have bought and sold several times. Looking at the chart below, I can see a really clear upwards trend channel, and within it, I can identify several trades that would have made money. A swing trader will never buy exactly at the bottom, or sell exactly at the top, and this isn't something you should ever expect to do. But you will buy very early on the way up, and sell very early on the way down, depending on the chart signals.

So, a good swing trader would have had at least four trades: from $95 to $102 (late December 2023), $103 to $116 (May 2024), $114 to $122 (July 2024), and $124 to $135 (late September 2024). Now those would only have delivered $39, against the $44 enjoyed by the investor. However, the swing trader would have been out of stock before November 7, and the awful crash would have occurred at $103. (That was the US election. The prospects for the cannabis sector stocks under a Trump administration are not great.) The investor would have suffered a very nasty hangover.

Besides, if you swing-traded IIPR, you would be able to put your capital to use elsewhere when the stock was crashing downward during the elections. Or you could even have reversed your position and gone 'short' on the stock, in which case you could have made another $20 of profit after November 7, while the investor was just watching the stock shown as red charting lines in their portfolio.

Shorting a stock is a trading strategy where a trader borrows shares of a stock and sells them on the open market at the current price, aiming to repurchase them later at a lower price. If the stock price *falls*, the trader can buy back the shares at the lower price, return them to the lender, and pocket the difference as profit. However, if the price *rises*, the trader faces potentially unlimited losses.

Of course, not all stocks show a great uptrend like IIPR. Some stocks are range-bound - that is, they move between the same swing high and the same swing low all the time, but they never really go anywhere. They are no fun for long-term investors, but as a swing trader, you can spot the opportunity to buy the share at the bottom of the range and sell it at the top. It really is that easy.

The example below shows Ark Genomic Revolution (ARKG) has gone nowhere since May, but it has set up a neat channel between about $23 and $27. The first time it traded the range, you wouldn't have seen it. But the second time - if you look at that big jump in early July, you would have entered the stock just after it gapped up, around $24.46, and come out probably at $26.46 just a few days later, after the upwards movement ran out of juice. So that's $2 a stock profit. Next time round, in August, there are possible entry points at $23.47, or around $24.50 if you are more cautious, and an exit around $26 at the beginning of September, so again, you're taking a couple of dollars quite quickly.

ARK Genomic Revolution ETF, 1D, CBOE O24.25 H24.25 L23.51 C23.51 -0.62 (-2.57%)
Vol 116.57K
SMMA (20, close) 24.83

And then again, in early November, there's a nice signal start to get in around $24.40, and I'd run it to about the same $26 level.

Of course, the thing that matters when you're trading channels like this is working out whether the stock is going to stay in the channel to make you your money or break downwards, in which case you need to get out quickly. So at the end of the chart, although ARKG has hit the bottom of the range, I don't see a signal telling me it's going back up. I will put the stock on my watch list, but I won't buy it unless I see some upward price action beginning.

And that takes *patience*, which is one of the things you need to learn if you're going to get good at swing trading.

How much do you need to get started?

The bad news is that you will need some capital to start.

The good news is that it might not be as much as you think. Imagine you wanted to run a Burger King franchise; you'd need to find a $50,000 franchise fee together with an investment of $300,000 upwards. That's a stretch for most people. You might borrow some of the start-up cost from the bank, but that might mean putting your house on the line.

On the other hand, you can start *swing trading* with a few hundred bucks in a brokerage account, though I'd recommend you don't start with much less than $5,000 if you want to do it properly. The problem with starting much smaller is that you won't be able to diversify; you'll only have enough capital for one or two positions, so you need all your trades to work out. If you have a number of different positions, you can afford for some of them to make small losses, as long as the others do what you expected - which is of course to make some nice profits!

Small orders can sometimes be difficult to execute at a good price, exposing you to the risk of slippage - that is, having to pay a bit more to get into the stock because the initial price is unavailable when the broker processes the order. It can also make your life difficult when you look at stocks that have high share prices, like Amazon at $211, Alphabet (parent of Google) at $177, or Berkshire Hathaway B shares at $468. However, choosing a broker that allows you to trade fractional shares isn't such a problem. Fractional shares are a 'slice' of a share, which you can buy from a broker which enables fractional shares to be traded; they're not traded on the exchange but part of a private transaction with your broker, but they do give you all the rights to dividends that a full share would, in proportion to the fraction that you hold.

I'll talk about position size later, but for now, just remember that to be successful in day trading, you never, ever bet the bank. You want to limit the risk on any trade to a small percentage of your total trading capital. Doing that when you have little money in your account means your trades will be small.

Let's be realistic about what you can make swing trading. Your returns will depend on the size of your trading book. For instance, if you had $5,000 initial capital, even if you made a 40% annual return in your first year, you'd only make $2,000. In fact, that's a big ask - most successful swing traders make between 10% and 40% annual returns. At 10%, you'd only have made $500 in your first year. So, this is not a get-rich-quick scheme.

The good news is that as you gain experience, if you stick with it, your trades should get more profitable, and your win rate should get higher; at the same time, you'll have more capital to trade as your profits fill your trading book. If you want to make a reasonable living out of swing trading, you'll likely need over $400,000 capital - but you don't necessarily have to put that all in at once. In fact, I'd suggest you scale your way up so that you face the steepest part of the learning curve with the lowest available capital. That way, you'll learn from small losses rather than big ones.

You may have looked at that $400,000 figure and gulped. Yes, if you're starting with $5,000, it's a long way away. You won't get there fast. But think what happens if you make a profit every year, you add a little capital from your savings account every year, you keep growing your capital steadily. Maybe it will take ten years to get to a level where you see really useful returns from your portfolio. But at that point, you'll have some "drop-dead money" if your boss turns out to be a jerk, if you want to take a sabbatical, or if you want to go full-time trading - and you wouldn't have that if you hadn't got into swing trading for the long haul. This is a marathon, not a sprint.

Or, maybe, you'll just have that little bit more in your retirement fund. But that little bit more could mean you can RV the winter out in Florida rather than hunkering down in chilly New Jersey.

Just to check your understanding, every chapter in this book will have a short multiple-choice quiz at the end. Don't worry; no one's keeping the score, and you'll probably find that you do pretty well in most chapters. If you don't, all that's telling you is to re-read the chapter, maybe after a couple of days, and see if it makes better sense. Sometimes, there will be more than one good answer, and I expect you to be able to find both or all of them! The quiz answers are on page 550.

Chapter 1 Quiz

1. Swing traders are likely to regard day trading as:
a) Hyperactive
b) Stressful
c) Time consuming
d) All of the above

2. How much capital does a day trader have at risk overnight?
a) None
b) 50% of their capital
c) 100% of their capital
d) Only the margin on their open positions

3. Which of these do you need to get started in swing trading?
a) Capital
b) Patience
c) A degree in math
d) Self-discipline

4. What kind of annual returns might you expect from swing trading?
a) 15-20%
b) 5%
c) 100-150%
d) Twice the return on the S&P 500

5. Which of these are good reasons to start swing trading?
a) There's a great subReddit on swing trading
b) Adding extra returns to an investment portfolio
c) It's more fun than sports betting
d) Eventually turning it into a full time income source

2

Chapter 2: What Can I Trade?

So far, I've talked about trading stocks. That's my specialty, and it is a good way to get started in swing trading. However, there are a number of different financial assets that you could trade, so in this chapter, I'm going to talk you through the various assets, their advantages and disadvantages, and the way they trade. The choice is up to you.

Stocks

Stocks represent an investment in a company that participates in its profits and may be rewarded by the payment of dividends in cash or in stock. You're buying a tiny percentage of the company's underlying business. That's why long-term investors are in the stock, and they represent a lot of the demand for stocks. Of course, as a swing trader, you're not really interested in the underlying business completely - but it's useful to know a bit about it.

Stocks trade on various markets. The main US markets are NYSE and Nasdaq, and they work slightly differently. NYSE is the New York Stock Exchange, the US's oldest stock exchange; Nasdaq, is an all-electronic exchange with a bias to technology stocks and is a relative newcomer having been founded in 1971. On NYSE, 'specialists' make a market in shares, while on Nasdaq various market makers offer prices via the electronic trading system. Effectively, as a retail trader you're not going to see a huge difference between the two systems.

You might also trade ADRs (American Depository Receipts). These are a way of owning foreign shares - technically, they are a bank-issued certificate of ownership; some have a one-to-one relationship, and others represent several shares. For instance, HDFC Bank of India has a ratio of *three* shares to every *one* ADR, whereas British American Tobacco (BAT) has a ratio of *one* share to *one* ADR.

The big advantage of ADRs for American investors is that they are quoted in dollars, so there is no currency exchange required, and that they are traded on US stock markets. The disadvantage is that some ADRs may have tight liquidity compared to the underlying stock, so that you'll find it difficult to get good prices when you buy or sell. Some ADRs also make a quarterly or annual charge for custody fees (money charged for managing an investment), though this probably won't affect you much as a swing trader since you're not going to own the ADRs for long.

Outside the US, large stock exchanges include Euronext (in Paris, Brussels, Dublin, and Amsterdam), the London Stock Exchange, Deutsche Boerse in Frankfurt, and the Tokyo Stock Exchange.

All stock markets require certain filings from companies that are listed on them, though the exact requirements may differ. There is also good pricing transparency, with trades being reported in a timely way. You can see the stock prices offered and be asked in real-time, and it's easy to access historical price and volume data.

However, you will want to choose the stocks you trade carefully. I'd suggest the following screens:

• Absolutely no penny stocks. Any stock with a share price under $10 is likely to have high risks for a swing trader. These stocks are often in declining industries or speculative loss-making stocks, which means there's a high possibility of unexpected upsets.
• Ensure the stocks you trade in are large and liquid. They should have a minimum market capitalization of $300 million (that's the value of the stock x the number of shares in issue) and trade at least $100,000 of value a day, otherwise you're going to find it difficult to place your trades. Some traders prefer to concentrate on stocks over $1 billion market capitalization.
• You need to trade stocks with a tight spread (the difference between the price at which market makers will sell you stock, and the price they'll pay for you to sell it back to them). For instance, if you're trading AAPL, you'll only pay a few pennies spread on the share price: the quote today is $242.30 to $242.44, just $0.14 or 0.06% of the price. On the other hand, if you traded CareMax on Nasdaq, the spread is $0.011 to $0.019, or 7.2% ($0.019 - $0.011 = $0.008 difference, then 0.008 / 0.011 x 100 = 7.2%). That means you'll need to make 7.2% on the trade just to break even!

If you stick to stocks with these characteristics you have a much better chance of trading them easily and successfully.

ETFs

Like shares, ETFs (exchange-traded funds) are also traded on the stock market. The difference is that an ETF is a product that has been structured to reflect the performance of a stock index like the S&P 500 or Nasdaq Composite, a sector index, or a commodity such as gold. But just like a stock, it also has a ticker symbol (i.e. VUG = Vanguard Growth ETF), and you can buy it through your broker.

Suppose you have a feeling that the biotech sector is going to go upwards strongly. You could go and buy every biotech stock you can find. Or you could check out all the stocks and wait till one gives you the right signal. But the ETF gives you another choice to check out. Effectively, the ETF lets you buy the whole sector as a package; in ETF-speak, it 'replicates' the index, whether physically (by actually buying all the stocks) or synthetically (through a contract with a counterparty). Suppose you made up a mini-sector of carbonated beverages, which consists of two stocks, Coca-Cola and Pepsi. You could trade either or both of these stocks, but you could also simplify your job by trading FIZZ. Or perhaps there would also be an inverse ETF, FLAT. (Please note, I made up FIZZ and FLAT. They don't actually exist.)

In fact, ETFs are far more useful than in this example, because most sectors don't have two stocks in them, they have dozens, and buying ETF gives you exposure to the lot. Like stocks, ETFs vary in size and liquidity, so make sure to check out the ETFs you're planning to trade. As well as trading stock market index ETFs, you could trade silver (SLV), gold (IAUM), or even pork (HOGS).

You can also trade ETFs that offer a leveraged return. For instance, Direxion Daily Gold Miners Index Bull 2x Shares (NUGT) offers twice the return on the gold sector. If the gold miners' index goes up a penny, NUGT goes up two. Of course the bad news here is that if the index goes down, NUGT will fall down twice as much as the index.

ETFs also allow you to go short of a sector or commodity that you think will fall. For instance, if you think the gold price will fall, you could buy DUST, the Direction Daily Gold Miners Index Bear 2x Share. It's worth noting the tickers NUGT and DUST; these ETFs do what they say on the tin, right? Another neatly tickered pair is GUSH and DRIP, a leveraged 2x Oil and Gas shares ETF and its 2x bear counterpart.

Direxion also offers a bear S&P 500 ETF if you think the stock market is headed down, allowing you to 'short the market' without selling short. Basically, you are *buying* the ETF, so you don't have to be able to sell short, but the ETF will make you a profit if the market goes *down*. This ETF, SPDN, is inverse (i.e. it's a risk *against* the market), but it isn't leveraged.

In fact, Direxion must have identified a little gap in the market because they now offer single-company inverse ETFs such as AAPD (bear ETF for Apple), AMZD (for Amazon), AVS (for Broadcom), and TSLS (for Tesla). I haven't tried these out, but they might offer an interesting opportunity for traders whose brokers don't allow short selling to trade downturns.

I wouldn't advise trading leveraged ETFs, though. They're likely to whipsaw against you (a sharp increase or decrease in price, which goes against the prevailing trend), and it's difficult to manage your risks effectively, particularly if they gap up or down at the open.

Currencies

The currency markets (Forex) are vast pools of liquidity where money circulates continuously - these markets never close! Trillions of dollars are traded every day by banks and big companies, hedge funds, and individual traders. However, you'll need to understand some important differences from the stock markets.

First, currencies always trade in pairs, and you have to know the pair you're trading. For instance, you might trade the yen against the dollar, but you could also trade the yen against the pound sterling or the euro. Some pairs are much more commonly traded than others, like 'cable,' the special term for sterling against the dollar, GBPUSD.

Like GBPUSD, each pair is given a six-letter denomination. So, the dollar against the yen is USDJPY. But you could also trade JPYUSD. What's the difference? Quite a lot! The first three letters are the numerator - the base currency, which is always worth *one*.

So with JPYUSD, the numerator is yen, so you are trading however many dollars to 1 yen. And because the yen is really small, you'll see the rate is around 0.0065. In other words, you're looking at 0.0065 cents to 1 yen.

The other way round, USDJPY, the unit is the dollar, so you're looking at how many yen you can get for 1 dollar. The answer is about 154 yen to 1 dollar.

So you can see that you need to be the kind of person who can get these things the right way around, or you're in trouble. If when you travel abroad, you end up asking your traveling companions, "Remind me, is the euro bigger than the dollar, or is it the other way around?" then the huge and liquid currency markets might not be for you.

On the other hand, if you have a good understanding of macroeconomics and a feel for the impact of interest rates, the currency market could be a good place to trade. One of my friends is in corporate treasury, so his day job is assessing how currency movements will affect the company he works for; he swing trades currencies in his spare time!

There are several ways of trading currencies. If you want to stick with a regular broker, the easiest is to trade currency ETFs. However, if you want to head for the currency spot market straight off, you'll want to open a dedicated currency account. Currency price changes are given in 'pips,' that is, the fourth decimal place - for JPYUSD, a pip is 0.0065 to 0.0066. You'll need to get used to thinking in pips and particularly in terms of the effect that a single pip will have on your trading position.

Unlike the stock market, there are no specialists or market makers; the currency spot market is a huge free-for-all. So make sure you choose a well-reputed broker. Such as ig.com or interactivebrokers.co.uk.

Cryptocurrencies

Cryptocurrencies arrived with Bitcoin, which was released in 2009, so they're a fairly new asset type. These digital currencies are created through blockchain technology and stored in a digital ledger; they don't depend on a bank or government to give them value. That has a certain appeal to people who don't trust the government to maintain the value of their currency.

Swing trading crypto has made some traders fortunes. It has bankrupted others. If you want to try your hand, you'll need to sign up with a cryptocurrency exchange such as Binance or Coinbase. Brokerage eToro also offers crypto as one of its products. On the whole, though, I would say crypto is an unforgiving marketplace to learn your trade. Start on stocks, build your skills, and then think about whether you want to move on to crypto.

There are a few disadvantages with crypto. First, cryptocurrencies aren't legal everywhere, and the regulation of exchanges is increasing - for instance, Binance has had to quit the UK market. Secondly, a lot of the exchanges are not transparent, and there have been quite a few exchanges that went bust - Mt Gox in 2014 and Alameda Research in 2022, to name the two most prominent. So make sure your money is safe.

Options

Options represent another interesting market for swing trading. Traded options on stocks are standardized so that they can be traded efficiently. You can buy either a call option (option to buy the stock at a certain price) or put option (option to sell the stock at a certain price). Buying a *call* option is a traded on the share price going up; buying a *put* is a traded on the share price falling.

Options have a number of complexities. Unlike shares, they are limited-life investments; every option has an expiry date, on which, if it hasn't been exercised (used to buy the shares), it becomes valueless. As the option approaches its expiry date, the price will change to reflect that fact. It might be 'in the money,' for instance, if the exercise price of a call option is lower than the share price. The exercise price, also called the *strike price*, is the price at which the option lets you buy or sell the share.

For example, suppose XYZ stock is trading at $122 per share on February 1, 2025. A trader purchases a call option with a strike price of $130, expiring on March 31, 2025, and pays a $5 premium per share. Since options contracts cover 100 shares, the total premium cost is $500 ($5 premium x 100 shares).

If XYZ rises to $150 by expiration, the option's intrinsic value is $20 per share ($150 expiration price - $130 strike price), resulting in a total value of $2,000 ($20 x 100 shares). After deducting the $500 premium cost, the net profit is $1,500.

If XYZ rises to $135 by expiration, the trader would have profited $5 per share ($135 expiration price - $130 strike price), but this would have covered their initial $5 premium cost per share - therefore, they would just break even.

Conversely, if XYZ stock stays below $130, then the option expires worthless, and the trader loses only the $500 premium cost. Who wants to pay a $130 option for a stock that's currently traded at a price lower than that?

Personally, I find there's too much advanced math in options trading, and I don't find the quote pages friendly - they show all the differently priced options in what is called the 'options chain,' so there is a lot of information to take on at once. But if you're a bit of a geek, this might just be the market that appeals to you.

Chapter 2 Quiz

1. Which of these is not a stock exchange?
a) Euronext
b) Deutsche Bank
c) NYSE
d) Nasdaq

2. A December 2024 call option on Amazon with a strike price of $210 will let you:
a) Buy Amazon shares at $210 at any time before December
b) Buy Amazon shares at $210 at any time after December
c) Sell Amazon shares at $210
d) Sell the option in the market

3. 'Cable' is abbreviated as
a) USDJPY
b) WIRE
c) GBPUSD
d) CHFEUR

4. Which of these can you swing trade through an ETF?
a) Gold
b) Currency
c) Stocks
d) All of the above

5. Where are ETFs traded?
a) On the stock market
b) On the options market
c) Via Blockchain
d) On the pork markets

3

Chapter 3: Grasping the Stock Market Environment

When you go shopping in a supermarket, everything is already priced. If a pizza says it's $5, it's $5, and that's not going to change. It's $5 all day today, and tomorrow - unless it gets reduced as short-dated stock. That's very different from the stock market, where stocks trade up and down all day and the price at the closing can be very different from where the stock opened.

There's another big difference from the supermarket, of course. Imagine if you could go to the supermarket and say, "Hey, I have a pizza and some burger buns I want to sell; what will you pay me for them?"

So, if you've been used to shopping with price tags, you're going to need to take a little time to get used to the way a financial market works. It's more like bargaining in a marketplace, or going to an auction.

Supermarkets only work one way; the supermarket sets the price, and sells things to customers. On the other hand, financial markets work both ways - you can buy and sell. And though the market makers fix the bid (buy) and ask (sell) prices, they don't 'set' the price like a supermarket. Instead, they adjust the prices they quote in relation to the demand and supply of shares in the market. If they see a lot of people are selling, they will adjust the price downwards; if they see a lot of the people buying, they will move their prices up. But the price reflects the interests of all the traders and investors who make up the market - the market maker is just trying to stay in line with what's happening.

Let's go back in time to the very early days of Wall Street and look at how things worked then. There wasn't even a stock exchange building; traders met and traded under a buttonwood tree. If you had stock to sell, you simply turned up and asked around till you found someone prepared to buy it, and you'd settle the price between the two of you.

In 1792 - after a major financial panic - the regular traders joined together under the Buttonwood Agreement to form a stock exchange and moved to the Tontine Coffee House as their offices. Their agreement was simple; the traders would only deal with each other, not with any outsiders; and they would charge a set 0.25% commission. That's why there is still a buttonwood tree outside the New York Stock Exchange - the only tree on Wall Street.

The New York Stock Exchange eventually acquired its own building. That's a bit irrelevant now that trading has gone online, of course, but the essence of the stock market is still the same as it was in the old days; a system that reconciles buyers' and sellers' requirements by changing the prices of stocks. In the financial market, we often call buyers 'bulls' and sellers 'bears' - no one knows exactly why.

Think about this system in a slightly more abstract way and you can see that it is driven by forces of supply and demand - sellers and buyers of stock. But what drives the buyers and sellers? There are several answers to this. Some are driven by mathematical models; some investors work out exactly what they think is the intrinsic value (the actual value) of a stock, so they will buy up to that price and sell above it for profit. Some are driven by asset allocation; that is, they have decided that they should have a certain percentage of their money invested in healthcare, so they look for healthcare stocks to buy in order to fill that allocation.

But often, investors are also driven by emotion. They see a stock price falling and think that something's going wrong - someone must know that the company is in trouble. Or they see a stock price rising and want to get on the bandwagon. That's where social media can be dangerous - Twitter and Reddit are likely to boost these emotions, sometimes without good and reliable information. We saw that with the huge bull run in Gamestop (GME), when the wallstreetbets subreddit inspired speculative trading in the company's shares.

The two big emotions of the market are fear and greed. Greed is about "I want to be rich" - fear is about "I don't want to lose money." Both these emotions get in the way of rational thinking. And once an emotion starts to power a market, it tends to draw in more and more people and gets stronger and stronger.

Fear starts with one investor who is feeling a bit stressed or a little bit concerned about the market - maybe thinking valuation are a bit too high, or feeling prices moved up too quickly and have lost touch with the real economy. This feeling of stress gets stronger, and some "early birds" sell their holdings. Other investors catch on and decide to follow them, and eventually, this starts a selling frenzy. In the case of the 1929 market crash, it ended with brokers jumping out of windows.

Greed starts with one investor seeing a bargain in a stock, and buying it up. Then others get in early, too. Many of these might be buy-and-hold investors working based on fundamental analysis information. Then others, including traders, notice the stock price has gone up. Momentum traders jump in, and they're joined by retail investors who are suffering FOMO (Fear of Missing Out) when they see the stock price has already started moving up. Sooner or later, everyone is buying the stock, and the share price is set for take-off - until one or two investors start feeling a little bit stressed. At this point, you can go back to the beginning of the previous paragraph on fear and "repeat the cycle" from there!

And of course, these emotions mean that markets tend to overreact. Bad news sparks fear, and so a tiny bit of bad news can make a stock fall hard and fast to a price much lower than is reasonable. On the other hand, as we saw in the tech boom of the late 1990s, when buyers get greedy, stock prices can head up way too high and fast. It's basic crowd psychology.

If you were being rational, not emotional, you would set the price of a share to reflect the company's earnings, the amount of growth you expected in future years, the value of the company's assets (like buildings, or brand names, or technology), and so on. It might also reflect how the share compared to other potential investments, such as other shares, Treasury bonds, or real estate. Then you'd likely have a market that didn't move much except when there was news that altered these valuation criteria.

But fear and greed mean that share prices are changing all the time, and often with big overreactions that create wild swings in the share price - the swings that *swing traders* use to make a profit.

This leads to the fact that stock markets run in cycles. A price trend will run until something stops it. For instance, a fast-growth tech stock might see its price keep moving up until one of the following things happens:

• It announces bad results, and investors start selling the stock because their assessment of its long-term profitability has taken a hit.
• One or two major investors or analysts think it is way overvalued and start selling the stock.
• Traders who have made a profit on the stock decide to crystallize their gains and sell. That is, they're sitting on a paper profit, so they decide they want to take the money.

At that point, if market participants get worried that suddenly there are more sellers than buyers in the market, the share price might take a dip. That dip is likely to carry on until there is a reason for it to reverse, which might simply be that short traders who have sold the stock decide they've made enough profit and decide to buy it back.

Look at any chart of the stock market (e.g. the S&P 500) or of an individual stock and you'll see how this happens all the time. There are big cycles that play out over a number of years, and tiny cycles that can play out within a single trading day. Look at the S&P chart for the last five years below. You'll see it's in an uptrend. But then you can see two 'waves,' one big wave rising till January 2022 and then falling back, then another big wave all the way to 2025. And within these waves you can see individual smaller waves, or spikes, rising and falling back. This chart uses daily prices, but if you downloaded a chart of hourly or even five-minute prices, you'd find even smaller cycles happening.

The particular interest of stock market cycles for swing traders is that these cycles are at least partly predictable. Remember that idea of walking along the shore? It's roughly every seventh wave that is the biggest. It might not be exactly seven, that's just folk wisdom, but if you watch the sea you'll find that waves come in sets, gradually increasing in size till the biggest, then decreasing in size till the smallest. The sea isn't just random; there is a pattern to it. In the same way, the stock market isn't completely random either. If you learn to read the patterns that stock market waves make, you'll be able to take advantage of them.

All stock exchanges, in fact, all financial markets, work this way. It doesn't matter whether you're trading stocks, commodities, T-bonds, options, spot currency, or futures; the crowd psychology that drives them is the same.

One way of looking at this is the Wyckhoff price cycle (seen in an example below). The cycle starts with a phase of *accumulation*, in which market participants are buying the shares. Gradually, they buy all the 'loose' shares in the market from eager sellers, and eventually, the price starts to move up. In the *mark-up* phase, prices continue to rise, with major investors still buying them. The third phase, *distribution* or consolidation, sees some investors selling out, while others are still buying. On a stock price chart, you'll often see a long period of the price going nowhere, just bobbing up and down slightly, as the buyers and sellers are equally matched. The final phase of the cycle is *markdown*. Now, everyone who wants to buy the shares already has them, and there are more sellers than buyers in the market. There might be a final push upwards before the share price starts to fall, and when it falls, it usually falls fast as holders of the shares get anxious.

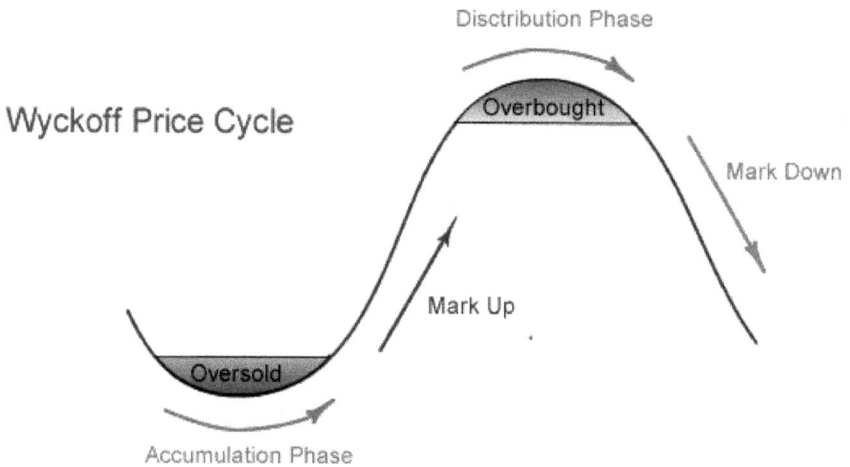

Wyckoff Price Cycle

Disctribution Phase

Overbought

Mark Down

Mark Up

Oversold

Accumulation Phase

At the end of the markdown, all the sellers are out, but very few investors are brave enough to get back in. So, the accumulation stage starts with just a few early buyers, and right at the start, there are a lot of eager sellers. It's only once buyers have soaked up all the ready supply that the price starts to move up - signaling the start of the mark-up phase. Another fresh stock market cycle is on its way!

The two main American exchanges are the New York Stock Exchange (NYSE) and Nasdaq. NYSE acquired the third major exchange, the American Stock Exchange, back in 2008, and it now trades as the NYSE American, covering mainly smaller capitalization stocks. What we used to call 'Wall Street' nowadays we really need to call 'American financial markets', because a lot of the action doesn't take place on Wall Street any more. NYSE's trading center and Nasdaq's servers (which, given that the market is electronic) are in New Jersey, and many of the participants in the market are scattered across the US. Hence, the historic Wall Street area is now a 'symbolic' center rather than where trading actually happens.

Trading, investing, or gambling?

Often, popular culture doesn't differentiate these three activities. You'll hear some people say, "The entire stock market is a gamble," or you'll hear others say, "Of course, I'm an investor, not a speculator." But in fact, trading, investing and gambling are three very different things.

Investing means placing your funds in a financial instrument, such as a stock or a bond, in order to gain long-term returns. You might get those returns in a cash payment, when the government pays you interest on a treasury bond, or a stock pays you a dividend. But you might also get those returns in terms of an increase in the value of your holding when a company grows its business, and therefore, the stock becomes more valuable.

Investors look at the fundamentals of an investment, for instance, the underlying business behind a stock. An investor in McDonald's will consider how fast its earnings are growing, how it competes against Wendy's and Burger King and perhaps Chipotle, what it might earn in the next few years and how much it might pay out in dividends. Investors are rational, and are interested in long term returns - though of course if a stock price increased fast, making the investment valued more highly than they thought was justified, they might sell, and look for a better way to employ their capital.

Gamblers, on the other hand, know that they are taking a chance. While a few people do make a living as professional poker players, most gamblers are dreaming of a big win, while losing small amounts of money all the time - they would probably be better off investing. A gamble may be pure chance - roulette, for instance, or may have a mix of skill and imperfect information - poker, where you can't see your opponents' cards, or horse racing, where 'the form' or past records do not have complete predictive value.

Gamblers often also run the risk of losing their entire stake. If you bet on a horse and it doesn't win, or you bet on black and it is red that comes up, you have lost the lot.

Gambling should really be something you do for fun. And if you do, then you should look at the money you lose as similar to money spent on eating out or going to the movies; it's entertainment.

Trading is something else entirely. It's not investing, because you are not in there for the long term - you want to get in and then get out relatively quickly at a profit. It's also not investing because while you might look at the fundamentals to ensure you're trading a stock with no hidden pitfalls, you're not buying it because of those fundamentals. You're buying it simply in order to benefit from short-term share price movements.

But it's not gambling. With a few very limited exceptions, traders don't lose their entire stakes (in fact, later on, you'll see how a big part of trading is about limiting your losses). Traders, like investors, are putting their money into something that has a real value; gamblers aren't.

Traders also do a lot of work to find potential winning situations and assess them in a rational way. Traders who trade on emotion or 'gut feel' rarely win. Swing traders use various logical and back-tested methods to find stocks which are likely to see strong movements in price, and calculate the risk and potential return before executing a trade.

Risks and return

I am going to give you an absolute rule here; there are two words I never want to hear you use. Never, ever say 'safe,' and never, ever say 'risky.'

There is no such thing as 100% *safety* in a financial situation and there are very few 100% *risks*. There are only different levels of safety and riskiness on the spectrum. In other words, something can be more or less safe, and more or less risky, but it can't be 'safe' or 'risky' as an absolute.

The reason I want you to never use those words is because, as a trader, you should always be thinking about the relationship between risk and return on any trade.

The only thing that is 'safe' is cash. But it will not give any return at all if it's sitting in your brokerage account.

Investing and trading both represent a risk to your capital. But by trading or investing you are looking to secure a return. In other words, you are running a risk in order to achieve a return.

Naturally, the risk should be proportionate to the return you expect to achieve. If you take on more risk you'd expect a higher reward - "danger money," so to speak. That's why venture capitalists who invest in start-ups expect to make a high return, because they're taking on a high risk as many start-ups fail.

I'll show you later how traders evaluate risk and return. But right now you should be getting used to thinking about the relationship between risk and return. And you should be stripping out of your vocabulary words and phrases like "risk-free," "a sure thing," "you can't lose," and so on.

Because you can lose. In fact, as a trader, you expect to lose on some of your trades. It's only by getting the risk/reward formula right that you manage to win more on the good trades that you lose on the bad ones.

By the way, the definition of the word risk is "the measurable likelihood of loss." In other words, you need to be able to quantify risk - to put a number on it. Just feeling apprehensive is not a measure of risk. A lot of your success as a trader will depend on your ability to quantify both downside risk and upside potential returns, and to be able to execute a trade on the basis of that analysis rather than letting your feelings run the trade for you.

Defining the basic principles for swing trading success

One of the main ingredients for success as a trader is focus. Rather than trying to learn everything about swing trading, and trade as many markets and assets as possible, you're better off trading one market, a select group of assets, and one kind of 'setup' that you really understand. You may *not* trade all that often to start with, and you may *not* be successful from the get-go, but stick to a simple formula, and you *will* find out how it works and how to take advantage of it.

On the other hand, if you chop and change every time you make a losing trade, you're never going to develop your skills and insight into the market.

Remember that you're an individual with your own set of skills, tastes and abilities. If you're a math geek, maybe you should be trading currencies or options. If you're not, stocks may be a better choice. If, when you read the chapter 6 on technical analysis, you find that there's one particular kind of chart pattern that you can see really clearly, start trading with that one. That will give you the kind of focus that makes for successful trading. Later, you can branch out a bit - once you have a bit more skill.

Another major ingredient is capital and position management. It's rather boring compared to double bottoms, ascending triangles, black crows, but it's the ingredient that makes for success in trading, a bit like yeast makes all the difference to a loaf of bread.

I'll go into detail later, but capital management is basically all about ensuring you never bet the bank. Often, traders go bust spectacularly when they fail to control the amount of risk they're taking on a single trade. Manage your positions properly, and you'll be able to take a string of losing trades without losing a big chunk of your capital.

And, of course, you need to always know your risk and reward ratio. Unsuccessful traders often think too much about the reward but don't clearly grasp how much risk they are taking on. Good traders make money because they always know that the odds are stacked in their favor.

The other ingredients - as with most things in life - are hard work and discipline. For instance, good traders have the discipline to close a trade at a loss as soon as they see that it's going against them. They don't hang around to lose even more money. And they work hard because trading is a business, not a hobby. You may not need to put in forty hours a week but you do need to check the market and your positions every day; if you can't commit to that kind of regularity, you may not have what it takes.

You'll also need to be able to cope with loss. Every good trader has the occasional run of loss-making trades, and you'll need to be able to take those losses on the chin. If not, you'll either end up too scared of losing money to trade well, or making unnecessary high-risk large trades to try to claw back your losses.

Chapter 3 Quiz

1. Which of these kinds of risks should you *never* take on your trading books?
a) A high risk for a high return
b) A low risk for a high return
c) A low risk for a low return
d) A high risk for a low return

2. What is a bull?
a) Someone who is buying stock
b) Someone who is selling stock
c) A kind of market maker
d) A type of cattle

3. Which of these attributes will not be particularly useful to you as a trader?
a) Discipline
b) Imagination
c) Focus
d) Ability to cope with loss

4. A successful swing trader is one who
a) Never makes losses
b) Makes more gains than losses
c) Wins more on their winning trades than they lose on their losing trades
d) Sometimes wins and sometimes loses

5. Which of these is not a phase of the Wyckoff market cycle?
a) Markup
b) Markdown
c) Accumulation
d) Decomposition

4

Chapter 4: Tools and Platforms for Swing Trading

You're going to need some basics to get set up. Particularly if you start by entering your orders after market hours, rather than trading full time, your requirements will be slightly less than those of a day trader. If you haven't been involved with financial markets before, this will all be new to you. But you shouldn't assume that you already have everything you need if you have an investment account with a broker. Some brokers don't offer all the functionality and tools you'll need for swing trading, so you must evaluate your existing broker. You might decide to take your trading portfolio elsewhere.

You also need to manage your costs, particularly if you are starting in a small way. Plenty of firms would love to help you spend your money on trading software, advice, subscriptions, and conferences. Some are reputable; others are less so. But even if a particular service is useful, you need to work out whether it will pay its way at your level of trading. A self-employed electrician and a taxi driver need an accountant, but they don't necessarily need to employ Deloitte or PWC!

Brokerage accounts

First of all, you'll need a brokerage account to swing trade; and you'll want to be quite specific in looking for the things you need and not getting too caught up with things you don't need. For instance, you don't need a broker to give you ideas for buying stocks or funds to help you manage your money. Full-service brokers will charge you a premium for their research, and they won't bring anything to your particular party. Nor do you need a named account manager or an in-person yearly review of how your account is performing.

You want good trading execution, which means you'll want to be able to give conditional orders, and you'll need a broker with some decent power in the market so that they secure you reasonable prices and timely trades. Most of the larger discount brokers will deliver - but be careful. I had one broker that always seemed to deliver my stock at a penny more than the market price, and always seemed to get me a price when I sold that was some way below the spread indicated on Nasdaq. I decided I'd track their prices for a month, and I realized I was losing quite a bit of profit due to their sub-par execution performance. I found a different broker.

You want a broker with low costs. If you're getting charged high account fees or high commission fees, that will drag down your performance over time. Some brokers even offer commission-free trades, while others offer a low flat fee per trade.

You'll need to do some detailed work to find the right tariffs. Some brokers offer different programs, so if you join at the 'frequent trader' level, you'll get cheaper trades than on the basic program, but need to make a certain number of monthly trades. Watch out, too, for 'hidden' costs. Some brokers make you pay a percentage on money taken out of your account, or have custody charges or inactivity fees.

You might also want to check out what other markets you can access through each broker. For instance, eToro will allow you to trade across international markets and offer cryptocurrency options. You'll want to check out the costs for those markets, too; don't forget that foreign markets will incur currency exchange costs as well as trading costs. The difference can be marked; one broker I looked at charges five times more for international trades than for domestic ones, and then adds a currency charge too.

You might want to check out brokers like E*Trade, Robinhood, TDWaterhouse or Charles Schwab. These will probably work well for you when you start out, but you could also consider a direct access broker like Interactive Brokers, TradeStation or CenterPoint Securities. These offer you the ability to trade directly with market makers or exchanges, rather than routing your order via the brokerage. E*Trade now provides direct access through its E*Trade Pro package, though not all brokers will do this.

Before making a decision, check out reviews of the brokers you are considering in financial media and the internet. The rankings change over time; for instance, if a broker launches a new trading platform which is more user-friendly, that could affect its score markedly. It's important, then, that you stay aware of the rankings, both when you're choosing your broker to start out, and later when another broker might be able to offer you a tariff or platform more in line with your needs.

Check bulletin boards, subreddits, and social media, as well as Google reviews for customers' recent experiences. I was put off by one broker when I read numerous reports of the same negative experience with accounts being suddenly frozen. In particular, you need to know that you have access to a phone line and a real person on the end of it if you have a problem with access. Check out whether customers have issues such as poorly executed trades, or even trade orders not being executed at all. This is the time to discover such problems - not when you have money at risk.

You might also want to check out a few extra useful functions that brokers might offer. For instance, if a broker offers great reports such as performance statistics, comparison with market benchmarks, or a tax reporting package, that might be worthwhile. Many traders underestimate the amount of work that their tax filings are going to require.

If a broker offers a good charting platform, that's a big plus point, mainly if it's linked to the trading function. On the other hand, research is not a big plus (unless you use it for your investment account); as a trader, you'll find that equity research is outdated as far as moving the market is concerned.

Opening a brokerage account is usually fairly straightforward, but you'll need to be clear about what kind of account you require. For a start, if you're married or in a relationship, do you want to open the account in your sole name or joint names?

You also need to think about whether you want a cash account or a margin account. A margin account will allow you to trade on credit. Usually, this doubles the amount you can trade so that if you have $100,000 in your account, you'd be able to trade $200,000 worth of stock. If you make a profit, this is good news because you'll keep 100% of the profit while only having put up 50% of the capital. That vastly increases your profitability. However, if a trade goes against you, the broker may issue a margin call, requiring you to add cash to your account. You'll also pay interest on borrowings, which is a cost you'll need to consider when planning your trades.

I'd recommend that you start out with a cash account. It's too easy to go overboard with a margin account. Once you've got more experience of managing your trades, and have a decent track record, it's easy to ask to change account type.

You also need to think about tax. If you open a regular account, you'll be liable for tax on all your trades. You can get around this, at least partly, by opening the Individual Retirement Account; an IRA will keep the IRS away from your profits! However, there are limits on how much you can put into an IRA, and you won't be able to access your capital till you are 59 1/2 unless you pay a stiff penalty. If you want to be able to spend your trading profits, you'll need a regular account.

Some jurisdictions offer other tax-efficient accounts. For instance, in the UK, there's the Individual Savings Account, which has a fairly large annual limit and no restrictions on taking money out (though you can't put it back in again). In France, the PEA offers significant tax advantages if it's held for more than five years.

Trading platforms

Long-term investors don't need anything particularly sophisticated as an ordering mechanism; they don't need to squeeze the last penny out of a trade, and if their order has to wait half an hour to be filled, it's not a disaster. On the other hand, if you're a trader, just one minute's delay could mean the difference between making a profitable trade and being left on the sidelines - or worse, when you come to sell, making a nasty loss instead.

So you need to find a trading platform that will allow you to enter orders fast, as well as to enter conditional orders - stop loss orders are particularly important, as they are your protection mechanism if a trade starts going wrong. You really need to try trading platforms out for usability; many brokers now offer you the chance to use a demo version before opening an account.

Some brokers offer their own trading platforms. For instance, Interactive Brokers has Trader Workstation; some traders find its usability isn't what it could be. TD Waterhouse's Thinkorswim is well regarded; some day traders find they outgrow it, but swing traders should find all they need on that platform.

Some brokers offer third-party trading platforms such as DAS; if not offered with a brokerage account, it costs $100 or more every month, so it's an extra well worth having. Many traders also highly rate RealTick EMS, eSignal, Cybertrader, and TradeStation.

With any trading platform, you need to look at how it manages watch lists and scanners. This functionality will save you a lot of time looking for potentially profitable situations. You might want to see if it offers alerts, or if you can customize the screens or chart types offered. You'll also want to think about how easily you can track your trading book using the platform.

However, the two must-haves for a trading platform are reliability and support. Particularly if you're trading lives, "four-nines" reliability is something you really can't live without, and you'll want 24/7 support, preferably by phone or by internet chat (outside the trading platform, because if it's not working and you can only access the chat within the platform, you're stuck).

Charting platforms

You'll also need to consider charting platforms unless your broker has a particularly good offering. You'll need live data, unless you're only setting up trades when the market is closed. Brokers may have good charting platforms but they might not include all the technical indicators that you want, or may not offer customization or scanning capabilities, and probably won't offer backtesting functions. While backtesting functions don't sound attractive, they can be very useful when you're assessing the profitability of new setups or attempting to improve your trading.

Thinkorswim offers a pretty good charting package; among third-party providers, TradeStation and Finviz are strong contenders. Meanwhile, if you're strapped for cash, Tradingview offers some high-end capabilities for free, though you can get even more if you pay for the premium service.

Many platforms offer a 30-day free trial. If you're considering paying for a platform, it really is worth taking the trial. You may find that, for whatever reason, you just can't get on with that particular platform. You should also check reviews before you make a decision. There's often good discussion on trade-related subreddits. Don't use Reddit for investment ideas, but do use it to get the lowdown on brokers and platforms.

In the screenshot above, there is a view of the Thinkorswim trading platform showing the different views that can be open at the same time. If, like most swing traders, you want to have some basic fundamentals to inform your trading, you'll find basic financial data on Yahoo Finance and Google Finance. Zacks offers basics for free and has some basic screening tools which can help you cut down the number of stocks you're looking at, though it will try to sell you a premium service, including a special number-crunching investment service. Stick with the free stuff. For free market news, Reuters is your best choice.

Trade journaling

When you start trading, you can keep your trade journal in a notebook or in a database on your PC.

The data you need to enter are fairly basic:

• The stock
• The date, time, and price of entry
• The date, time, and price of exit
• Your stop loss and profit target
• Capital at risk (i.e. the difference between your entry price and the stop loss)
• Profit or loss on the trade
• The reason for the trade (e.g. head and shoulders formation, confirmation from moving averages and RSI)
• And possibly your frame of mind (feeling a bit overconfident this morning, not seeing many convincing trade ideas today).

It's also useful to have a note of the market level and trend at the time, so you know whether you were trading with the trend and how strong that trend was on the day.

These pieces of information will let you look back at the end of the week or month and see which trades worked well, and which didn't. You'll be able to pick up on trends in your trading, and to see what your best (and worst) trades had in common.

But if you go full-time, you're going to want to manage your time more proactively, and that's where journaling software comes in. TraderVue, TraderBench and Edgewonk all offer the ability to automate your trade journal. That means the grunt work of entering the size and price of your trade, working out the percentage of your capital at risk, noting down the market conditions at the time, and recording the share price chart, are all done for you. That saves you time and means you can't manually enter incorrect data.

Profit calendar

Even better, the journal software can carry out analyses for you to let you know your win rate, returns, and profitability. Most will also perform backtesting on different strategies, and of course, you can still add your own notes.

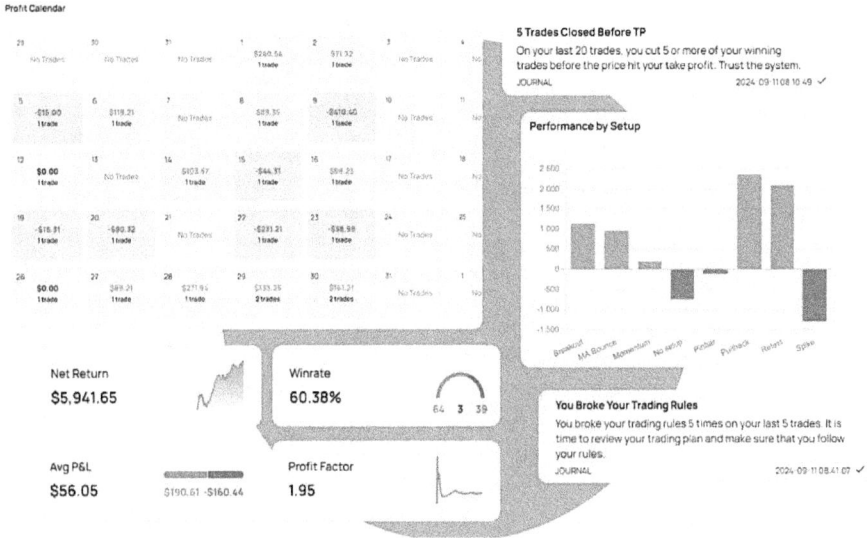

Here's a view of Edgewonk above. What I like about it is that it tells you in casual language what you're doing - "you broke your trading rules"!

It also shows you performance by setup, so that you can see which trading strategies are working best for you, and which are not working at all. It's actually done quite a lot of the hard work of analysis, and now it's just up to you to decide what action you need to take.

Where will you work?

Many swing traders get started on the kitchen table after dinner, but I don't recommend it. Ideally, you need a workstation where all you do is trade. That might simply be a closet with a desk and chair installed, a laptop, and a little task lighting, or it might be at the end of your home office with two big screens and a fast computer.

You'll want to ensure you have reliable internet access (this becomes more important when you're trading live) and, if possible, that you have an alternative if the internet goes down, like a phone app. Ensure your smartphone is not on the same network as your internet service.

You're really going to want a second screen or even three screens so that you can look at charts and the quote page at the same time. Tabbing back between pages will frustrate you and sometimes lead to errors, for instance, forgetting what time frame you're using for your charts.

You'll want to take a look at your computer's specification. You'll be doing a fair bit of data crunching and showing a lot of graphics, so it needs to handle a lot of data quickly. It could be time to upgrade. Best to trial it with a demo trading platform and a chart package or website open - if it's not fast enough or freezes when it's displaying too many tabs, you need that upgrade before you start trading for real. And don't forget to have an external hard drive or cloud storage so you can back up all the data on your computer every week (at least).

A few other things that I find useful are a legal pad or notebook in easy reach, with a mug for my pens and pencils so they don't get lost, and an old-school electronic calculator that I can use for really basic calculations without having to touch the computer. If you're trading live, you might want to have a TV tuned to a business channel - not too loud; you want to be able to ignore it and only 'tune in' if you hear particular stocks' names mentioned.

Managing watchlists and scanners

Suppose you wanted to find stocks to trade that had good earnings growth, modest debt, and market capitalization over $1 billion. You could start by checking out stocks you already knew, like Alphabet, Meta, Microsoft, and Amazon. Or you could start at the top and work down, stock by stock - A Consulting Team, A Mark Precious Metals Inc, ASV, A-Power Energy Generation System, A123 Systems… That would be crazily time-consuming.

Fortunately, you don't have to do it. You can use a stock screener to exclude all the stocks that don't fit your criteria. So, for instance, you could pick the following criteria:

• Share price > $10 (to exclude all the penny stocks)
• Market capitalization > $1 billion
• Earning per share (EPS) growth < 5%
• Debt to equity < 1

Let's see what that does to Nasdaq. The default screen starts with 3,353 stocks in total. Excluding penny stocks more than halves this, leaving 1,553 stocks that we could look at. Excluding lower market cap stocks gets us down to 893. Adding the requirements for 5% earning per share growth more than halves that number to 405 stocks while adding the requirement for a strong balance sheet with less than 1 debt-to-equity ratio gives us just 325 matches.

That's still a lot of stocks, but its 3,028 fewer than we started with (3,353 - 325 = 3,028). The stock screener certainly saved us a lot of work.

However, our work isn't finished. Some of those stocks will just be motoring along nicely, while others are at a standstill. We want to find stocks with strong share price movement in prospect. So, depending on what kind of situation we're looking for, we could use share price movement to look for prospective stocks rather than look at 325 separate charts.

If you're looking for stocks in a long-term uptrend, you could look for those trading toward the top of their 52-week range. On Zacks, there's the option to select "Price as % of 52 Wk H-L Range"; select 90% to get stocks which are towards the top of the range. Some of those might have spiked recently, but others will likely show 12 months of solid upward trend. Now, there are just 68 matches here in the example below.

Equally, you could search for stocks that have seen price increases or decreases of a certain amount in the last week, month, or 12 weeks; or for stocks that are beating the market, i.e. that have performed better than the stock market index ("Relative Price Change (YTD)" - try different values till you get a set the size you want.

At this point, you need to hit the charting program of your choice and start looking for chart patterns that look interesting. I'll tell you more about that later. And at the end of that work, you'll have a watch list of stocks that look like they could move pretty quickly.

You don't necessarily have to make the same choices. You might want to look for stocks trading in the top 80% of their 52-week price range, yet has dipped, so you can find situations where you can take advantage of a continuation of the uptrend. Or you might want to look for stocks trading towards their 52-week lows but which have shown 10-20% price upticks in the last month, hoping that the downward trend will now reverse. A scanner is only as good as the use you make of it.

It takes a little while to be able to formulate your requirements in quantitative terms to enter into the scanner, but you'll soon get used to it.

Having taken the time to do the scans and formulate a watch list, you've searched the whole market for situations that fit your trading style, without missing the situations that haven't been flagged up on social media or in the news. You've done so efficiently, and you've reduced the 3,000+ stocks on Nasdaq to about a dozen that will repay your watching them like a hawk, so you've gained real focus (remember, focus is one of the ingredients in the successful swing trading cake).

If you have a good trading platform, you'll be able to save your scans so that you can quickly run them every day to see if any new stocks have entered the net. You'll also be able to save your watchlist, for instance, by displaying all the charts on a summary page to quickly see if any of them have set up the conditions for a profitable trade.

Chapter 4 Quiz

1. Which of these things should not put you off a broker?
a) No telephone support
b) 15-minute delayed pricing
c) A clunky trading platform
d) Zero commission

2. Why might a new graphics card for your PC be a good investment?
a) You need to have pretty colors in your trading platform
b) You need to display multiple price charts in real-time
c) So you can play Grand Theft Auto after you've finished trading
d) Because it will make your PC worth more if you need to sell it

3. Which of these should you record in your trading journal?
a) The market trend when you traded
b) The chart formation or indicator that signaled the trade
c) The volume of stock traded in the market
d) How you felt on the day

4. What does a margin account let you do?
a) Buy stock on credit
b) Trade without putting your own money at risk
c) Trade currencies
d) Trade fractional stock

5. Which of these do you really need at your workstation?
a) Coffee
b) Two or more monitors
c) An executive toy
d) A cat on the desk

5

Chapter 5: Preparing for the Market Day

Most people think the swing trader's day starts when the opening bell rings. It doesn't. It doesn't even start in the pre-market in the early morning hours.

It starts with the closing bell. As soon as the market's closed, it's time to get to work.

Okay, you don't have to start that very moment. There's time for you to get home from the day job, if you have one, have a cup of tea or eat a snack, and then get to work. But all you need is the moment the market has closed.

This is the time to find your winners for tomorrow; look for the best opportunities and refine your watch list.

Some stocks may have broken out of the patterns you thought they were establishing. You can take these ones out of the watchlist. Check through the other stocks that fit your stock screen to see if any of them are beginning to make price trends that could give you a good trading opportunity.

Stock Screener ˅

| Market | US ˅ | Watchlist | Red list ˅ | Index ˅ | Price ˅ |

| Sector ˅ | Analyst Rating ˅ | Perf % ˅ | Revenue growth ˅ |

| | | Overview | Performance | Extended Hours | Va |

	Symbol 12			Price	Change %	
	TSLA	Tesla, Inc.		174.92 USD	−0.42%	2
	MA	Mastercard Incorporated		487.83 USD	−0.04%	3˙
	ORCL	Oracle Corporation		131.66 USD	+1.87%	
	TM	Toyota Motor Corporation DR		251.10 USD	+1.78%	‹
	BAC/PO	Bank of America Corpor... P		20.38 USD	+0.84%	

The Tradingview stock screener, as shown above, will give you a basic watchlist. It has a set of defaults, but you can customize it to show stocks that you have identified as good opportunities. By setting up a watchlist, you're making your job much easier, cutting out the market noise to concentrate on the meaningful signals.

Check for stocks 'in play'. They are likely to see strong trading tomorrow. They may be in play for various reasons; an earnings announcement by the company or a rival, a takeover bid in the sector that means there might be a bid for this one too, news affecting the sector (e.g. a strong run in the oil price, legalization of cannabis in a new state, or bankruptcy of a rival).

The easiest way to check for stocks in play is to look for stocks that had a very high volume day yesterday. If you're trading live, you might also pick up stocks with high volume in the pre-market. You're looking for high relative volume, well above the usual amount traded daily. One way to find these stocks is to type Relative Volume > 2 into a stock scanner.

Apple below, for instance, shows a correlation between price spikes upwards and downwards and big volume. The volume average is pretty constant, but you can see big volume spikes in June and September, and slightly less marked spikes in March and then again in August.

Check if there has been any news affecting your stocks. For instance, if a company issued a profit warning, that might destroy the case for trading the stock. Or perhaps it gives you an opportunity if you think the stock price overreacted to the bad news. Often, the news goes together with high volume - a clear sign of a stock in play.

You need to understand the basic news. You don't need to understand the details. A stock market analyst or a long-term investor will want to dig into the details of an earnings announcement: which parts of the business did well, whether there were any weaknesses, whether profitability increased, what happened to cash flow, and so on. As a swing trader, you just need the basics;

• The company's got a lot of Russian business, so sanctions will hurt;
• It's an airline, and oil prices just increased; that's bad news;
• Earnings are way up, surprised on the upside, and the company raised guidance;
• All the bank's user data has been hacked, that's going to have a big impact;
• The product launch is on time, and everyone's excited about the product.

The reason why you don't need to understand the details is because what you care about isn't the details - you just care about the fact that the stock has been put in play. Investors have to reassess the stock in light of the news, which means that the share price is going to move as they decide the stock is worth more (or less) than they thought it was. As a swing trader, it's the share price movements that are your opportunity.

This is also the time to think about your performance. Check any trades that were executed yesterday. Were any of your automatic entry orders executed? Were any stop losses activated? Was there any automated profit-taking? Take time to assess where this leaves the stock; has it completed the pattern you expected, or might another profitable trade be made in a few days?

It's good to take a couple of minutes to think through any completed trades. If you made a profit, did you take as much as you could have? What happened after you exited the trade? If you made a loss, remember that because you are trading on the basis of probabilities, there always will be losses, but look for any human error in the equation, for instance, having set the stop loss too tight and been 'bounced' or 'whipsawed' out of the trade before it came good again.

This isn't the right time to think about your trading strategy; it's just about yesterday's trades. You don't want to keep tinkering with your strategy. That would be like McDonald's rewriting the recipe for their burgers every time they sell one! The time for doing that is in a regular weekly or monthly review.

Check all your open positions to ensure you understand how much of your capital is at risk right now.

Finally, check whether there is any expected news tomorrow, such as economic news releases such as jobs data, a Fed report, or company news releases. It's also useful to be aware of the expiration days of the options. CBOE has an options expiration calendar for the whole year, also available on the Options Industry Council website, which can lead to volatility in the stocks concerned. Or you can get the calendars from macroption.com/options-expiration-calendar - they show the next two years and the last one, too.

The last thing you'll want to do is to check over the charts yourself and set your target profit and stop loss levels. Now, you can enter automatic orders for trades tomorrow. Suppose one of your stocks has given a signal that will be confirmed if the price rises above $15, then set a buy order that will be activated if the stock reaches $15.05. Then, if the stock behaves the way you think it will, you won't miss the trade, but if it doesn't confirm the pattern, the trade won't execute.

Automatic trades are particularly useful for part-time swing traders, but even if you trade live, they're a valuable way of ensuring that you don't miss a move. Even if the phone doesn't ring, you might be concentrating on another stock at the time and miss the right entry point. If a price move happens fast, and you don't get in at the right price, you run the risk of being 100% right about the move and making precisely 0% on the stock.

An example of being right but trading wrong? I was following a great situation in German property stock Vonovia. It's a huge land owner in Germany, but the stock price had been beaten down by worries about its debt at a time when interest rates were going up. I thought the stock was worth more and had relatively little risk. And I missed not one, but two good opportunities. The arrows on the chart below show you - three white soldiers, then a gap up, then three white soldiers in late March and then in late April. There was some really fast price action, and I missed out both times. (In my defense, some family stuff was going on at the time, which took my mind off trading.)

Worse, I felt too keen to make a profit out of Vonovia, so the next time I saw the three white soldiers in July, I jumped in fast and maybe didn't pay enough attention to historical resistance lines. That hurt!

This all sounds like a lot of work, but once you get up and running, you can do most of it pretty fast. The key is establishing a good workflow and a good process, and concentrating on the handful of patterns that you understand and succeed with. As you continue, you'll probably build your own customized scans and refine them with experience, and you'll get better at focusing straight away on the 5-10% of stocks that give you a decent chance of a good swing trade.

More on stock scanning

The stock screens I mentioned in the last chapter gave you some raw material to work with. But to focus on a daily basis, you'll want to use a technical analysis-based stock scanner. Your trading platform or charting software likely contains one; if not, there are a number available online, some paid-for, and some free, like stockmonitor.com and chartink.com. Personally, I like tradingview.com, and I've also heard good things about pocketoption.com.

Scans that you could use include:

• 10-day moving average greater than 50-day moving average (10MA > 50MA): this will find stocks that have started to rise faster over the past few days.
• RSI under < 20 - this will find stocks that may be oversold, and are ready to bounce.

Using two different indicators will really focus on potentially profitable situations:

• "Golden cross," where the 55-day moving average is less than < 200-day moving average, AND the 50-day moving average is greater than > 200-day moving average. That catches stocks where the 50-day MA has just crossed over the 200-day to the upside, showing the beginning of an uptrend. (We're at the bottom of the dip because the 55-day is still headed down, while the 50-day has started to move up.)
• Refined RSI scan: RSI is less than < 20.

Again, you're going to have to think through how to express the visual signals of a chart in quantitative formulas, but once you get used to it, you'll soon be able to formulate your own scans.

Alternatively, sites like stockmonitor.com have ready-made scans for popular technical formations. You can even find candlestick formations such as shooting stars or engulfing patterns (explained in the next chapter). However, these ready-made scans often throw up four or five pages of results. As you gain experience, you'll want to customize these scans to include your own 'take' on chart formations, exclude penny stocks, etc.

StockMonitor   FEATURES   QUOTES   BLOG   FREE SCREENERS ▾   PRICING   LOGIN   SIGN UP

Stock Screener Home

Popular

Golden Cross (50MA cross up 200MA)
Death Cross (50MA cross down 200MA)
Oversold + Momentum Rising
Overbought + Momentum Falling
Oversold RSI + Stochastic
Overbought RSI + Stochastic
PSAR Switch Up + Momentum
MACD cross and RSI above 55
RSI Cross Up and Volume
Price Broken 52 Week High
Price Broken 52 Week Low
Hammer
Shooting Star
Engulfing Pattern

Moving Average

Price / Gaps / Breaks

Oscillators

Trend Indicators

Volume

Golden Cross (50MA cross up 200MA) results

Technical stock screener for Golden Cross (50MA cross up 200MA) results.

Ideas for the best stocks to buy based on data for Nov 18, 2024.

Register FREE to see today's results

Symbol	Price	Change	High	Low	Volume
BTCS	3.26 ▼	-1.09 (-25.06%)	4.19	3.1501	4,345,021
BXC	122.76 ▲	+2.37 (+1.97%)	123.54	120.20	53,560
CHD	110.29 ▲	+1.27 (+1.16%)	110.41	108.31	1,361,717
DDOG	125.97 ▼	-0.12 (-0.10%)	127.50	124.835	2,802,880
DNN	2.27 ▲	+0.18 (+8.61%)	2.33	2.16	34,991,005
FTXL	87.24 ▲	+0.93 (+1.08%)	87.27	85.955	27,815
GEOS	12.62 ▼	-0.07 (-0.55%)	13.08	12.46	34,245
GTLB	59.96 ▲	+0.09 (+0.15%)	60.07	58.47	1,314,418
HEES	57.75 ▼	-0.66 (-1.13%)	59.095	57.14	179,519
HSAI	4.23 ▲	+0.15 (+3.68%)	4.28	4.10	221,040
INTU	678.81 ▼	-9.06 (-1.32%)	688.12	675.795	1,574,680
JBL	128.29 ▲	+0.03 (+0.02%)	129.36	127.45	795,191
LNKB	7.22 ▲	+0.06 (+0.84%)	7.27	7.16	23,223
LSTR	183.12 ▲	+0.30 (+0.16%)	184.915	182.7344	110,297
MNTX	5.73	+0.00 (+0.00%)	5.76	5.725	55,791
PEN	240.48 ▲	+2.64 (+1.11%)	241.82	235.305	643,266

This is how stockmonitor.com shows stocks with a potential golden cross formation. It finds these by screening for stocks where the 50-day moving average has crossed the 200-day moving average and simply displays the basic data. You now need to go check the stock charts to determine whether any of these are good tradeable opportunities, though I wouldn't bother checking out the stocks with penny prices, like BTCS, DNN, HSAI, UNKB, MNTX - as you can see in the screenshot above. Penny stocks have large spreads, are often thinly traded with only a couple of specialists or market makers, and are often prone to manipulation. For instance, 'pump and dump' operations when a stock is 'pumped' on forums, and then the manipulators 'dump' by selling out ahead of the crowd.

Some often-forgotten basics

Sometimes, textbooks appear to forget that traders are human beings. So, some basic self-care will pay dividends in the long run.

Remember that focus is a key ingredient in swing trading success. Obsessively calling up more and more charts all night and not getting to bed till the early hours is counterproductive. Set yourself a basic target, like finding 6 good situations. If it takes you ten minutes, that's fine. And set yourself a time limit, too; say, 30 minutes if you have a day job, maybe a couple of hours if you're full-time. Only find as many situations as you can actually trade; finding two hundred if you're only going to trade ten is counterproductive. Less is more in this game!

Remember, too, that you'll need a good night's sleep, whether you're heading off to your day job or trading the market open live. Whatever it takes to get your mind nicely quiet, do it: for some people it's meditation, for others, it's playing pinball or Grand Theft Auto. You might do Tai Chi, or spend time playing with your dog or cat. Don't go to bed thinking through your watchlist or replaying today's bad trade!

Chapter 5 Quiz

1. When does the swing trader's day start?
a) When the opening bell rings
b) When the closing bell rings
c) With the first trade
d) Five o'clock in the morning

2. Why should you review the previous day's trades?
a) To check your orders were correctly executed
b) To check whether your basic setup was correct
c) To see whether you set stop losses too tightly
d) All of the above

3. What external events do you need to be aware of for tomorrow?
a) Economic news
b) Options expiry dates
c) Corporate news
d) All of the above

4. Why use a technical scanning program?
a) It's cleverer than you are
b) To cut down the number of stocks you need to look at
c) It has access to information you don't
d) Because it's there

5. Which of these websites does not offer stock scans based on technical data?
a) Stockmonitor.com
b) Iguana.com
c) Tradingview.com
d) Pocketoption.com

6

Chapter 6: Technical Analysis Simplified

Technical analysis is the analysis of share price action to establish the probability of future share price movements. For most people, it means looking at charts, though as I've shown you, you can express chart data as mathematical formulas to use a stock screener. What you're looking for, whether visually in a chart or through a stock screen formula, is a particular pattern establishing itself.

Remember that I said, "to establish the probability of future share price movements." You can't predict them, but you can work out how likely a particular pattern is to occur and the size of the potential price swing.

Why does this work? It works because the market is driven by crowd psychology - fear and greed, FOMO and panic. It works because of the stock market cycle that I already talked about. These cycles leave traces in the share price chart, and by analyzing those cycles, you can find out where a stock is right now and look at where it is likely to go next.

Trends, support, and resistance

The first time you look at a stock price chart you see just chaos. Ups and downs and ups and downs all over the place. Take another look, and you will usually start to see a pattern in the ups and downs. The stock price will only go up to a particular point, then it will backtrack, then it will go up to the same point, and backtrack again. Or maybe it will keep 'yo-yo-ing' up again every time it gets down to a certain level, as if it's bouncing off an invisible line.

Sometimes, you'll see that the share price is marching up a hill, although it bounces around a bit. It's like an airplane in turbulence; it might go up and down in the air pockets, but it will get to its destination, however bumpy the ride.

These patterns become very obvious once you look at charts for a while. But why do they work?

RESISTANCE

SUPPORT

CHANNEL

← TREND LINE:
MATCHES ALL THE LOWS

HOW NOT TO
DRAW A TREND LINE

Take a look at Berkshire Hathaway above. In 2024, throughout March, April, and May, every time the share price got to about $420, it fell back again. In fact, later in May, it didn't even make it that far, falling back every time it touched $416 or so. If you were to draw a line across the chart at $416, that would show you a *resistance* level. Imagine a kind of drywall ceiling; you could punch through it, but you'll need to shove really hard to do it.

Once you're through, it's difficult to stop the upwards move. And you can see that in the chart, in July and early August. When Berkshire Hathaway shares finally got through that barrier, they just keep going higher!

Something is making people more likely to sell than to buy at just that level. It might be a level at which the shares begin to look expensive on certain valuation criteria (that's why the fundamental analysis is always worth checking for a swing trader). It might just represent the place at which buyers who have made a neat profit decide to get out. And the second time, of course, there will be people who bought at the resistance level, held on to the shares until they make their money back, and now want to sell. That's how resistance levels get started. They're not necessarily rationally backed, but they are levels that stick in the minds of market participants.

Shell PLC, 1h, NYSE O66.46 H66.52 L66.33 C66.33 −0.14 (−0.20%)
Vol 48.71 K
SMMA (20, close) 66.07

In the example above, Shell doesn't show much resistance level, but it seems to have established a *support* at around $64.50. You can see that it has flirted near that level twice in September, once in late October, and once in mid-November, and until now, it's always bounced off it. Quite often, it's had a little bounce, fallen back to the support level, and then motored away again, which is called "testing the support" - this can offer you a second bite at the cherry if you missed the initial bounce.

Why does this work? The share price falls as sellers are the majority. At a certain level, all the sellers who want to sell have sold their stock. That leaves buyers with the balance of power. And to some extent, since traders are all looking at the same charts, it's also a self-fulfilling prophecy. Anyway, it works… until it doesn't.

When it works, the share price will bounce up, and you can open a trade by buying the shares to make a profit out of the upswing. When it doesn't, the share price will usually send a clear signal, and you can take advantage of that to initiate a short trade by selling the stock.

The support and resistance lines that I showed you were horizontal. But you'll also find lines that run diagonally across the chart.

For instance, I can see two clear trendlines when I look at Netflix stock above. You draw a trendline by linking higher highs or lower lows. In this case, the share price keeps making higher highs, and it has even established a steeper trendline over recent months after a bit of consolidation during September and October.

On the other hand, if you look at Biogen stock below, you can join up the lower lows and see that it has been continuously in a downtrend for a good long while. Worse, the share price has just broken through the trendline on the downside, which suggests it could fall quickly. Trendlines work in this respect just like support and resistance lines; the harder a stock has to work to break them, the more violent the next movement is likely to be.

Note that the more 'touches' a share price makes with the trendline, and the longer a trendline continues, the stronger the signal that trendline is sending. The first two touches count for nothing - they make the *trendline* in the first place - but after that, every time the share price touches and bounces off, the trendline gets stronger. The same goes for support and resistance lines.

Let's take trendlines a bit further. You can link up all of the swing highs and all of the swing lows, so you have a line on both sides of the share price action. I've done that with IBM below. The result is what's called a channel. You can see IBM stayed within the channel from August through to late October, but when it gapped down on bad third-quarter results on October 23, it broke through the channel to the downside and then kept going. Again, when a stock breaks through a line, it tends to push onwards in the direction of the breakout.

Volume

The market doesn't send signals only through the share price. It also sends signals through volume, that is, the amount of stock traded. If a stock is at a standstill, very often you'll see very little volume; no one is really interested in buying or selling, and nothing's happening (you also see low volume in a real bear market, like 1989). On the other hand, if there is a lot of stock being traded, it shows there is a lot of interest in the stock - and makes any signal that the market is giving through the price more likely to be accurate.

Think of volume like decibels (dB). If there's no volume, the market is speaking very quietly. You might see a signal in the charts, but the market isn't really making a big thing out of it. It might not be that great of a signal. On the other hand, if there is suddenly a big volume day trading twice the usual amount of stock, the market is shouting at you; any signal given by the price chart is likely to be a reliable one.

If the share price is going up on high volume, it means there are a lot of buyers around, and the market makers are pushing the price higher because they need to be able to buy stock to meet that demand. That gives the share price real power.

That's why most share price charts show a volume bar chart beneath the main price chart. You might want to look back at the charts you've already seen, and look at the volume bar and the way volume matches (or doesn't match) big price movements.

The Realty Income chart below shows a massive increase in volume at the same time as a big dip in price, around 18-19 December. I think that this might be typical of a news-related dip, perhaps around a disappointing earnings release. To check it out, I looked at Realty Income's investor news - but there's nothing there. So, what else might have affected the stock? Aha - there was an announcement from the Fed that said further interest rate cuts were likely to be slower. That was bad news for the market, but particularly for interest-sensitive REITS (real estate investment trusts), which explains the price action and the high volume.

Technical indicators

While price and volume give useful signals, using technical indicators based on mathematical processing can refine and enhance those signals. Some technical indicators give their own signals, while others are useful for confirming the signals you see in a price chart.

Moving averages simply smooth out the bumps in the price action. Creating a moving average is simple; you simply add the prices of, say, the last five days, and then *divide* by five. So, for instance, if the price in the previous five days was $55, $50, $55, $56, $57, the moving average will be $(55+50+55+56+57)/5 = 273/5 = \$54.60$. If the price goes up to $60 tomorrow, then the first $55 drops out, and we have a new moving average of $(50+55+56+57+60)/5 = \$55.60$.

That's a simple moving average (SMA), and you can add a few mathematical bells and whistles to smooth it out further and get an exponential moving average (EMA). Basically, the formula for the EMA gives greater weight to the most recent changes and lesser weight to those that happened longer ago. Of course, you're not going to sit and calculate it - charting software does it much faster.

There are various levels of complexity in using moving averages. Let's look at what you can do in increasing order of complexity.

First, you can compare the share price and the moving average. If the share price is trending upward, the moving average will be trending upward, too. Look at the beginning of January 2024 for Salesforce below. Even though the share price falls, the 20-day moving average never turns downwards; it just flattens out a bit. But when the share price falls through the moving average in April, it just keeps going down. The same happens late in May, as well.

Now, look at the right-hand side of the chart. It seems to me like there's a good chance the share price might go back down under the moving average in late November. It's not a signal yet, so I'm not going to trade on it, but I might just put the Salesforce stock on my watch list.

Secondly, you can compare two moving averages with each other. One will be shorter, the other longer term. For instance, in the example below you could use 9-day and 20-day, or you could use 50-day and 200-day moving averages. Where the moving averages cross over each other, you're likely to see the share price swing. However, this often is used as a lag indicator - it tells you what's just happened, but its predictive value isn't always that high.

The third and most complex way of using moving averages is to analyze them further, subtracting the long-term from the short-term MA to get the Moving Average Convergence Divergence indicator or MACD.

This indicator is what's known as an oscillator that moves around a zero line. It gets its own chart, as you can see in the example below, underneath the price and volume chart, which shows a MACD line, a 'signal line,' and a histogram (the signal line is a moving average of a *moving average*. It's like moving average squared). The MACD above the zero line shows an uptrend, and the MACD below the zero line shows a downtrend.

What you're going to look out for is when the MACD crosses the signal line. Not necessarily every time because you're going to have to look at other price indicators, but this can give good alerts when combined with the price chart. For instance, the small downturn in early January comes right after a MACD cross. So does the upturn in September.

Another interesting indicator is the Relative Strength Index (RSI). It measures the strength of a price movement by taking an average of the price movement on days that close up, and an average of the price movement on days that close down, and dividing them both. Again, this is an oscillator, but instead of oscillating around a zero line, it oscillates between 0 and 100.

If it showed 0, it would mean that the stock had been falling continuously - every single day during the period that the RSI covers, which was down. Conversely, if it showed 100, it would mean that the stock had been rising every single day.

Let's just look at a fundamental example of a 14-day RSI. First, we take the *average* gain of all the up days and the *average* loss of all the down days. So, let's say we have an average gain of 1% and an average loss of 0.8%. The formula is tough to understand even though it looks deceptively easy; RSI = 100 - [100 / (1 + [Up / Down])].

The calculation goes through the following steps:

1. Up days - 1%
2. Down days - 0.8%
3. Divide Up days by Down days (1% / 0.8%) = 1.25
4. 100 divided by (1 + 1.25) = 44.4
5. 100 - 44.4 = **55.6 RSI.**

I prefer to let the charting software take the hard work instead!

Again, RSI gets its own chart underneath the price chart, as shown in the example below. The first thing to look at is where the RSI stands. If it's over 70, that means the stock is 'overbought'; there has been a lot of buying, and the share price movement could be getting close to exhausting buyers' demand. If it's under 30, the stock is 'oversold', that is, the stock has been falling and is getting close to taking all the sellers out of the market. If you see a chart pattern that suggests a breakout to the downside (some people call that a 'breakdown'), and the RSI is under 30, then you have confirmation that the price is most likely to break out downwards.

Salesforce, Inc., 1D, NYSE O319.00 H322.70 L316.00 C321.24 −1.01 (−0.31%)
Vol 1.57 M
SMMA (20, close) 300.53
RSI (14, close) 60.81

However, although the RSI can be used for confirmation purposes, it also gives quite good signals. Track the RSI, and you can see that where it actually crosses from one side of the 30 line to the other at the end of May, that's a really good signal of the beginning of the uptrend. The latest movement, that sharp move down in November 2024, could be the beginning of a downtrend. However, look at November 2023 on the far left of the chart; the RSI moving out of the overbought zone appeared to predict a downturn, but in the event, the signal failed. By the way, you don't want to pick up the signal when the RSI enters the overbought or oversold zone - you pick it up when it starts to come out of the zone.

The stochastic is an oscillator that's quite similar to the RSI, though the relevant zones for the stochastic are < 20 for oversold and > 80 for overbought. It's quite a sophisticated little indicator which compares the daily high or low with the closing price and uses this to finesse the moving average. The idea is that if there's a strong uptrend, you should have closing prices close to the highest price of the day (and the opposite for a downtrend).

The stochastic has two lines rather than the RSI's one, so you can finesse your reading further by looking for situations where the stochastics exit the overbought/oversold zone and one line crosses the other at the same time. The chart below shows stochastics used with different indicators.

The stochastics are the two lines at the bottom of the chart, with the RSI in the middle and the price chart at the top. The share price is in a downtrend, and is close to an important support level. The stochastic is in the oversold zone, below 20, and it looks as if it is moving up and could exit the zone soon, which would be a bullish signal. Volume is currently low, suggesting the bearish trend doesn't have a lot of momentum behind it - no one is actually selling anymore.

The Bollinger band show the standard deviation of price movements from the moving average - that is, how far the price has swung from the trend. Usually, the share price stays inside the bands. You might want to think about buying when the price is towards the bottom of the bands and selling when it gets towards the top - and, of course, the stop loss will come into play if the price falls below the bottom band.

But you should also look at the width of the bands. They'll sometimes follow the moving average quite closely, but at other times, they'll widen out or narrow down. If they narrow down to a 'squeeze point,' that's often a signal that the price is going to move very fast and far. Generally, you'll want to trade expecting a move in the direction of the current trend.

I've stuck three big flags in the chart above where I think the Bollinger bands suggest a price movement. What do you think might happen next?

Let's run through what's happening each time. The first flag shows the bands squeezing up, with a high volume of trading, so things could move either way. What you get here is the beginning of a strong upwards trend. The second flag shows another significant tightening of the bands at a point of price consolidation, followed by another strong uptrend - resuming the existing trend.

The third flag shows another squeeze point, after a downwards leg. I would probably want to focus on that part of the chart and look for chart patterns, such as a flag or pennant, to tell me which way the price is going to break. It seems to have started another strong move upwards. So Bollinger bands won't necessarily tell you everything you need to know, but they will suggest a strong move is coming - and that's something a swing trader can make money out of.

P.S. In Class 5 of the free bonus #1 companion masterclass, I demonstrate some practical ways of how you can use some of the indicators discussed in this chapter with real life chart examples. I would highly recommend you watch the free masterclass video after you finished reading this entire chapter by visiting: www.az-penn.com.

Chart patterns

We've looked at trend lines and indicators; now, I want to introduce you to meaningful chart patterns. You may find that some patterns don't really stick in your mind, while others you instantly hook onto - and that's fine; as a swing trader, you'll always do better by trading the patterns that you instinctively understand. Later on, take another look at the ones that you found more tricky - they may make more sense to you once you've got a bit more experience under your belt.

The box

The 'box' was invented by dancer and trader Nicolas Darvas. It's a neat way to trade during a strong uptrend - don't use it when the market is falling or trading sideways.

You're looking for a stock that has just made a new 52-week high, and then establishes a narrow trading range as a consolidation. Your setup is the box - your signal is when the price breaks out of the box. It's important with chart patterns that you understand you're looking for the setup, first of all, then watching the stock till the breakout occurs. You don't trade the setup; you trade the signal. The box I like in the example below is that tight little box over late October and early November. Look for the breakout - if you bought the stock when it broke out of the box, you would have had to hold on to your stock for a little while, but you then would have benefited from some good upward price movement in mid-November.

Warning: the Box is very easy to read with hindsight, and it's tricky to get it right. Practice makes perfect!

You can set your stop loss at the top of the box when the price breaks out upwards. If it's a genuine breakout, the price won't fall back into the box; if it isn't, you want to be out of that trade.

Double top / double bottom

This one is a classic chart reversal pattern with a couple of interesting variations, too. The price rises, makes a first peak, and then falls into a 'valley,' and rises again to make a second peak, then falls again (illustration is below). This is your setup pattern - you watch it form, but you haven't traded it yet. To be a proper double top, the two peaks need to reach roughly the same height, though they don't need to be the same shape - one can be spiky and the other 'round,' for instance. The pattern might take a couple of weeks to form, or even longer.

DOUBLE TOP

The bottom of the valley is the place you need to watch. The signal to enter the trade when the price falls below the bottom of the valley, giving you confirmation that the pattern is complete. This is where you buy. Your profit target should be equal to the difference between the tops and the valley, which I've drawn as X. Your stop-loss could be placed just above the second peak - that's what some traders do, since if the price goes higher than this, the signal has failed. However, I prefer to apply solid risk management instead, and since I have calculated my profit target, I set the stop-loss where the return on the trade equals my risk. So that's halfway towards the second peak. Remember, sometimes risk management trumps the chart. If the chart suggests a stop-loss, which gives you a way too high risk for the likely reward, you need to insist on a tighter stop-loss.

Below is an interesting double top: Meta, owner of Facebook and Instagram. It's not obvious at first, but you need to look at the extreme right-hand side of the chart. The first top is quite easy to see, starting just above 'Dec' on the chart, but the second top (end of Dec/start of 2025) is just a little spike. However, it's not the shape but the price levels that are important when you're looking at this pattern. There's a critical support level at $580, and the stock tops out at about $630 ($632 on December 10 and then again on January 7). I could enter next time it hits around $580, sell at $630, and expect about $50 in profit.

Head and Shoulders

The head and shoulders pattern (the big W) is a key reversal pattern that is often found right at the top of the market, as the uptrend changes to a downtrend. The share price forms three peaks, with the middle peak of the three, higher than the other two (it's like a left shoulder, the 'head' in the middle, and a right shoulder. In the illustration example below, the blue line drawn is the 'neckline').

HEAD & SHOULDERS TOP

So basically, the pattern works like this: the stock price ends a long uptrend by falling, usually on high volume (forming the left shoulder), then tries to rally on lower volume, indicating a loss of confidence, then falls (forming the head), rallies again not reaching the previous high, then falls again (forming the right shoulder), another sign of loss of confidence.

To trade the head and shoulders, you need to draw a 'neckline' at the bottom of the shoulders and a line across the tops of the shoulders. I added an extra line to show the top of the pattern, too. Your signal comes when the head and shoulders pattern is complete, and the price breaks down through the neckline. In the example below, if you traded overnight, you would have gone short at $41 on December 16 and taken your profits in just one day as the stock fell to $37.83.

Your profit target with a head and shoulders is the distance between the two lines (the neckline and top of the shoulder) - here, you're looking for about $4 because the neckline is just above $41 and the shoulders are about $45.

You'll often see that a head and shoulders start with strong volume and then see volume gradually ease off. That reflects the fact that the uptrend is running out of conviction - buyers are no longer chasing the share price up. If, as well as this, you see the breakout downwards occur on high volume, you have a really classic signal, and it's time to trade!

Naturally, an inverted head and shoulders are just the same, only upside down (the opposite of a W). You'll find this one at the bottom of the market, and when the price breaks upwards through the right-hand resistance line, it's time to buy.

Flags and pennants

Flags and pennants are created when a share price starts to consolidate after a strong trend. You can easily see the 'flag' or 'pennant' shape if you draw the top and bottom trendlines for the consolidation; if you end up with a roughly rectangular box, it's a flag; if it's more triangular, it's a pennant. The best ones are tight ones, where the stock price practically shades the entire area - if you see a lot of white space, it's probably a trade to ignore.

Flags and pennants usually form against the trend - for instance, in an uptrend, a flag will be horizontal or slightly downsloping. They will only take a couple of weeks to form. You should also note that a flag needs a flagpole! That is, the price trend leading to the flag should be quite steep. Illustrations for the bullish flag and bullish pennant are shown on the next page.

TARGET

x

ENTRY

STOP

BULLISH
FLAG

TARGET

x

ENTRY

STOP

BULLISH
PENNANT

You want to place your trade when the price breaks out of the flag or pennant, and you should be trading in the direction of the trend. Your profit target is the distance from the bottom of the flagpole to the top of the flag, added to the low from which the price breaks out. So, for example, if the flagpole starts at $25 and the top corner of the flag is at $31, with the bottom corner of the flag at $27, then your profit target is $27 + ($31-$25) = $27 + $6 = $33.

Here's another good example from Tradingview below. There's a nice pennant forming in GOOGL and trader hariyanto has indicated the likely profit by comparison with the 'leg' running up to the beginning of the pennant. However, I'd prefer to limit myself to looking at the width of the pennant when it starts, as shown in the schematic example on the previous page. So while hariyanto is looking for a $37.83 profit, I'm just looking for $21 (from $181 on December 10 to $202 on December 17). Still, the pattern looks good, and there's a clear stop around $188 - drawing a support line under the pennant will show you that if the price goes through that level, there's no more support until further down.

GOOGL bullish Pennant chart pattern. Bullish Pennant TP: USD230

And here's a flag example below. This time, it's a bullish flag for TSM. There's a good, strong support line on the bottom of the flag, and the price looks as if it could break out. There's $17 of profit (the start of the flag, $194 to $211 on 16th to 17th October), and the downside is about $175 on October 3. However, I would set a much tighter stop-loss, just a bit below that top line, perhaps around $196. If the price falls below that level, it will likely trade back into the channel, and the breakout has probably failed, so I don't want to hang around. Remember that a stop-loss needs to help you exit a position *when the signal has failed.*

These examples are an excellent reason for putting Tradingview on your bookmark list. Some of the examples are good, and some are not so good, but I find it's always worth taking a look at the ideas. Once you get really good, perhaps you'll decide to put some of your own good ideas up on Tradingview.

By the way, if you're still unsure on bullish flag and pennants, I would definitely suggest you watch my free bonus #1 companion masterclass because in Class 3 I demonstrate examples of both patterns with real life charts – which will hopefully help your learning!

Symmetrical triangles

You can trade ascending and descending triangles, too, but I rather like symmetrical triangles because they can go either way. A symmetrical triangle happens when the trendlines along the peaks and valleys of the share price converge. As with flags and pennants, the more the triangle is 'filled in' by share price movement, the better. The trendlines get closer and closer, and your signal is when the price breaks out of the triangle, preferably on high volume. Trade in the direction of the breakout.

ASCENDING
TRIANGLE

DESCENDING
TRIANGLE

Above is an example of Bitcoin - a symmetrical triangle. You can see the two trendlines converging, forming a symmetrical triangle on either side of a horizontal line. You can predict *that* the price will break out, but you can't predict *which side* it will break out, upwards or downwards, so you really need your stop-loss in case you guessed wrong.

Your profit target can be found by measuring the open side of the triangle where it began to form, and adding that price movement to the price at the point of breakout.

Here's an example below from the bulletin board at Tradingview - an Indian stock, Bajaj Finance. It has not only drawn a clear ascending triangle but also a good close support level that should limit any losses. As soon as the price closes above the top of the triangle at R 8000 (assuming that it does so), it will be time to buy and wait for a strong upward movement.

BAJFINANCE - Ready To Bounce from LongTerm Support Area

A condensed guide to candlesticks

Let's talk about candlestick charts. Rice traders invented this special type of chart in Japan. It gives you four pieces of information in every candlestick:

• The opening price,
• The closing price,
• The highest price touched in the time period,
• And the lowest price touched in the time period.

It's the fact that it delivers so much information that makes the candlestick chart very powerful. With normal charts, you don't get to see the high/low inside the session, only the open and close.

The candlestick has a body, which represents the difference between the open and closed prices. A white (or green) candlestick represents a price that rose during the session, while a black (or red) candlestick represents a price that fell. You'll mostly see green and red used now that we don't have to live our lives in black-and-white media. Examples are shown on the next page.

But what makes candlesticks so useful is that they also have whiskers - known as 'shadows' or 'wicks' - extending out from the body to the top and bottom. These show the range of prices in the time period covered by the candlestick - in a daily chart, it will be a full trading session, but you could also look at half-hourly, five-minute, or one-minute candlesticks. As a swing trader, the *daily* chart is your go-to.

Bullish candlestick

Bearish candlestick

If you think about it, you might have two days where a stock opens at $43 and closes at $44.

• First day: opens at $43, trades up to $43.50, and then to $44.
• Second day: opens at $43, falls to $38, then eventually regains $43 and just manages to close at $44.

If you looked at a regular share price chart, they would look like similar days. But in fact, they're very different. In one of them, the stock goes up very slightly. Nothing interesting happens. But the other day, sellers hit the stock hard and sold it all the way down to $38, but it's resilient; the bulls came back into the market, and the stock actually closed up. That's interesting because it shows that the bulls were able to resist selling pressure - they pulled back in the tug-of-war. That suggests there's a stronger upward momentum than with the other trading day.

Chart experts pay attention to several different kinds of candlesticks. A really long one can be bullish (green) or bearish (red); one of these coming after many smaller candlesticks of the opposite kind will often signal a trend reversal. Another particularly important kind of candlestick is the spinning top, and particularly the doji.

A *spinning top* is a candlestick with almost no body but very long wicks; it shows a moment of indecision in the market when the bulls push the price way up, and the bears push the price way down, but neither bulls nor bears ultimately win the day. The price closes pretty much where it started. In other words, bulls and bears are at equilibrium - for the moment. It won't take much of a push to get the stock moving one way or the other. Illustration is shown below.

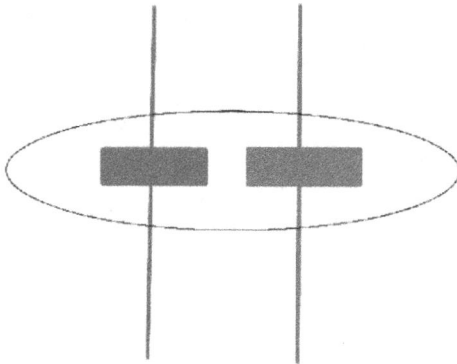

SPINNING TOP

The hourly chart below shows quite a few indecision candlesticks, but the best example of a spinning top is the eleventh candlestick from the left. That one is well-balanced, and the top and the tail are equal.

The doji is a spinning top, but it's characterized not just by the long wick, but by having almost no body at all. It sometimes looks like a cross (as shown below). The really interesting thing is when you see a doji with just one very long wick, and the other one short - it shows that all the buying or selling pressure was on one side. The hammer doji has a long wick on the downward side - it shows that the bears sent the stock down as far as they could, but it still managed to bounce back. This often ends a downtrend - it's the last big tug in the tug-of-war as far as the bears are concerned, and they have no more to give.

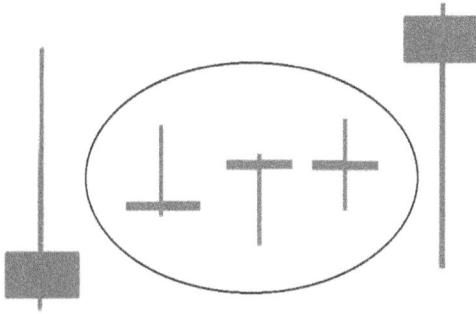

DOJI

But while a single candlestick gives you good information, candlestick patterns give you even more. A *doji* that happens in the middle of a long sideways move isn't interesting; it's just a doji. But a hammer after a long downtrend is a very interesting sign. It's the context that gives it meaning. In the chart below, Brent oil has a big signal after a downtrend - the two dojis that have been drawn in a box show a short-term reversal upwards.

The *shooting star* is the reverse of the hammer doji, with a long upwards wick - and it is often the signal that an uptrend is going to reverse. Illustration is below.

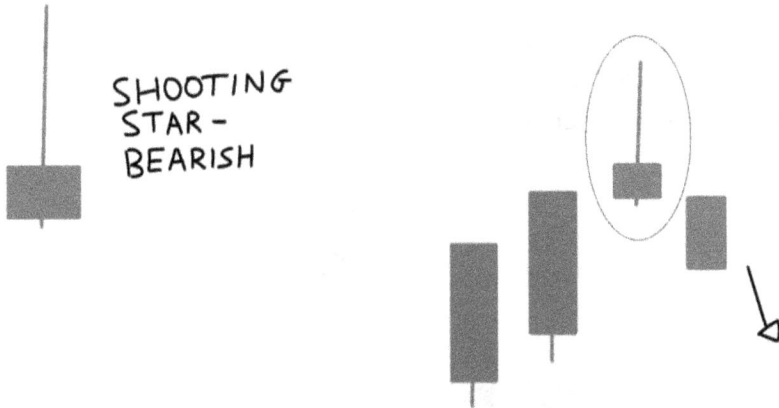

SHOOTING
STAR -
BEARISH

So, in the real-life example of Micron Technology below, you see an uptrend, and then you see a shooting star. That suggests the uptrend will reverse, and the shares will fall, so you'll want to short the stock.

Engulfing pattern

The engulfing pattern can be either bullish or bearish. It's a short candlestick, followed by a candlestick of the opposite sort that is deeper and taller than the other, 'engulfing' it. So, for instance, a set of quite short bearish candlesticks might see the last one followed by a bullish engulfing candlestick that starts below its bottom and rises well above its top.

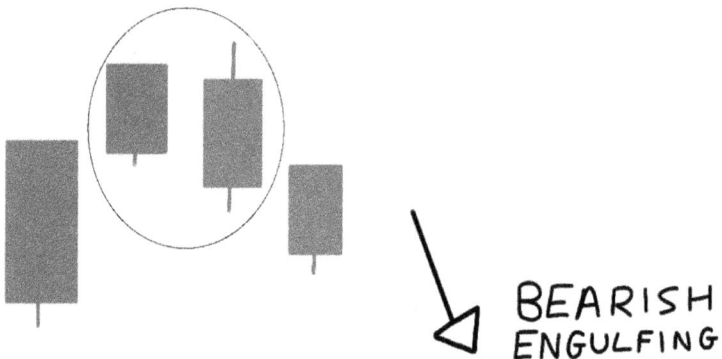

BULLISH
ENGULFING

BEARISH
ENGULFING

Think that through. The bearish candlestick that starts the pattern (the third one in the bullish engulfing chart) shows a day on which the price fell a little from the open to the close. Then, the bullish engulfing candlestick, the next day, shows that the price opened lower, but there was enough buying interest in the market to push the price past the previous day's high - a big move that likely marks a decisive change in direction.

A good engulfing pattern (bearish or bullish) must be backed up by good volume. If the engulfing candlestick doesn't show markedly higher volume, you must be wary of it. You'd probably also want to check out RSI and MACD indicators.

A big advantage of the engulfing pattern is that it already shows you your stop-loss, which is the bottom of the engulfing candle if you want a tight stop or of the first candle in the pattern (the shorter candlestick in the circle I drew above, which is engulfed by the other) if you think a looser stop would be justified.

Below is a real-life example of SBA Communications Corporation. The very last two candlesticks right at the end of December 2024 show a bullish engulfing pattern. But you might want to consider how this fits into the rest of the chart; where are the resistance and support levels? What's happening to the Bollinger bands? Would you trade on this signal?

So, just taking you through that, you can see some support levels around $187 from May to July, and there looks to me to be a resistance level around $215. So, from where we are now, there's more upside than downside, which is good - the risk-reward ratio is a good one since we are risking a fall of just $8 ($195 to $187) for a potential gain of $20 ($195 to $215).

But the Bollinger bands don't really help me here; they maintain the same width and relationship with the moving average, not squeezing up at all. I think I might want to do a bit more work on this one, maybe looking up the RSI and a couple of other indicators.

Evening star

The evening star is a doji with an excellent win rate, though it is relatively infrequent to find. It is a reversal sign after an uptrend. One long bullish candlestick is followed by a gap up to a doji and then a gap down to a bearish candlestick. This is the setup; don't trade till the pattern is completed. As you see in the illustration below.

Evening Star Candlestick Pattern

Star ────▶

Gap down

Gap up

Long first body ──▶

Strong finish into first candle body

Evening Star Characteristics:
1. Long first candle body
2. Second candle star: short body gaps away from preceding candle
3. Third candle body closes into body of first candle

The opposite is the morning star, marking the reversal of a downtrend and the start of a rise in the share price (see below). You may even find a morning doji star or evening doji star, which is just this pattern with a doji rather than a regular candlestick in the middle.

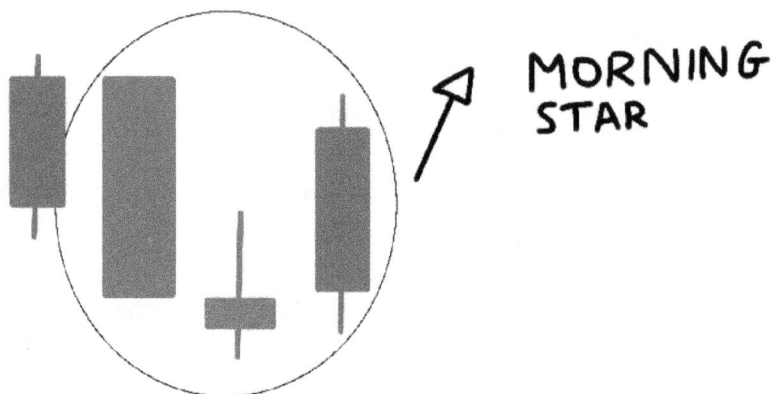

MORNING STAR

Confirmation and your profit target and stop loss will often come from looking at the support and resistance lines; trade once the price breaks through resistance.

So here's a real-life doji morning star below. You can see a big downtrend from about December 14 - oh look, there's a nice signal from the three black crows there on 14, 15, 16 December! - and then if you follow it right to the bottom, there's a tiny little doji around December 21, followed by a big bullish candlestick. But this trade fails. On the other hand, if you look back to October 28, there's a downtrend followed by a doji, then followed by a morning star. This trade was a good one; you would have entered the trade at around $5.52 and you would've gotten out at $5.60.

MFM:Daily Nov 14, 2024 O: 5.58 H: 5.595 L: 5.56 C: 5.57

However, I've found morning stars often show quite short-term price moves. They don't usually give me a really big swing, but they're a useful way to make small profits.

Three black crows and Three white soldiers

Three black crows happen when an uptrend is broken by three descending bearish candlesticks, typically fairly similar in size. It usually indicates a reversal of the uptrend. (Three black crows in a downtrend might be significant, but the signal is much more ambiguous.) Wait till the pattern is complete and make a short trade on the open to take advantage of a collapse in the price. Below is an illustration for the three black crows.

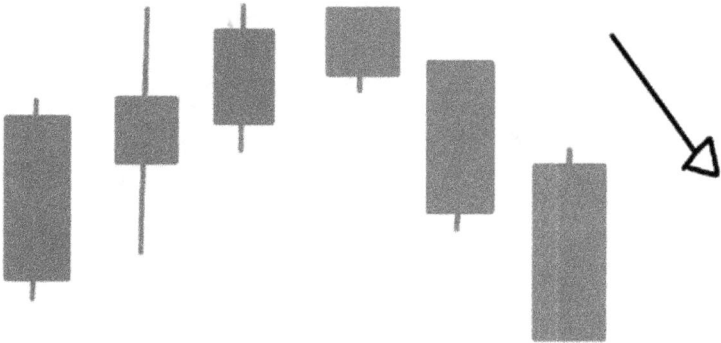

THREE BLACK
CROWS

Three white soldiers as shown below is just the reverse of the three black crows - a downtrend broken by three ascending white candlesticks.

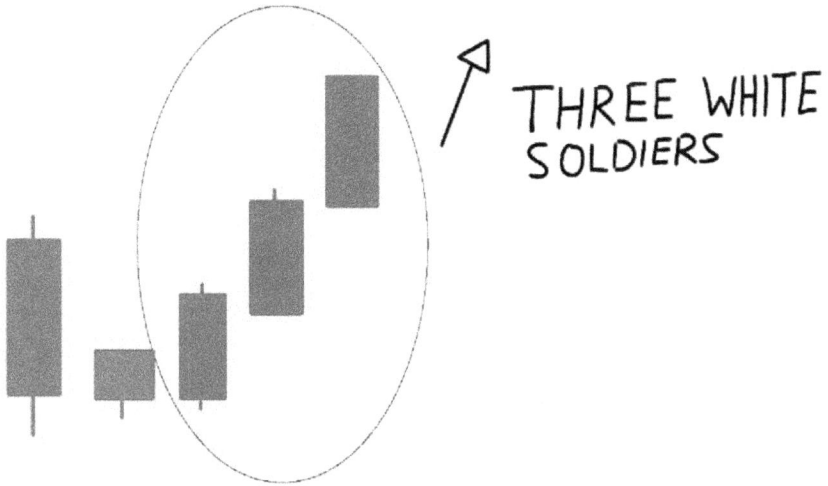

THREE WHITE SOLDIERS

The crows and soldiers need to be a reasonable size; if you get three almost-dojis, ignore them.

Below is a stock that's had its fair share of three black crows. I've drawn *rectangles* around each series. The first rectangle set of black crows are classic, quite large candlesticks moving downwards, and if you'd traded after the third candlestick, you would have been easily in the money. The same goes for the third rectangle set of black crows.

But the second rectangle is a set that doesn't work out. In fact, if you look at them carefully, you can see that the second candlestick body starts above the lowest point of the first candlestick, so although you have three bearish candlesticks in a row, it's not quite a classic three-black crow formation. That said, if you had gone short at $8.22, the bottom of the last of the three 'crows' candlesticks in the third rectangle, you would have easily been able to activate a stop-loss and exit the trade without losing too much. That's the good thing with soldiers and crows - they don't often reverse catastrophically, so they give you relatively low-risk trades.

Belt hold

This reversal pattern works either way. After an uptrend, a black (or red) marabozu appears. A marabozu is a long-bodied candle with almost no wicks. That is, the market went from the opening price all the way to the closing price, but it didn't go further up or further down. It's a very powerful candle. After a downtrend, it will, of course, be a green marabozu. See the illustration below.

GREEN MARABOZU -
BULLISH

RED MARABOZU -
BEARISH

The belt hold is very common but doesn't always work. You need to select the best opportunities by checking the breakout day volume: if the marabozu happens on above-average volume, it's a good signal, if not, sit it out.

A chart from Tradingview below shows a bullish belt hold as the very last candlestick in the chart, just above where it says July 18. This is a great chart for you to consider because the author shows all their workings - for instance, the fact that volume is rising, the triangle pattern, and a bullish engulfing pattern the day before, which the belt hold confirms. Your charts should look like this also once you've finished illustrating them!

If you want to read up in a lot more detail on candlesticks and charting, Thomas N. Bulkowski's books are very useful. Bulkowski has backtested the different chart patterns and candlestick patterns to see how often they occur, how often they work out, and how much profit they generate on successful trades, which is fantastically useful information.

Chapter 6 Quiz

1. Which of these is not a chart pattern?

a) Head and Shoulders

b) Wash and Go

c) Double Top

d) Double Bottom

2. Which of these is not useful for trading?

a) The Trend line

b) The Support Line

c) The Resistance Line

d) The Maginot Line

3. Why do chart patterns work?

a) They are magic

b) They reflect the psychology of the crowd

c) Advanced mathematics can detect patterns in nature

d) They are sometimes a self-fulfilling prophecy

4. Which of these is not a candlestick pattern?

a) Morning Star

b) Evening Star

c) Evening Standard

d) Morning Doji Star

5. Which of these is not a candlestick?

a) Doji

b) Marabozu

c) Spinning Top

d) Grasshopper

7

Chapter 7: Getting to Know Fundamental Analysis

The last chapter looked at technical analysis, which evaluates the probability of future price action by looking at historical price patterns. In this chapter, I'm going to take you through fundamental analysis, which looks at the business behind the stock.

Day traders don't bother with fundamental analysis, for the most part. They don't care; they're not even going to hold the stock overnight, so they are focused solely on the next few hours or even minutes. They might trade if they see an opportunity after a stock.

But as a swing trader, you should probably know how to run the basic numbers. You *won't* need to go all the way through the annual report, as you would as a long-term investor, but you'll need to know how to get the gist of the earnings report and how to focus on stocks with a good underlying story.

Where to get your data

One great thing about today's stock markets is that it's rather easy to get your hands on financial data about the companies behind the stocks you trade. Part of the deal with the exchange on which stocks are listed is that the company will put out regular earnings reports, and report any material changes in the company's business, i.e. 5% or more impact on earnings or the balance sheet.

A good place to look is EDGAR, the Securities and Exchange Commission's online financial reports database. It's not particularly pretty, but it has all the raw information that you need, and an awful lot that you don't. Go to sec.gov/search-filings and search using a company name or ticker symbol.

The basic filings for US companies are the 10-K, 10-Q, and 8-K. The 10-K is the annual filing with the company's earnings for the year; it includes a full profit and loss account, balance sheet, and cash flow statement, together with some analysis of how the company performed during the year, and, usually, guidance on how it expects to do next year. This is your basic go-to document to find out everything about a company that's new to you.

You can see Oracle's 10k in several formats at:
investor.oracle.com/sec-filings/sec-filings-details/default.aspx?FilingId=17631592

The 10-Q is the quarterly earnings release. It can be less detailed than the 10-K, particularly in the discussion of operations - you'll get complete financial statements, though. The 10-Q is basically a *news* item - if you were an analyst, you'd read through last year's quarterly reports, but as a swing trader, you just need to look at recent ones and read the top two or three lines.

See one of Oracle's 10-Q quarterly reports at:
investor.oracle.com/sec-filings/sec-filings-details/default.aspx?FilingId=18036350

The 8-K is the 'miscellaneous' report and covers any event that affects the business. That might be an acquisition, disposal, bankruptcy, a major new product release, or approval; it might confirm that there have been rumors about or come as a complete surprise. It will be timely; directors only have four days to get a release out once they realize one is needed. And here is one of Oracle's 8K filings, this time from the SEC's website and not Oracle's own. This was quite a big deal, the acquisition of Sun Microsystems.

You can access Oracle's 8K form here:
sec.gov/Archives/edgar/data/1341439/000119312509083550/d8k.htm

While an 8-K could arrive at any time, 10-Qs and 10-Ks are generally planned well in advance, and you'll see them on the NYSE and Nasdaq earnings calendars. Most finance websites and some broker sites also have earnings calendars for you to check. Most companies also put relevant data on their websites, and financial news sites like Reuters will also carry the basics of company earnings releases. Plus, if you're looking for historical figures, you can get them on Yahoo Finance, Zacks, Google Finance, and other sites in a standardized format. Swing traders should probably avoid companies with upcoming earnings announcements, which add an unquantifiable risk to your trades.

One site I find very easy to use is MarketWatch's earnings calendar at marketwatch.com/tools/earnings-calendar. You can choose to see all the companies reporting on a particular day, or you can search for a company of interest, and it shows the forecast income per share and (if the result is out already) upside or downside surprises.

For instance, an earnings announcement could move the share price in any of these ways:

• Earnings are above or below expectations, so the share price gaps up or down;
  • The earnings *outlook* is more cautious than expected, so the share price falls;
• The *mix* of business is different from expectations; for instance, if a car maker's electric vehicle business does worse than expected because that's the long-term growth business, even if petrol cars do well, the stock might still fall;
• *Margins* or *prices* fall, which could hit the stock even if earnings meet expectations.
• News about a major customer, product, or competitor comes to light in the earnings statement or during the analysts' conference call - for instance, a major customer is in bankruptcy proceedings.

So, there are many different ways that an earnings announcement could play out. Remember that a lot of information is being released, all at the same time - that's a high-risk time to trade.

Basic finance

The first thing everyone's interested in is a company's earnings. When you see a financial report, go straight to the *income statement* (or profit and loss statement). Generally speaking, there are three figures that are crucial.

1. Revenues (sales or turnover). If a company can't increase its sales, it will run out of line sooner or later. Unless there are special reasons, like a disposal or a major disruption to the business (COVID-19 was an example), you'll want to see revenues increase.
2. Operating income. This is the basic profit once all the costs of running the operations have been taken out - the costs of production, marketing, and management, for instance - but not the cost of funding the business. This is the basic profitability of the company.
3. Net income, which is operating income after interest on debt has been paid, and tax has been paid. This is the income that 'belongs' to shareholders. You'll also want to look at net income per share to see how it's portioned out; if the company raises net income by 30% but issues 50% more shares, each share will have lower earnings. You have a net income that's a third bigger, but has to be divided between half as many more people than before.

Oracle's *income statement* below includes all the basic figures, but it also shows a useful breakdown of the business between different sources of income. As you get more expertise, you'll be able to see how some companies give you good quality, useful breakdowns of the business, while others are much less forthcoming.

CONSOLIDATED STATEMENTS OF OPERATIONS - USD ($) shares in Millions, $ in Millions		12 Months Ended		
		May 31, 2024	May 31, 2023	May 31, 2022
Revenues:				
Cloud services and license support		$ 39,383	$ 35,307	$ 30,174
Cloud license and on-premise license		5,081	5,779	5,878
Hardware		3,066	3,274	3,183
Services		5,431	5,594	3,205
Total revenues		52,961	49,954	42,440
Operating expenses:				
Cloud services and license support	[1]	9,427	7,763	5,213
Hardware	[1]	891	1,040	972
Services	[1]	4,825	4,761	2,692
Sales and marketing	[1]	8,274	8,833	8,047
Research and development		8,915	8,623	7,219
General and administrative		1,548	1,579	1,317
Amortization of intangible assets		3,010	3,582	1,150
Acquisition related and other		314	190	4,713
Restructuring		404	490	191
Total operating expenses		37,608	36,861	31,514
Operating income		15,353	13,093	10,926
Interest expense		(3,514)	(3,505)	(2,755)
Non-operating expenses, net		(98)	(462)	(522)
Income before income taxes		11,741	9,126	7,649
Provision for income taxes		1,274	623	932
Net income		$ 10,467	$ 8,503	$ 6,717
Earnings per share:				
Basic		$ 3.82	$ 3.15	$ 2.49
Diluted		$ 3.71	$ 3.07	$ 2.41
Weighted average common shares outstanding:				
Basic		2,744	2,696	2,700
Diluted		2,823	2,766	2,786

[1] Exclusive of amortization of intangible assets, which is shown separately.

Everyone will be asking questions about how fast the company is growing and how much profit it makes from every dollar of revenue. You'll want to compare growth this year versus growth last year, and you'll also want to calculate the operating income margin. This is simple: *operating income divided by revenues x 100* gives you the percentage. If the operating margin goes down significantly, you'll want to see an explanation in the report - otherwise, it might just mean the company has lost control of its increased costs. Or it might mean it's had to discount its products heavily.

The second statement is usually less important: *the balance sheet*. This shows what the company owes and owns, and it's a snapshot taken at the end of the financial year. There are two sides - assets and liabilities. The assets include long-term assets like machine plants, offices, or server farms and short-term assets like cash, inventory, and accounts receivable - that is, credit extended to customers that will eventually be paid in cash. See Oracle's balance sheet below:

CONSOLIDATED BALANCE SHEETS - USD ($) $ In Millions	May 31, 2024	May 31, 2023
Current assets:		
Cash and cash equivalents	$ 10,454	$ 9,765
Marketable securities	207	422
Trade receivables, net of allowances for credit losses of $485 and $428 as of May 31, 2024 and May 31, 2023, respectively	7,874	6,915
Prepaid expenses and other current assets	4,019	3,902
Total current assets	22,554	21,004
Non-current assets:		
Property, plant and equipment, net	21,536	17,069
Intangible assets, net	6,890	9,837
Goodwill, net	62,230	62,261
Deferred tax assets	12,273	12,226
Other non-current assets	15,493	11,987
Total non-current assets	118,422	113,380
Total assets	140,976	134,384
Current liabilities:		
Notes payable and other borrowings, current	10,605	4,061
Accounts payable	2,357	1,204
Accrued compensation and related benefits	1,916	2,053
Deferred revenues	9,313	8,970
Other current liabilities	7,353	6,802
Total current liabilities	31,544	23,090
Non-current liabilities:		
Notes payable and other borrowings, non-current	76,264	86,420
Income taxes payable	10,817	11,077
Deferred tax liabilities	3,692	5,772
Other non-current liabilities	9,420	6,469
Total non-current liabilities	100,193	109,738
Commitments and contingencies		
Oracle Corporation stockholders' deficit:		
Preferred stock, $0.01 par value—authorized: 1.0 shares; outstanding: none	0	0
Common stock, $0.01 par value and additional paid in capital-authorized: 11,000 shares; outstanding: 2,755 shares and 2,713 shares as of May 31, 2024 and 2023, respectively	32,764	30,215
Accumulated deficit	(22,628)	(27,620)
Accumulated other comprehensive loss	(1,432)	(1,522)
Total Oracle Corporation stockholders' equity	8,704	1,073
Noncontrolling interests	535	483
Total stockholders' equity	9,239	1,556
Total liabilities and stockholders' equity	$ 140,976	$ 134,384

On the liabilities side, you'll find current liabilities, which include everything that *needs* to be paid but hasn't been paid yet, such as payments from customers who have ponied up in advance and overdrafts. You'll also find long-term liabilities, most of which will probably be represented by long-term debt. You'll also find shareholders' funds - this is what belongs to shareholders once the company's other liabilities have been paid.

That's all a bit theoretical, and the bare numbers won't necessarily mean much to you. So here's what you need to look for:

• Cash - the more, the better!
• Current assets that are a higher sum than current liabilities - better if they're one and a half times more.
• Watch out for big increases in inventory - that could mean sales are not going fast enough to sell the stock.
• Watch out for big increases in accounts receivable, a possible sign of a company giving customers extended credit to shift the product. (Accounts receivable represent customers who haven't paid for the product or service they used yet.)
• Net debt - all the debts shown in the balance sheet *minus* available cash. You'll want to compare it to equity, and a good way to do this is the debt/equity ratio - simply divide debt by equity. I'm not going to give you a target 'good' ratio, as it differs by sector - banks and real estate companies have higher debt than most other companies, for instance. You'll want to compare your target company's debt/equity ratio with other companies in the same sector. Lost your calculator? Don't worry — the debt/equity ratio shows up on many finance websites, and it's already calculated for you.

For instance, on Morningstar, as you can see in the screenshot below, the 'Key Metrics' page for Chevron Corp (CVX) shows Debt to Equity as the last figure on the balance sheet summary (highlighted in red). Morningstar also calculates gross and operating margins for you, as well as book value per share. This is all on the Morningstar free level, so you don't need to pay for it.

| Financial Summary | Growth | Profitability and Efficiency | Financial Health | Cash Flow | 5 Years ∨ | As Originally Reported ∨ | | |

Income Statement (in B), except ratios)	09/30/2024	12/2023	12/2022	12/2021	12/2020	12/2019
Revenue	194.01	196.91	235.72	155.61	94.47	139.87
Revenue Growth %	-4.19%	-16.48%	51.48%	64.71%	-32.46%	-11.98%
Gross Profit	57.92	60.39	73.98	48.31	24.46	30.53
Gross Profit Margin %	29.85%	30.67%	31.39%	31.05%	25.91%	21.83%
Operating Income	21.91	28.23	39.95	16.18	-6.10	0.10
Operating Margin %	11.29%	13.32%	16.95%	10.40%	-6.45%	0.07%
EBIT	25.45	30.05	50.19	22.35	-6.76	6.33
EBIT Margin %	13.12%	15.26%	21.29%	14.36%	-7.15%	4.53%
EBITDA	41.59	44.61	65.00	39.25	9.40	24.13
EBITDA Margin %	21.44%	22.65%	27.56%	25.22%	9.95%	17.25%
Net Income	18.68	21.37	35.47	15.63	-5.54	2.92
Net Profit Margin %	8.62%	10.87%	15.11%	10.06%	-5.89%	2.03%
Basic EPS	9.14	11.41	18.36	8.15	-2.96	1.55
Diluted EPS	9.10	11.36	18.28	8.14	-2.96	1.54
Normalized EPS	11.05	13.04	19.18	8.29	-0.39	6.18
Dividends per Share	6.40	6.04	5.86	5.31	5.16	4.76

Balance Sheet (in B), except ratios)	09/30/2024	12/2023	12/2022	12/2021	12/2020	12/2019
Total Assets	259.23	261.63	257.71	239.54	239.79	237.43
Total Liabilities	102.20	99.70	97.47	99.60	107.06	92.22
Total Debt	25.64	20.84	23.34	31.37	44.32	26.97
Total Equity	157.03	161.93	160.24	139.94	132.73	145.21
Cash And Cash Equivalents	4.70	8.18	17.68	5.64	5.60	5.69
Working Capital	2.47	8.87	16.14	6.95	3.90	1.80
Shares Outstanding (Bil)	1.87	1.87	1.90	1.92	1.93	1.88
Book Value Per Share	87.61	86.93	83.79	72.80	66.40	76.62
Debt To Equity	0.16	0.13	0.15	0.22	0.33	0.19

The third statement in the results is the *cash flow*. Basically, the balance sheet and income statement use something called the accruals basis to record revenues, for instance, when they are earned - whether the customer has paid or not. So a company that gave customers credit and never chased them might have a net income of $45m but actually not have seen any of the cash due to customers not paying up. Oracle's cash flow statement is below:

CONSOLIDATED STATEMENTS OF CASH FLOWS - USD ($) $ in Millions	12 Months Ended		
	May 31, 2024	May 31, 2023	May 31, 2022
Cash flows from operating activities:			
Net income	$ 10,467	$ 8,503	$ 6,717
Adjustments to reconcile net income to net cash provided by operating activities:			
Depreciation	3,129	2,526	1,972
Amortization of intangible assets	3,010	3,582	1,150
Deferred income taxes	(2,139)	(2,167)	(1,146)
Stock-based compensation	3,974	3,547	2,613
Other, net	720	661	220
Changes in operating assets and liabilities, net of effects from acquisitions:			
Increase in trade receivables, net	(965)	(151)	(874)
Decrease in prepaid expenses and other assets	542	317	11
Decrease in accounts payable and other liabilities	(594)	(281)	(733)
Decrease in income taxes payable	(127)	(153)	(398)
Increase in deferred revenues	656	781	7
Net cash provided by operating activities	18,673	17,165	9,539
Cash flows from investing activities:			
Purchases of marketable securities and other investments	(1,003)	(1,181)	(10,272)
Proceeds from sales and maturities of marketable securities and other investments	572	1,113	26,151
Acquisitions, net of cash acquired	(63)	(27,721)	(148)
Capital expenditures	(6,866)	(8,695)	(4,511)
Net cash (used for) provided by investing activities	(7,360)	(36,484)	11,220
Cash flows from financing activities:			
Payments for repurchases of common stock	(1,202)	(1,300)	(16,248)
Proceeds from issuances of common stock	742	1,192	482
Shares repurchased for tax withholdings upon vesting of restricted stock-based awards	(2,040)	(1,203)	(1,093)
Payments of dividends to stockholders	(4,391)	(3,668)	(3,457)
(Repayments of) proceeds from issuances of commercial paper, net	(167)	500	0
Proceeds from issuances of senior notes and other borrowings, net of issuance costs	0	33,494	0
Repayments of senior notes and other borrowings	(3,500)	(21,050)	(8,250)
Other, net	4	(55)	(560)
Net cash (used for) provided by financing activities	(10,554)	7,910	(29,126)
Effect of exchange rate changes on cash and cash equivalents	(70)	(209)	(348)
Net increase (decrease) in cash and cash equivalents	689	(11,618)	(8,715)
Cash and cash equivalents at beginning of period	9,765	21,383	30,098
Cash and cash equivalents at end of period	10,454	9,765	21,383
Non-cash investing activities:			
Unpaid capital expenditures	1,637	588	731
Supplemental schedule of cash flow data:			
Cash paid for income taxes	3,560	3,009	2,567
Cash paid for interest	$ 3,655	$ 3,250	$ 2,735

If you haven't come across the term before, a very easy example of accrual is if I sell you a box of oranges (that cost me nothing) for $10, and you promise to pay me next week. I will record this in my accounts as $10 revenue. But because you haven't paid me, I must record accounts receivable of $10. So, while my profit and loss account shows a $10 profit, my cash flow account cancels it out with the increase in accounts receivable, showing $0 cash generation.

The cash flow statement lets you see the flow of cash in a company. There are a few big things to look at here.

• Cash flow from operating activities is, if you like, the company's salary it's how much the company has to live on for the year.
• Capital expenditure (capex, for short) - money spent on the company's long-term assets. This might reflect a new manufacturing or processing facility, purchases of software licenses, or new real estate. Some companies have very lumpy capex; that is, they have to spend a lot at once, and they don't see the impact on their profitability for quite a while. Mining and oil companies, for instance, have very lumpy capex.
• Acquisitions or disposals. If the company got a huge amount of cash from selling off an unneeded factory site, you'd want to check that its operations were still generating plenty of cash before that one-off item. Or, if it bought out a regional rival, you'll want to check what the cash flow looked like before that acquisition.

You'll generally want to see cash from operations following net income. If a company that seems to be growing nicely as far as its income statement is concerned is seeing no growth in its cash flow from operating activities, that might mean there are problems in the business. Maybe it has loosened its credit terms and is selling to customers who don't pay on time. Maybe it is piling up stocks of a product that isn't selling. Or perhaps it is growing too fast, and its inventories and receivables have increased rapidly.

For your information, in my free bonus #2 - Company Valuation Simplified Masterclass, I walk you through some of the financial statements discussed in this chapter and share my real-time analysis on a company called Vesta. It would be practical for you to watch this masterclass to gain a better idea on how to think like an analyst. Please visit www.az-penn.com to watch the class.

Expectations

The stock market is driven by investors and traders making predictions about the future. The past is only a guide to what could happen - what matters is future expectations. So when you look at an earnings statement, you need to have a page open on your broker's website (or a finance website) that shows you agreed expectations among analysts for what a company might make.

Zacks shows sales and earnings estimates and how many analysts' forecasts have been used to reach the consensus. That way, you know whether the forecast comes from just one analyst or whether there's a fair amount of research available.

You can view Detailed Earning Estimates for Primerica, which is in the screenshot on the previous page, by going to this link below:

zacks.com/stock/quote/PRI/detailed-earning-estimates?icid=quote-stock_overview-quote_nav_tracking-zoom-left_subnav_quote_navbar-detailed_earning_estimates

Generally, companies get a reputation for the relationship between expectations and the results they come out with.

• Some companies almost always beat expectations. In this case, if they come out with earnings that are 'just' in line with expectations, the shares might actually fall.
• Some companies usually have earnings in line with predictions.
• And some companies have a bad reputation for cheating investors by having earnings wildly short of the mark.

It's worth discovering what kind of stock you're trading!

One date that you need to be aware of is the date a stock goes ex-dividend. This is the date on which buying the stock no longer gives the right to the next dividend payment.

Because you no longer get this as soon as when you buy the stock, the share price is adjusted downwards by the amount of the dividend payment. For instance, if Oracle is paying a $0.40 dividend, and the ex-dividend date is October 10, on October 11, the stock price will be reduced by $0.40 by the market makers to allow for the dividend. I.e. a $10 stock would be reduced to a $9.60 stock.

Particularly if you are trading a stock that pays a high yield, you need to be aware of ex-dividend dates - they can make a nasty hole in your trade. When the dividend is paid, the share price will adjust, and if a stock is paying 7% in dividends, the price might be 7% down the next time you look! For a stock like Microsoft, with a dividend representing less than 1% of its share price, the damage will not be as noticeable.

Talking business

Of course, it's not just numbers that make a company. Fundamental analysis also includes a lot of other factors. For instance, a pharmaceutical company needs to have both blockbuster drugs that are currently selling well and new drugs in development to replace drugs coming off-patent. If it doesn't have the latter, sales will fall off a cliff sooner or later. Look at a restaurant group and assess how much room it has for growth, how well it compares with its competitors, and whether the concept attracts customers or loses them to other formats such as fast casual, fine dining, or drive-through.

Here are a few issues that have hiked or crashed share prices over the years:
• Apple stock rose 16% in the month after the release of the iPhone in 2007, and 13% in the month after the release of the iPad in 2010.
• Chipotle shares crashed after the company was implicated in a spate of food poisoning incidents.
• Robinhood shares fell after the SEC issued a Wells Notice recommending enforcement action for alleged violations of the securities laws. To be fair, Robinhood also has another major problem, having hired too many staff and failed to control its costs.
• Numerous tech stocks and even data farm REITs have risen as investors assess the likely impact of Artificial Intelligence on their profits over the long term.
• Auto stocks have generally fallen as the disruption of moving to electronic vehicles leaves them fighting on two fronts in a weakening market. Market share wins and losses often move share prices for stocks such as Ford, Stellantis, and Tesla.
• Oil stocks and gold miners often see their prices rise when wars and global trade disputes threaten to cut supply.

You might want to consider a retail stock; for instance, what demographic is it selling to? Is it doing so successfully? Are younger shoppers going elsewhere? Does the sales season seem to have bigger discounts every year? Are its outlets well located and well maintained? Sometimes, it's obvious that a retailer is losing its way quite a while before the earnings releases really show it.

You might also consider what Warren Buffett calls a 'moat': a major advantage that stops rivals from competing effectively with the company. For instance, Boeing and Airbus pretty much have a monopoly of aircraft sales to commercial airlines; Estee Lauder has a brand name that is incredibly valuable; Abbvie has immunology and aesthetics drugs that lead the field. Companies that establish and defend their moats are solid; companies that have no moat have to compete hard on cost and can lose market share fast.

How shares are valued

Shares can be valued in one of two ways: intrinsic or comparative. The intrinsic valuation looks at the likely long-term prospects for the business, and what that means in terms of cash flow to shareholders, and uses a discounted cash flow model to assess what those future cash flows are worth today. The comparative or relative valuation is derived by finding similar businesses to serve as a comparison and looking at comparable ratios such as the price/earnings, price/revenues, or price/cash flow ratios.

Valuing a company on an intrinsic basis is hard work, as it requires forecasting the company's cash flows five or more years into the future. On the other hand, comparative valuations are simple to calculate using publicly available information such as the share price, earnings per share, and company revenues.

If a well-known analyst comes up with a new intrinsic valuation model that states a value very different from the current share price, that could move the market. However, you don't really need to know how to create the model.

If you're looking for a basic idea of whether shares are expensive or cheap, use the comparative method. So, for instance, let's compare Coca-Cola and Pepsi.

Coca-Cola (ticker symbol KO) is trading at $62. Its earnings over the last twelve months (TTM, or trailing twelve-month earnings, which is the sum of the most recent 4 quarters added together) were $2.41, so it's PER, or Price/Earnings Ratio (P/E ratio) is $62 / $2.41 = 25.7.

Pepsi (ticker symbol PEP) is trading at $159 and has a TTM of $6.79, giving it a P/E ratio of 23.4.

If you buy KO now, you'll have to hand over 25.7 times what it earns - another way of looking at it is, if it earned the same amount every year for 25.7 years, you'd just get your money back in terms of earnings per share. On the other hand, you only have to wait 23.4 years for PEP to earn your money back. Now, that's completely theoretical - the money is not 'yours,' and in fact, you're hoping both companies will grow their businesses over that time - but the fact is, PEP is cheaper than KO, nearly 10% cheaper.

Finding trades with fundamentals

You might want to find stocks that are in an uptrend. One good way to do it is to look for a growth sector. Look at the prospects of different industries. Which sectors are doing excellent, and which sectors are seeing companies collapse?

Some sectors are cyclical. For instance, extractive industries often have a glorious time when commodities prices are going up. Then, they invest in opening new mines or oil wells so that the next time commodity prices dip, there's way too much production capacity, and they start to lose money. This happens repeatedly, so you want to know where they are in the cycle before you decide to trade the shares.

You might want to look for a cheap valuation in a sector. You can go to fullratio.com and check the P/E ratios of different industries, for instance. Right now, oil and gas, residential construction, auto manufacturers, and marine shipping are cheap. But of course, there might be a reason for that - they might not be growing their earnings; in fact, their earnings might even be falling. You'd need to find out how fast stocks in the sector are growing.

Alternatively, you might want to trade shares in the fastest-growing sectors. So head for S&P's website and their release of S&P 500 Sector Earnings and Revenue Data for the latest quarter. That will show you which sectors are forging ahead and which are not. Go to spglobal.com/market-intelligence/en/news-insights/research/sp-500-q3-2024-sector-earnings-revenue-data.

You might also use stock screeners to find shares that, irrespective of sector, fit your preferred characteristics. So, for instance, you could look for shares with earnings growth of more than 10% if you think that growth stocks provide a more attractive trading potential, because they are more likely to have positive catalysts like good corporate news, and more likely to attract both short and long term investors.

Or, if you wanted to find good value, you could look for stocks with a P/E ratio of less than two-thirds of the S&P 500 (right now, that would be around 20 times earnings). Let's just unpack that. The S&P is valued at 30 times earnings which you can find on Macrotrends or Gurufocus. Basically, if the company earned the same every year for the next 30 years, that's how long it would take for those earnings to 'pay back' your initial investment. But if you buy a 'value' stock, your theoretical payback will come in just 20 years. Because of this lower valuation, there is a lot of room for the stock price to rise without the stock becoming expensive on a fundamental basis.

Or you might want to find companies with a high return on capital employed (ROCE) so that you have access to the most profitable companies in the stock market universe. A high return on capital means those companies are investing their money to make better profits than other enterprises, so they are very high-quality profit generators.

Whose advice to follow

Plenty of Wall Street analysts get quoted in the media. Lots of amateur analysts post on Reddit, on Motley Fool, Seeking Alpha, or brokers' bulletin boards. And there are plenty of commentators on TV, like Jim Cramer. I reckon you'd like to know which of them are worth following, right?

So I'll tell you. None of them.

Analysts are quite careful about what they write; they don't want to upset companies. So they might say 'hold' a particular stock, but when they phone an important client like a big pension fund, that 'hold' would more likely be expressed, "I think you could probably invest the money better in something else." There are always more buy-and-hold recommendations out there than sell recommendations - even in a bear market.

TV commentators aren't so careful. But they also may not be quite as expert. And if you're listening to one, then so are millions of other people, all of whom could hit the markets at tomorrow's open. It's good to be aware of what's going on - if you see a run in a stock, it may just mean it was featured on TV yesterday - but don't try using the media as a source of ideas.

In the same way, it may be worth knowing that there's a lot of talk about a particular stock on Reddit. You then know that retail interest could push the stock. But I wouldn't pay much attention to what people say - particularly to information-lite comments like 'next stop $200' or 'gotta be a buy.'

Where analysts are useful, if you have the time and the interest, is in explaining businesses in depth. If you have the chance to get an analyst's initial report on a stock, which will be a pretty chunky document, it can make for interesting reading. Once you've read it, you'll have a good understanding of the company, the business environment in which it operates, and the kind of comparators that the market uses to value the shares. As for the recommendation, I'd just ignore it - if it's more than 24 hours old, it's already old news!

Ratios you need to know

One of the things that has made me relatively successful as a trader is having all the basic ratios at my fingertips. The secret? Just practice, practice, practice. Calculate your ratios till they stick permanently in your brain cells. Here are my top 18 ratios that you should really get to know.

1. Income per share = *Net income / Average number of shares*

Simply divide the company's net income by the *average* number of shares in issue. Why use the average? Because shares issued halfway through the year, for instance, are only entitled to half the year's income. This is usually done for you in the SEC filings, but it does not harm to check!

2. Gross margin % = *Gross profit / revenue x 100*

Take gross profit (that is, revenue *less* the cost of goods sold), and divide it by the revenue; multiply by 100 (to get the percentage figure). For businesses like retail and wholesale, this is a really important figure; a decline in gross margin might mean a fashion company has to get rid of unsold stock at a discount, for instance.

3. Operating margin % = *Operating income / revenue x 100*

Divide operating income (income before interest and tax) by revenue and multiply by 100. This shows how much operating profit the company makes on each dollar of sales. If the company can push up prices or reduce costs, the operating margin will increase, so the trend in the operating margin will show how well the company is being managed or whether competition in the sector is becoming tougher.

4. EBITDA margin % = EBITDA / *revenue x 100*

This is similar to operating margin, but you use EBITDA (earnings before interest, taxes, depreciation, and amortization). So it's EBITDA, divided by revenue, times 100. Depreciation and amortization are ways of spreading the cost of a long-term asset over the years that it's expected to remain in service. For instance, if you buy a computer you expect to last five years, you'd take one-fifth of the value against your profits each year - another example of accrual.

You could call this the 'cash earnings' margin, earnings without the biggest non-cash expense. This is quite useful for companies that charge high depreciation because they are heavily invested in assets with a relatively short life (such as computers or vehicle fleets).

5. Interest cover = *EBIT / interest expense*

Divide EBIT (earnings before interest and tax) by the interest expense. This shows how easily the company can cover its debt service requirements. If the interest cover is below 1, the company can't pay its debt service charges. If it's a relatively high number, the company won't have a problem. Remember to exclude one-off items from the EBIT calculation. For instance, if the company disposed of a big office building, you'll want to exclude that, as you can't expect such a source of funds every year.

6. Debt to equity ratio = *Total liabilities / total shareholders' equity*

Total liabilities are *divided* by shareholders' equity (one of the major elements on the balance sheet, as it shows the amount that 'belongs' to shareholders rather than being funded by banks). This shows the relationship of equity to debt in the company's finances. If it is above 1, the company is more highly leveraged (that is, has a greater reliance on debt to fund its operations), so that shareholders' equity is not enough to pay all the company's liabilities; if it is below 1, the company has lower leverage (its less reliant on debt to fund its operations).

7. Free cash flow per share = *Free cash flow / total outstanding shares*

You divide free cash flow (the **cash flow from operations**, *less* capital expenditure) by the number of shares. Free cash flow adjusts earnings to take account of acquisitions, disposals, capital investment, changes in working capital (inventories and accounts payable or receivable), and depreciation/amortization. This is particularly interesting to compare with income per share - if a company has *high* income per share but *low* free cash flow, you need to know why. It may have problems, for instance, customers who are not paying on time, or huge unsold inventories, perhaps because of expired products. Or it may have spent too much on capex and it's been getting too little profit from its investment.

8. Dividend cover = *Net income / dividend paid*

Divide the net income by the dividend paid. This shows how easily the company could continue to pay the dividend if, for some reason, earnings were to fall. If the cover is 2 times, the company has significant firepower left; if it is below 1.5 times, the dividend may not be safe if earnings stumble.

9. Book value per share = *Shareholders equity / total number of outstanding shares*

If you take the shareholder's equity and divide it by the total number of shares in issue. This shows how much of the company's value is attributable to each share. It benefits asset-rich companies like property companies/REITs and infrastructure companies. It is one of the major valuation methods for REITs since you are buying a bunch of real estate assets rather than an operational business.

10. Return on equity % = *Net income / shareholders equity x 100*

You divide net income by shareholders' equity, and multiply by 100. This ratio shows how much profit the company generates for each dollar of shareholders' equity. This will reflect how efficiently the company uses its tangible assets (i.e. anything it owns that is physical, such as offices, plant, vehicles, or servers), and the mix of debt and equity finance used to fund its operations.

11. Return on assets % = *Net income / total assets x 100*

You divide net income by total assets, and multiply by 100. This shows how much net income the company makes for each dollar of assets - how efficiently it uses its tangible assets to generate profit.

12. Price earnings (P/E) ratio = *stock price / earning per share*

Divide the stock price by the earnings per share (EPS). This is the most basic ratio for valuing stock - the higher the ratio, the more highly valued the share. If a stock is valued at a P/E ratio of 5, you will 'earn back' your investment in five years; if it's valued at a P/E ratio of 27, it will take 27 years. That's a theoretical payback - not a real one.

13. Price revenue ratio = *Market capitalization / total revenues*

You divide the market capitalization by total revenues. For loss-making, newly profitable, or turnaround companies, this can be a better comparator than the P/E ratio; loss-making companies won't have a P/E ratio, and companies that are still turning around will have what appears to be a very high P/E ratio because their profits are still low compared to their income. Comparing price to revenue allows you to compare these companies with profitable companies in the sector to understand what they *should* be worth when they become equally profitable.

14. Price to book value = *Share price / book value per share*

Divide the share price by the book value per share (or market capitalization *divided* by total shareholders' equity). This shows the relationship between the share price and the total value of the company's assets. If it is below 1, you buy those assets at a discount - the share price is below the assets per share.

15. PEG (Price Earnings Growth) ratio = *P/E ratio / expected EPS growth rate*

You divide the P/E ratio by the expected percentage of EPS growth. The PEG ratio shows how the company's P/E ratio relates to its growth prospects. A PEG below 1 usually shows that a stock is undervalued since its growth is higher than the price-earnings ratio, giving you a quicker 'payback.'

16. Dividend Yield % = *Dividend per share / share price x 100*

Divide the dividend per share by the share price and multiply by 100. This shows the cash return to shareholders. This is an important metric for income stocks like REITS and mature companies like Johnson & Johnson. Many investors (both retail and institutional) buy these stocks for income, so the yield is a key metric for their decision to purchase the stock.

17. Asset turnover ratio = *Net sales / total assets*

Divide net sales by total assets. This shows how efficiently the company uses its assets to generate sales. For instance, with retailers, how quickly they can sell and replace their inventory is a major part of this ratio, since inventory is likely to be quite a big part of assets, and accounts for the major direct cost of goods sold.

18. Inventory turnover ratio = *Cost of goods sold / average inventory*

Divide the cost of goods sold by average inventory (which is the inventory at the start of the year + the inventory at the end of the year, divided by two). This simply digs further into asset turnover to show how efficiently the company is cycling its *inventory* into cash - so it doesn't show how efficient the company is at using its fixed machinery or real estate, which also impacts asset turnover.

Chapter 7 Quiz

1. What is EDGAR?
a) A database that gives the number of shares issued by every stock exchange listed company
b) A database of corporate earnings releases and other filings
c) A charting program
d) A database of all trades executed on the New York Stock Exchange

2. Which of the following screens would work to find growth stocks in an uptrend?
a) Net income per share growth > 10%, share price > 20-day moving average
b) Net income per share growth > 15%, RSI > 60
c) Net income per share growth > 15%, share price > 20 day MA, share price > 50 day MA, 50 day MA > 20 day MA
d) Net income per share growth > 10%, relative volume > 1.5, share price > 50 day MA

3. Which of these events would require an 8K to be issued?
a) The company makes a significant acquisition
b) The company loses a significant contract
c) The CEO gets fined for driving while intoxicated
d) The SEC fines the company for breaches of securities law

4. Which of these is a good sign?
a) A rapid increase in inventories
b) An increase in accounts receivable
c) An increase in cash flow from operations
d) An increase in current liabilities

5. Which of these is not a way to value a share?
a) Price / earnings ratio
b) Price / revenues
c) Price / employees
d) Price / cash flow

8

Chapter 8: Plan Your Trade and Follow Your Plan

People often think of the life of a trader as watching the screens, spotting an opportunity, and paddling into the market as if the trader shoots from the hip, like a stock market Clint Eastwood or John Wayne.

The truth is very different. That's true for all traders, even swing traders. A good trade needs to be planned in detail before you trade - in fact, it should be planned in detail before the chart confirms the move you want to trade. In other words, you're always going to look for shares that are to give you a good trading opportunity at some point in the next few hours or days, and you should have your trade fully planned out with entry price, target profit, and stop loss before that opportunity arrives.

In fact, you're more like a sniper than a gunfighter. Cool, calm, lying in wait, and only shooting once the perfect opportunity presents itself.

In this chapter, I'm going to talk about how to plan your trades. In the next chapter, I will go into more detail about how to manage your risk. If you get your planning wrong, or you just don't bother to do it, then you're putting yourself on the road to failure.

Profit targets

A buy-and-hold investor usually doesn't have a hard and fast profit target. Maybe they have an initial target price, but they're likely to hang on to the shares as long as the company keeps growing its earnings and the reason they bought it remains valid.

Swing traders, though, need a profit target. Otherwise, how could you calculate your risk/return ratio? That is part of planning your trade - the stop loss controls your downside, while your profit target allows you to plan your exit.

Many chart patterns will show you where your profit target needs to be. For instance, in the head-and-shoulders patterns, the distance between the neckline and the head gives you the profit you should make. In other cases, you may see a support or resistance line that the price will hit if it moves the way you want it to; that's a good place to exit because the price might bounce off it.

You might also use Fibonacci retracements. These are based on mathematical patterns that recur with impressive regularity; 38%, 50%, and 62% are the 'magic numbers,' the levels at which experience shows that prices often turn. If you're lucky, your chart package can overlay a Fibonacci grid on top of the regular share price chart to show you these levels. They work as support/resistance lines, so if the share price is coming up to it, then it's likely to bounce off or perhaps consolidate around that line - it's time to exit your trade.

Above is an example of a Fibonacci grid applied to a chart: first, the highs and lows have been extended into horizontal lines. Then, treating the lower line as the base (=0), the share prices representing each of the Fibonacci levels have been calculated and drawn. They fit pretty well with the support and resistance levels shown.

You should keep re-evaluating the position all the time. Other technical indicators might tell you when to exit the trade. For instance, in a long trade, I will sell if the shares close below the 18-day or 9-day moving average or the MACD gets into overbought territory. Equally, if I see shares break below a support level or trendline, that's time to head for the exits. And if I've ridden an uptrend, but the candlesticks are getting shorter and shorter, and volume is decreasing, that suggests the bulls aren't pushing the market as strongly as they were - again, time to exit.

You might decide to exit your trade in stages. For instance, when your trade is 10% up, you might sell half your stake as a *partial sale*, letting the rest ride and setting the stop loss at the same price as your partial sale so you don't make any losses. There's more paperwork to do, of course, and you'll also pay a bit more commission this way, but many swing traders like to do it to lock in their profits.

Finally, you'll probably find that a stock refuses to move sometimes. It won't make you a profit, it won't trigger your stop-loss, and you could use your capital much better elsewhere. Give yourself a time limit - mine is three weeks; yours might be shorter or longer depending on how active a trader you want to be.

Round numbers are very dangerous. Let's stick with the Coca-Cola trade from the previous chapter. If I buy at $63 and have a stop loss at exactly $62, that's a round number, and many other people will likely have stop losses at that level. If you place your stop loss at $62.20, you'll get out before those guys - but you might get out too soon if the share price is just bouncing around a bit and ends up rising to where you thought it would. If you place your stop loss at $61.80, you're going to miss out on small turbulence, and only get stopped out if the trade is really going wrong - that would be a more suitable stop loss placement.

In every case, *avoid* those round numbers. In particular, avoid the roundest of round numbers, like $100. Better to put an order slightly below or slightly above.

Creating a business plan and process

If you want to be a successful swing trader, you're going to have to treat trading like a business. Not a hobby, an obsession, a craze, not 'fun' - a business, just like any other. And that's the same whether you are trading in your spare time from a laptop, or full time from a dedicated workstation in your home office.

First of all, you need to have a good routine. For part-time swing traders who have a day job, that's going to be an evening task, but even full-time swing traders should keep the routine of doing a market post-mortem every day once the market has closed. Full-timers might add checking the market opening as well.

Every closing, you'll want to quickly review the market fundamentals. Yes, you'll want to see if the Nasdaq and the S&P 500 closed up, down, or sideways, but there's more to it than that. You'll also want to check some other statistics;

• Advances vs declines,
• Stocks hitting new highs vs stocks hitting new lows,
• And the percentage of stocks above and below their moving averages.

While the closing level (i.e. the last price recorded) just gives you a single piece of information, the closing price, these other data will show you what's going on inside the market and making it move. For instance, if the market goes up but there are more declines than advances, then it's likely that it was just a handful of big stocks moving the market higher. That makes the advance rather unpredictable. If you can see that, then you know something that people just looking at the headline figure don't know - and that can give you a big advantage.

Find a good stock market news page, perhaps on Reuters, Marketwatch, or your broker's site, and pull that up to ensure you haven't missed any major news. Major companies' results, big political decisions (such as the imposition of tariffs on imports or changes in the corporate tax rate), and economic data are all things you need to catch up with. You'll also want to see the major movers among the big stocks, such as if all the techs are up, for instance, or if oil stocks have been plummeting.

Why not try out one of these stock market news sites:

• marketwatch.com

• investing.com

• thestreet.com

And it wouldn't do any harm to look at the major index charts to see if you can spot any patterns emerging. After all, if you think Nasdaq has just completed a head and shoulders formation, and the next step will be a downward breakout, you probably don't want to be opening any long trades tomorrow!

It really helps, of course, if you can somehow customize a single webpage or screen to give you all this data together. It might take a little time to set up, but it will save you time in the long term.

The next thing you want to do is to review all your open positions and then review your watchlist. Have any trades been stop lossed out? Have closing orders on any profitable trades gone through? Did automatic trades open any new positions?

Take a good look at the charts to assess where you are with your trades. In particular, look for any new patterns that are being established, and check the RSI, volume, and moving averages. If you have a stock that you bought for a breakout upwards to $61, and it's got to $60.50, but the RSI is telling you it's overbought, and volume was only half what it was the day before, well that's telling you that the upwards momentum is weakening. It might be time to enter a sell order even though the stock hasn't quite got to your target price.

Review your watchlist. If you see a confirmation signal from any of your watchlist stocks, then it's time to enter the trade. Don't forget to enter at least two orders: your purchase order and your stop loss order. The latter is the one that will save your butt time and time again, so don't miss it out!

That's it. If you have spare time, it's worth running a scan to see if any new ideas emerge. If you don't keep scanning for new ideas, you'll run out of good trades sooner or later. However, this is something that you can leave for the weekend if you are short of time.

As musicians and athletes know, it's better to practice half an hour daily than save it all up for Saturday morning. If you are trading part-time, it's better to have a quick *daily* review than a weekly in-depth assessment. If you want a holiday, take a proper holiday. That means no trading. If you need to set a timer to ensure you get everything done in 20 to 30 minutes, do it - that will focus your mind.

Every week, you'll want to review your performance. You probably already have a feel for how you are doing, but you need to go through the numbers in detail and draw conclusions about how you can improve in the future. Get out your trading journal (or power up the software) and take a look. In particular, you will want to analyze the following factors:

• Your total number of trades. Do you think you could have done more? Did you miss profitable entry points on some potential trades?

• Your win ratio. If 50% of your trades lose, that's about what you would expect from random coin-tossing, but you can still be profitable if your stop-losses work well and your profits on the other 50% of trades are good. However, ideally, you should improve your win rate as time goes on.

• Your total returns on winning trades, your losses on losing trades, and the aggregate. You'll want to compare your returns to your total trading capital; if you make $540 this month, that's great news if your total capital is just $5000, but if you have a $100,000 retirement account to trade, maybe $540 return is not so impressive.

• The setups that made money for you. Maybe you always make more money on continuation trades rather than reversals or vice versa; maybe your candlestick ideas work out, and your chart patterns don't do so well. Setting up this feedback loop through weekly reviews lets you refine your strategy and focus on the kind of trades that you're best at.

Were there factors in any trades that didn't pan out as expected? For instance, was your order only partially filled, limiting the profit you could make on the trade? Were you stop-lossed out by a temporary dip in the price before the stock rose, taking you out of what should have been a profitable position? If that happens often, you need to loosen your stop-losses a little; stocks often test the support a couple of times before cutting loose.

If you made a loss but the trade was perfectly executed, that's fine. Remember, when you're swing trading, you are assessing probabilities, not trading on certainties, so it's inevitable that you will sometimes make a loss. Your job is to ensure that you control those losses and regard them as one of the costs of doing business.

At the end of the week, look at what happened to stocks in which you closed out your positions. Are you exiting trades too early or too late? That is, did you take a profit and then see you could have made even more, or were you up by 10% and then saw the shares fall back, so you made a smaller profit?

Above all, you must ask the following question: Are you sticking to your plan?

By the way, while your trading journal tells most of the story, it doesn't tell all of the story regarding your business. How many stocks did you scan? How many failed to produce good signals? How many did you add or subtract from your watch list? How much time did you put into the process? It might be worth jotting down some basic information like this to check if you're using your time effectively.

Walking through the trade

Here, I will take a single trade setup, but I will show several variations on how things pan out from there.

So, first of all, I've gone through my watchlist today, and I've found this potentially interesting situation in the chart below - ODD stock with three very clear white soldiers (or green soldiers if you have colored candlesticks, I suppose). Look at them right there on the right-hand side of the chart. I've looked for confirmation from the RSI, which stands at 62. There is plenty of interest, and it is not in overbought territory, so that looks okay. I also note that the share price broke through its 30-day moving average with the first of the 'green soldiers,' which is a good sign. So, I'm looking for the shares to break upwards.

ODDITY Tech Ltd. - Class A (ODD) Stock Price

48.05 ▲ +2.49 (+5.47%) Open: **45.86** Vol: **1.19M** Day's range: **45.62 - 48.15** Nov 25, 16:00 EST
IEX Real-Time Quote

| type a symbol | Display ▾ | Time ▾ | Draw ▾ | Indicators ▾ | Free Stock Screener |

ODD:Daily Nov 21, 2024 O: 40.73 H: 43.35 L: 40.29 C: 43.12
MA(30) 41.03

RSI(14) 56.28

2. Sep 9. Sep 16. Sep 23. Sep 30. Sep 7. Oct 14. Oct 21. Oct 28. Oct 4. Nov 11. Nov 18. Nov 25. Nov

ODD Technical Analysis

Buy/Sell Signal   MA Levels   Momentum Indicators Levels

What's the upside? This isn't an easy pattern to put a definite upside on, but I think if the price moves, it will be fast, so I will look for a rise that matches the three white soldiers' length ($41 to $48), so that's gonna be another $7 upside from $48 to $55.

And what's the downside? The next big support level is $40. But in fact, I can set a tighter stop-loss than that because if the stock goes back below the body of the last candlestick, I'll know the three white soldiers pattern has failed. So I will set my stop there, at $45.83, the bottom of the last candlestick on the chart.

I've now assessed the upside and the downside, so that lets me work out my risk/return ratio.

The upside is $7. The downside is $48 *minus* $45.83, that's $2.17. So, I'm risking $2.17 to get $7. That gives me a risk/return ratio of 1:3.2, i.e. risking $1 to get a $3.20 profit. That's more than acceptable.

For interest, let's find out where the risk/reward ratio is 1:2, which is the absolute minimum I'm prepared to accept for a trade to be viable. If the reward is $7, then at 1:2, the risk would be $3.50. So that means I could bid up to my stop-loss plus $3.50, which is $45.83 + $3.50 = $49.33.

However, I don't want to chase this trade. It's not the biggest stock on the market, and I want to make sure I can cover any slippage. So, I'm prepared to buy only up to a buy limit of $48.54. Why not $48.50? I want to make sure I don't use a round number; lots of unwise traders will probably put orders in at $48.50, and market makers might mark the price up a bit before my order can get filled.

Why did I calculate how far I could push the buy price if I'm not going to use every cent I can? Ultimately, trading is about risk management, and sometimes, you will decide you want a larger margin. However, you should never accept a *lower* return than $2 for every $1 you risk.

By the way, when you're working out all these calculations, it can really help to use a spreadsheet rather than just a calculator. If the price changes, you can plug in new prices instead of recalculating everything from scratch. But make sure you label your cells clearly ('buy price,' 'expected profit,' 'stop loss'), or you could get yourself confused… and that could cost you money!

Sometimes, you may see a chart where the share price is already slightly higher than you'd like. You certainly can place a buy order below the market price, hoping to take advantage of any small dip in the share price. For instance, if you see a chart pattern where a share price has already made an upward breakout and is a bit beyond an optimal buy price, you can place the order nearer the support line. Quite often, share prices will test a support line before the breakout becomes definitive, so this gives you a second bite at the cherry.

Now that I've set my buy limit, I will not chase the shares. No second thoughts, no raising the limit to $48.60 if it opens too high. And no changing the stop loss either; I'm going to put it at $45.83, as I said, and if it gets there, the position is sold, that's it. So, as it were, I have set my risk/reward ratio in stone. Whatever happens, I have a trade where I know the potential outcomes.

So now I can enter those orders, and they will execute automatically if the conditions are met.

What happens tomorrow? Let's look at the different things that *could* happen if I set my buy limit to $48.50.

• The stock gaps up at $49.50 and keeps going. If this happens, then my buy order never gets filled. There's no trade - if I bought the share that high, I would run far too much risk for too little profit.
• The stock opens at $48.20, filling my buy order. Now, suppose the shares trade around $48.50 all day. And the next day. And the day after that. After a week, it will be time to give up because the positive momentum has disappeared. In that case, I will just about break even. It didn't work out.

• The stock opens at $48.20, and my buy order is filled. Then it starts to fall, stops at $46, and comes back up, then at $47.50, falls back again, and starts heading down further. At $45.83, my stop-loss is executed automatically. I have lost $2.37 per share ($48.20 - $45.83), but I have lost exactly what I expected to lose if things went wrong, and I know that the risk/reward of the trade was acceptable, so that's just a cost of doing business.

• Or perhaps everything goes right. My buy order is filled out, and I am rewarded by white soldier number four! The stock shoots up. In the following days, it kept going, and a week later, it got to that $56 level where I spotted some resistance. What do I do now?

I need to do some work before I can answer that question. I want to look back at the longer term. Maybe there's a higher resistance level if the $56 level is broken? That would give me another target.

But it turns out that there is not. $56 is close to the all-time high, so asking for more might be greedy. I can check this out by taking a look at the share volume. If that's still high, maybe there's more to shoot for. But if it's falling, it means the bulls are running out of steam. In that case, I'll definitely want to make an exit - and given everyone else can see the $56 level too, I won't get greedy; I'll set my sell limit at $55.95 so that if there is a selling madness, I will already be out of the stock.

Things might be different. If, for instance, I see another resistance level around $63 and good volumes continue, then I might scale out by selling half my position and letting the rest run. At this point, though, I would also need to increase my stop-loss. I should bring it up to $55.95 so that I still have a good risk/reward ratio on the remaining position, and that I've locked in my profit.

If the stock was in a very hot sector, I might decide not to scale out but to leave the whole position working for me. But I would still bring my stop-loss up to $55.95 or thereabouts, locking in a profit. I would also keep checking indicators like the RSI and the 20-day moving average to spot the first signs of the stock running out of juice.

Improving your trading performance

You shouldn't change your strategy because of one losing trade or one trade where you could have made more profit if you had run your position a little longer. Remember, you are not working based on certainties but on probabilities, so inevitably, you will meet less-than-optimal outcomes for some trades. However, you can improve your trading performance by looking back on your trades in aggregate - whether you are averaging the right amount.

Maybe your decision to get out of a share at a 10% profit when it went to make 20% was right. Perhaps that further run was just a fluke. If the share reversed course dramatically shortly afterwards, you may have not made the most profit - but you also haven't seen a paper profit turn into a real loss after the share price collapsed.

Maybe when you were stop-lossed out of a share that tested its support line, you had set your stop-loss too tight. And then again, maybe you hadn't.

You can't know about individual trades. But if you see that on a significant percentage of all your trades, you got stop-lossed out of what should have been a profitable trade, or exited your position before the stock price increased another 20%, then probably the problem is you, and not the market. Go back, look at the charts, and see if you made any mistakes, such as not recognizing support and resistance levels, or failing to see that there was still high volume pushing the share price upwards and the share price was still way above the moving average, which was trending upwards. Work out if there is anything you missed. Would checking another indicator have helped, maybe?

Annual returns

If I ask another swing trader what their annual return was, and they don't know, they're just swing trading cowboys - rank amateurs. You might have made 20% on your last trade or lost 1% on it; I don't care - it's your annual returns that show whether you're a successful swing trader or not. I know some traders have entire years when they are down - usually if the market has changed dramatically; but usually, they'll show a reasonably consistent run of overall figures.

The annual return is your big comparative figure. It's what you can set against the performance of the S&P 500 or Nasdaq, to see whether you are beating the market. (If you're not, you need to improve - or quit trading.) It's the figure that can tell you how you compare to other traders - eToro publishes its top traders' records, so you can take a look at them. It's the only way to tell whether you are really doing okay.

It's also the way to work out if you're improving. Hopefully, if you start swing trading now, in three years, you'll see that your annual returns are increasing.

If you are fortunate, you have a trading journal system that automatically calculates your annual return. If not, you'll need to do it the old-fashioned way, with a calculator or a spreadsheet. The basics are simple - but adjusting for increases in the capital you have to trade, taxes, commissions, and other expenses can take some doing.

The simplest calculation would be if you started the year with $5,000 and just traded with that - adding no money and making no withdrawals. You take the difference between the closing and opening values, and divide it by your initial stake. So suppose you end the year with $5,542, that means you made $542 in the year, and your return would be 10.84% (which is, $542 / $5,000 x 100).

Suppose you end the year with $4,026, then you lose $974, and your annual return would be -19.48%. Better luck next year!

But if you were increasing your capital throughout the period by keeping your profits in your trading book, you'll really need to use the *average trading book*, not the starting value, to calculate your return. So, there's a little finesse to add here; instead of dividing your profit by your initial stake, you divide it by the average of your initial stake and your closing stake. In this case, that's $5,000 + $5,542 / 2, which is $5,271, so now your return comes in a little lower at 5.42%.

However, things can get much more complicated. Many swing traders add money to their trading books as they gain experience. Once you're up and running, you might also withdraw some of your trading profits to live on, or take a nice vacation, or help finance a new car or house. So, your return needs to be calculated on the value in your trading book after that event.

Suppose I got a bonus mid–year, and doubled my initial stake from $5,000 to $10,000, while making the same trading profit of $542? If I applied the simple method, it would look as if my annual return was $10,542 - $5,000 = $5,542. Then divide $5,542 by $5,000 = 110%. But of course, it wasn't! So, we need to adjust the results.

The best way to do this is the time-weighted return method; that is the way most mutual funds and money managers use when reporting their returns. To do this, for example, you need to break the year's performance into two distinct periods - the return when you only had $5,000 in the account and the return when you had $10,000 in the account. Then, you need to calculate the profit and the return for each period.

Then, you multiply those returns to arrive at the growth for the year as a whole. The math is complicated, and I'm not going to run through it here; and if you're not great at advanced math, you're going to be relieved to find that apps and websites like rateofreturnexpert.com/time-weighted-return-calculator will do the job for you automatically. (Some trading journal software does as well.) You just need to be aware that the simple method of calculation needs to be adjusted for additions and withdrawals.

Some investors prefer to use a dollar-weighted method. However, it's not particularly useful for traders because it can't cope with large negative returns, and it's the nature of swing trading that, occasionally, you'll have a loss-making period to report.

Suppose you have calculated your five-year return but want an average annual return to compare to other traders? You would need to annualize those returns. To do that, you need to create a fraction, dividing the time period you want to convert the return to by the actual time period over which it occurred. In other words, you are creating a fraction that will convert the figure for one time period into the figure for another. For instance, if you want an annual return, the first part of the fraction (the numerator) will be 1. You then need to divide it by the number of years for which you have returns; in the case of 5 years, the number would obviously be 5, but if you have a quarter's returns, you'd need to use 0.25 instead. So your annual return over 5 years needs the fraction 1/5.

Now, you need to take your return and add 1 to your return percentage; for instance, if you had a 10% return, you'd need to express that as 1.10, and 62% would give you 1.62.

Now, things get complicated because you need to use a scientific calculator (the one in Windows is okay) to raise the return to the power of the fraction. Then subtract 1 and convert it to a percentage.

This little trick is well worth applying when you read that a certain trader "made a return of 102% over five years."

All these calculations involve hard number crunching. However, it's easy to set up a spreadsheet that can do all the work for you. I'd suggest that if your broker or trading platform provides a returns calculator, you check it against a spreadsheet, at least initially, to make sure it applies all the right bells and whistles to give you a useful number.

Benchmarks

As a swing trader, you're aiming to accelerate past the market and make a significantly higher return. So, you'll want to look at the various market benchmarks. You might just see whether the S&P has gone up as much as the value of your portfolio, but that's not really scientific. Instead, use the FTSE Russell index return calculator for US stocks or the BNY Mellon index performance tables for international stocks to find the total returns (including dividends) for any given period.

The FTSE Russell indices show the total return of the market. The Russell 3000 includes 98% of the total equities available in the US, which is a really broad index. It is adjusted every year to ensure that it's still representative of the market as a whole. However, you might want to finesse things a little, as the index is broken down into different sub-indices, and you need to make sure you use the right benchmark. If you're trading only the biggest stocks, you'll want to use the Russell 1000, or 'Large Cap Core,' for instance, because it includes only the 1,000 biggest companies by market capitalization. You'd use the Russell 2000 if you were trading smaller stocks because it focuses on the 2,000 smaller companies of the '3000-strong' Russell Universe instead of the top 1,000. So, in each case, you're comparing your returns with the returns on a similar universe of companies.

In the same way, if you trade UK stocks, you'll want to compare your return with the FTSE 100 or maybe the FTSE All-Share - again, depending on which index has constituents most similar to the stocks that you trade.

Chapter 8 Quiz

1. Why should you avoid round numbers when creating a stop-loss order?
a) Because if you use a round number, you will be competing with a lot of other orders
b) Because round numbers aren't Fibonacci levels
c) Because odd numbers confuse the IRS
d) For luck

2. Which of these would be an acceptable position size?
a) 2% of your total capital
b) 5% of your total capital
c) 18% of your total capital
d) 100% of your total capital

3. You currently have positions in Tesla, Amazon, Apple, Meta, and Microsoft. How can you get more diversification?
a) Trading a Japanese market ETF
b) Trading Samsung
c) Trading Chevron
d) Trading Twitter

4. How can you set a good profit target?
a) At the next resistance level
b) At a Fibonacci retracement level
c) Some chart patterns show the expected profit level
d) Doubling the stop-loss price

5. If you enter a trade and the share price quickly falls through your stop-loss, which of these would be appropriate actions?
a) Sell the position, and open another trade
b) Sell the position
c) Sell the position, and cry
d) Sell the position, and take the day off

A.Z Penn

9

Chapter 9: Managing Your Risk

One of the most important elements of planning your trades is managing your risk. It's not rocket science; working out and controlling your risks is pretty basic math. The real difficulty is having the discipline to follow your system. There's always an excuse - "It'll come right if I wait a bit," "I can't give up now," "If I hang on, I'm sure I can do better" - but you need to stick to the system, or you've lost.

Risk management is what limits your losses. Whenever I hear about some poor guy who lost half a million on Robinhood, I think, "There goes another guy who didn't do his risk management." (For some reason, it's always men. Maybe women are a bit smarter in this particular regard.)
Rule number one of Swing Trade Club is... don't bet the bank. Do not, do not, do not, ever, bet the bank.

I'm going to look at position sizing for individual trades. You can think of this in a couple of ways:

• First of all, in terms of your total capital tied up in a trade.
• Secondly, in terms of your total at risk in that trade.

You should have a rule for the sizing of trades according to both of these criteria. I'm not going to tell you what the rule should be because it will be different depending on the kind of assets that you trade. But it should be a pretty small percentage.

As a long-term buy-and-hold investor, you might have several investments, each at 10% of your total portfolio, and you could actually be pretty well diversified. You'd also be fully invested or close to fully invested. And that would be fine.

But as a swing trader, you run more risk. So, I'd suggest you get used to thinking of using only a small portion of your total capital and total risk percentage on a single trade. Otherwise, it's easy to get almost wiped out by a succession of losses. Your trading rules on position size are there to protect you - like guardrails on a cliff-top walk.

The second rule of Swing Trade Club is to have a stop-loss. That could be a stop-loss order with your broker, or it could be a stop-loss level in your head or written down on your notepad, but the important thing is that if the share price hits your stop-loss, you must exercise it. I'd suggest that if you are just starting swing trading, it's best to have a stop-loss order with your broker (if a broker doesn't offer stop-loss orders, don't use it for trading).

There is one certainty in swing trading: you will have losing trades. That's why risk management is so important. If you minimize the loss that you make on losing trades, you have much more chance that you'll make a profit overall.

Position sizing

Position sizing is all about the question, "How much can I afford to lose?"

I'm going to suggest that it isn't all that much. When I look at the total risk on a particular trade, I don't want it to be more than a single percent of my capital. Ten trades would then equal a maximum of 10% at risk, which is quite enough short-term risk for me.

The total at risk isn't the total amount of stock that you're purchasing; it's the maximum you are prepared to lose before you give up on that trade and exit the position. In other words, it's your purchase price *minus* the stop loss price.

So if you have a $100,000 trading book, and you apply the 1% rule, your total at risk for a position would be $1,000.

Suppose you saw an interesting trade in Coca-Cola at $63. The chart suggests it will break upwards to $66. You set a stop loss at $62. How much can you trade?

Your risk per share is $1 ($63-62) - so you can buy 1,000 shares ($1,000 maximum risk in a single position *divided* by $1). Those shares would be worth $63,000 - but you would only be at risk for $1,000.

That's a very chunky position, though, and it would mean (unless you were using margin) that your opportunities for other trades would be very limited. So, you probably want to think about your total trade size as well as your at-risk position. This depends on how many chunks you want to cut your trading book into.

Some traders really try to finesse this using different formulas, but it's a lot easier to stick to a single percentage. I use 5% because it's easy to calculate, and I'm usually trading big-cap or liquid stocks. But you might decide to use up to 8%, although it's probably best to get some experience before moving up to this level. Or if you're trading smaller cap stocks, you might go for smaller positions to manage your increased risk, say 2 or 3%.

You can do these two calculations in either order. You can set your at-risk amount for the trade, then apply your position size rule, or you can apply your position size rule and then check your stop-loss level, which would give you a loss equal to or less than your maximum at-risk rule. You'd choose to do it the first way if the chart shows you where your stop loss needs to be, for instance, just below the support line if you're trading an upward breakout, and the second way if the chart is not conclusive.

I suspect nearly every trader has had the horrible experience of seeing a trade go wildly right, watching the position rack up profits minute by minute - only to see the stock plunge and the trade finish at zero profit. But there is a way you can avoid this.

Simply raise your stop loss as you go. For instance, if I'd bought Coca-Cola at $63 and seen it rise fast to $69, then I'd want to raise my stop-loss from $62 to $68 or maybe $68.50 - so that if the stock started to fall, I'd automatically be stopped out with a juicy $5.50 profit per share ($68.50 - $63).

Some brokers will even let you run a trailing stop-loss, which tracks the share price upwards. It will automatically be activated if the share price falls a certain amount, so you need to be careful to set it wide enough that small variations in the stock price don't set it off.

As I mentioned, some traders try to finesse this rule by varying the amount traded according to various formulas. There is a version called 'fixed-fractional,' which adjusts for the relative risk of the trade. However, I think this just plays to your own subjectivity and is very dangerous.

Why shouldn't you increase the amount you trade if you have a particularly good gut feeling? One good reason is that you are playing a game of probabilities. You shouldn't be making any trades at all that you don't feel have a likelihood of coming out ahead, but on every trade, however cast-iron the chart pattern is, there's a small probability that it will go wrong.

There's another system known as the Martingale - it's more popular with gamblers than it is with traders, though. With this system, you double up to recover a loss you made in an earlier trade. After every loss, you double your trade amount.

I don't recommend it. In fact, if you have a run of losing trades, the right thing to do is usually to take some time out. Do the math; with a 5% position size, five losing trades would wipe you out. So, 1) a 5% fixed position size loss, 2) doubled up to 10%, 3) doubled up to 20%, 4) doubled up to 40%, 5) doubled up to 80%, and the next double up wouldn't be possible because you're wiped out by those five losing trades.

Of course, you might miss the stop-loss level with any trade, even with a stop-loss trading order already placed. Sometimes, when a share falls in a fast market, it is difficult to get your order filled. You might be a good few pennies out. But most of the time, the stop loss system works - and the fact that your position size is limited will allow you to take a slightly worse hit in the event that your stop loss is filled at a lower price than you'd expected.

Finally, you might want to limit the total amount of your capital at risk at any time. Suppose you only decided to risk 10% of your capital - that's the maximum you could lose in a day. If you use the 1% at-risk rule for each position, you'll have room to run 10 different positions at the same time. Remember, you need to reassess your at-risk amount; on some trades, if they have performed well and you have ratcheted your stop-loss level up to the entry price, you'll have zero risk.

There are several other things you can do to reduce the risks you run. I've already talked about some of them, so very quickly, let's sum them up;
• Trade only in liquid stocks.
• Trade only in stocks with tight spreads.
• Avoid micro caps, which are much more prone to having their share prices manipulated.
• Don't trade in advance of an earnings release.

Risk/reward

Position management is part of the risk management job, but it's not all of it. Remember that the risk/reward ratio has a major effect on your profitability.

Imagine that I gave you the choice between two kinds of risks.

• In one, you risk $100 and get $25 if you win.
• In the other, you risk $50 and you get $25 if you win.

It's easy to determine which risk you'd want to take, though they both stand to win the same amount. And I then offered you the chance to risk $100 to win just one dollar? I suspect your response would be shocking.

You need to do this risk/reward analysis for every trade you make. If you only stand to win the same amount that you have at risk, you will need to win more than 50% of the time to make any money at all. On the other hand, if you always risk one dollar to get three, you can lose more trades than you win and still make a profit.

In my example of a Coca-Cola trade, the risk was $1, and the reward was $3 – that's a 1:3 ratio. That's not a bad trade at all. You could lose 60% of your trades and still make a profit, though not a huge one. I suggest you try to make all your trades come out at 1:2, 1:3, or better. You're a swing trader; try finding real swings, not tiny price movements!

Diversification

Diversification is 'not putting all your eggs in one basket.' It's easy to see how it works for investors - but how does it work for swing traders?

• Try to have 5-10 positions at any one time. Not more than 20, because you'll lose focus if you do.

• Don't have all your positions in the same industry. If you have long positions in Alphabet and Amazon, try to pick something other than Microsoft or Meta for your next trade - like Ford or Johnson & Johnson instead.

• If you can diversify geographically, for instance, by trading Topix, FTSE 100, or CAC40 ETFs (Japan, UK, and France), that's a great idea.

• You might also want to think about trading some commodities through ETFs. Gold, silver, or 'soft' commodities could be a useful diversification if stock markets aren't moving. Remember to check you are buying a physical gold ETF, though, not a gold mining shares ETF.

Chapter 9 Quiz

1. Which of these securities is an adequate diversification for a big trade in Alphabet?
a) An SPX ETF
b) Apple
c) Amazon
d) Bristol Myers Squibb

2. What is the one certainty in swing trading?
a) That you will lose - at least some of the time
b) That you will lose all your money
c) That you will lose your self-respect
d) That you will lose track of time

3. Which of these position sizing systems should you never, ever use?
a) Fixed position sizing, e.g. $1,000
b) Fixed position sizing, 2% of portfolio
c) Martingale
d) Fixed position sizing, 5% of portfolio

4. What is the advantage of a trailing stop-loss?
a) Exactly the same as a regular stop-loss
b) It is automatic, so it ensures you take losses early
c) It will lock in your profits when the share price has already risen
d) It will stop you losing money in the first place

5. How much risk should you take?
a) All of your account balance
b) As much as you like
c) Only 1/2 to 1/3 of the potential reward
d) None

10

Chapter 10: Strategies that Work

Finding strategies that work is the long-term aim of every swing trader. Some traders find them out for themselves. Others search every website and book they can find hundreds of strategies, and play them all till they have weeded out the ones that don't work for them and can concentrate on the ones that do. Other traders start with just one trading strategy that they get to know inside-out, then add another and maybe get up to a handful of tried and tested strategies that support a flourishing trading business.

You know that traders need to focus. But let's admit it, we're all different. A Greek poet once said, "The fox knows many things, but the hedgehog knows one big thing." Whether you're a fox or hedgehog, you know better than me, but here are a few strategies that can get you started. Why not try them all out? Then, stick with the ones that work best for you, at least for a while.

By the way, while it is not an absolute rule, you will find that with most of these strategies, *the trend is your friend*, and you'll likely have the best success with them if you are trading in the same direction as the trend. Of course, there's no trend to trade within a range-bound or sideways market, so you'll have to pick the right trades!

Buy the dip with the MA

If the market is trending upwards, however strongly, there will still be times when the share price falls back, taking a breather. How will you know when the stock has got its second wind and is ready to start running again?

To buy the dips accurately, you must track the 50-day moving average. The share price will often fall back towards this MA, which acts as a moving support line.

It's not flawless, so let's discuss how many times you could have used it with Broadcom stock above. In March 2024, the share price fell back to the 50 MA (the blue line), it fell just slightly lower, and then moved up super strongly. Not a lasting move, though. In April, twice, the price passed through the line on the downside, and if you'd tried to buy on the dip here, you probably would have been stopped out, but the second time (early May), there was a chance to take a $10 profit ($131 to $141), and then again in June the buy the dip strategy would have worked out well, especially with that spectacular gap up on June 13!

A gap up is when the share price opens way above the day before, leaving clear white space on the chart. A gap usually happens when there is news that affects the company, such as an earnings announcement or news of a takeover. Market-makers will view the news before the market opens, and mark the stock price up or down accordingly.

In late July, the share price tests the 50 MA and falls straight through. At this point, the uptrend looks like it might be under pressure, but the price bounces back again. It takes a while for things to settle down, so I would *not* have traded on the MA here - MA is a rather weak indicator, and there's a lot of other stuff going on.

But by October, things are settling down, and the 50 MA is moving upwards, so when there's another test of the MA just above where it says November, I'm interested in buying it. There's a nice big bullish candlestick as the price bounces off, which gives me confidence, so I buy at $174, the top of the candlestick. I don't manage to sell out at the top, but at $180, halfway down the first bad day, I've profited $6 a share, less my costs. Not a bad trade.

As you can see, this strategy isn't flawless. You need that strong uptrend, which is why the first half of 2024 worked out better than the second half here. And you need to confirm, ideally, with indicators like RSI and volume. But when it's working, this is a simple and good strategy, and you can usually go to the well several times with the same stock.

Of course, the 50 MA works as a resistance level in a downtrend, so you can 'short the bumps,' so to speak.

The Golden Cross

This is another MA-related strategy, and it's a real classic. It's the first pattern I ever learned! I learned it from an old guy with little half-moon specs who was well past retirement age, but his accountancy firm kept him on board for dealing with small clients like my dad. I thought that was "granddad wisdom," like telling you to eat your greens or that homework had to be done before playing soccer, so I ignored it for years. I wish I had listened to him! It's a classic for a good reason - it's a trade that works and can be super profitable. But only use it in markets where there is a strong trend.

The Golden Cross needs two MAs. One of the moving averages needs to be longer than the other. You then look for the short-term MA to cross over the longer-term MA to the upside.

You might want to look at 50 and 200-day MAs. This produces relatively few but very strong signals, which is why it's the classic pairing for this strategy. However, you might also look at shorter pairings - day traders often do. A 9 and 21-day pair can be good for *swing* traders. Whatever pair you choose, stick with it, don't tinker with the settings, and ensure you have paper-traded or back-tested it properly before trading real money with it.

You can see on the right hand of the chart that a golden cross just happened at the start of December. You can see the 'orange' short-term moving average moving up and eventually crossing the rather static 'green' longer-term MA. Remember that moving averages are lag indicators, so the initial upward move already happened. What will be crucial now is to see the share price advance further and the short-term moving average to continue up and not slacken. So, I want to see plenty of confirmation from other indicators.

Golden crosses have a very good profit when they are right, but they give many misleading signals. So, when you play a golden cross, you need to set a tight stop loss and keep a close eye on the slope of the moving averages after you initiate the trade. Here, I'd probably choose to put my stop-loss around $223 or $224, the level of the last retracement back in May, but I could even set it at $228, the bottom of the second of the very recent three white soldiers pattern (three of the last four candlesticks, right at the beginning of December) which would mean that pattern had failed. Assuming I'm buying around $232 right now, the $228 stop-loss gives me a risk of $4 a share, and my target is for the shares to get close to the previous highs, around $240, within a few weeks. Risking $4 to get $8 is a 1:2 ratio, not the best, so I'd need to check some other indicators first.

There are a couple of other exit rules that help you know just how long to hold on: if there is a 'death cross' (the opposite of a golden cross), you get out immediately, and if the share price falls back to and breaks through the 50-day moving average, you exit. Those will help you know how long to stay in while making a profit.

But if you have doubts about how this strategy can play out, just look back at that last golden cross in February. If I'd bought just after it, around $225, I would have benefited from a really quick run all the way to $244 in late March!

There are various ways to refine your golden cross strategy to rule out horrifying false signals. For instance, you could add a requirement that the RSI is in the oversold zone (under 30) before the golden cross, and buy only when the RSI exits the oversold zone.

Swim the Channel

This strategy works both during a trend and when the market is range-bound. You are looking for a stock that has established a fairly clear channel between two lines - one line linking the highest highs, and the other, the lowest lows. Nvidia stock below certainly fits the bill here.

Remember, of course, the first couple of times the share price bounces around, you won't make anything from it because it's still establishing the channel. But once the channel is established, it's time to trade. So, on October 14, when the price in Nvidia turns down away from the upper blue line, I'd want to enter my first short trade. That worked; the price fell from $138 to $131, though it only went halfway down this time before the move ran out of steam. And my stop-loss would have been pretty tight, as a break out above $140 would be a definitive move above the channel.

There's another touch of the top trendline in late October, and here again, the move down is only part way into the channel: $143 to $138 or thereabouts. In fact, I might have tried holding on and letting the price go back up to $139 before selling since, although the price is trending down, it hasn't established a reversal or a downtrend signal. But that's the kind of call you'll only want to make once you have a lot of experience. In any case, the stop-loss here can be tight, making a reasonably small trade profitable.

Run forward to October 31, and the share price has fallen to the bottom of the channel. That's a chance to go long at $132. An immediate run to $136 makes a first profit, but if I hung on to the shares a bit longer, there's a run all the way up to $149. I'd want to manage that with a trailing stop loss, of course - but not following it too tightly, perhaps, to avoid being stopped out by relatively small movements down.

But the channel now seems to have fallen apart, and the share price has broken right through the bottom trendline and fallen further. I think that's the last time I can swim this particular channel, but as you can see, it gave me plenty of opportunities along the way.

The Python Squeeze

I always like to look for shrinking Bollinger Bands. They don't tell you which way a stock is going to break out of their grip, but when it does, it will be a very strong movement. So, you must keep looking and be ready to trade when the chart gives the signal. Or, of course, to have placed orders that will execute when it happens. Bollinger Bands often come before one of these signals:

• Break above or below resistance/support
• Breach of either of the Bollinger Bands (i.e. the price line goes through the upper or lower band)
• Candlestick signals, such as Three White Soldiers, engulfing pattern.

I got really excited when I saw the USAP chart below in late October. That's a really tight Bollinger Band squeeze going on there all the way through November and December!

However, I always check the fundamentals before committing to a trade. When I did, I found that Luxemburgish industrial conglomerate Aperam has made an all-cash offer to acquire USAP. That's why the share price is headed nowhere, and unfortunately, it makes this potentially very profitable chart pattern completely useless in this particular case.

The thin end of the wedge

Among the chart patterns I have learned to enjoy is the descending wedge or triangle. Like some of my other favorites, it's a channel formation that is shrinking fast. Look at the chart of VNQ below. It's not quite perfect, but there's enough fit, and I liked how it moved.

You can see that those two blue lines I drew on the chart would end up joining together at about $93.50 pretty soon unless something else happens. So it's then a waiting game from about November 11 to see which way things will break. In a descending pattern like this, where the bottom is flat, it's very often upwards. Confirmation comes when, on November 21, the price closes above the line at $95.65.

What happens next shows why you don't want to put your stop-losses too tight. After a short upward move, the share price fell back to test the line - which was descending - at $95.45. If I'd put a really tight stop-loss, I would have been taken out of the trade before the explosive breakout and gap up move. So it pays to be aware of that and set your stop-losses a bit wider than normal with this pattern. If you're right up against the thin end, you could even set the stop-loss on the bottom line of the triangle, which is where failure is really obvious. You might even want to set an order for a short trade there, too, to catch the breakout downwards.

I also like the risk/reward ratio for this trade. If the price fell through the upper trendline, it would be back in the consolidation zone, so it's unlikely to run far or fast until it hits the lower trendline. But when it breaks out, it's likely to go far and fast. All the odds are on the correct side!

And you can see that the breakout is a pretty direct run here, in just a week (25-30 November), all the way back to the three-month high. Given that I can see quite a big consolidation zone earlier in the chart (mid-to-late September), where the stock failed to break decisively through $99, I'm not going to ask for a lot more, but that's a neat little trade.

There's just one thing that isn't ideal about this trade. It's a bit full of white space. Typically, I like to see the triangle really full of candlesticks, as if someone decided to scribble in it while testing a dried-out ballpoint.

Trade the failure

Most traders assume that if your initial trade fails - either because the chart pattern doesn't complete, or because it does, but you get stopped out fast - that's it, game over.

But I don't like to turn my back on all the work I did to find the chart pattern. I try to turn my mind to a little recycling. If the pattern has failed, does that mean there's a reversal or a breakout that I wasn't expecting?

For instance, with the descending wedge, if a breakout upwards fails, then it's quite likely that the share price will break downwards. So, as well as closing the failed trade, I want to keep watching to see whether the share price will fall through the bottom trendline. That would give me the signal that the breakout is going to happen downwards, so I'd then enter a *short* trade to take advantage of it.

Here's an idea from Tradingview below. You can see how, just at the end of 2019, CADJPY (the Canadian dollar / Japanese Yen currency pair) broke through a resistance line but then failed to continue the breakout. Where the price breaks through the resistance to the downside, you could make a short trade to capitalize on the collapse.

Often, "failed trades" have surprising energy. Well, it's surprising till you think it through - if the move in one direction failed, then that means there is a lot more power pulling in the other direction!

However, it isn't easy to look for failed breakouts. Most often, you'll trade a breakout and then see it fail. So, you simply reverse the trade.

Ride the waves

There are much more advanced candlestick readers than I am, but I have found a strategy that I enjoy and it plays out quite well for me.

I'm looking for stocks in a little dip within a long-term uptrend. I want to see a nice dip, and the stocks go on my watchlist.

What I'm waiting for is for the big bearish candlesticks to die away, for the dip to shallow out, and eventually to get one of the following patterns:

• Morning star or morning doji star,
• Three white soldiers,
• Bullish engulfing pattern,
• Or belt hold.

The advantage of proactively finding the stocks and then watching them is that I know the setup is right. There are plenty of ways to find these 'dippers,' such as using StockMonitor's 'Consecutive Losers 10 Periods' filter.

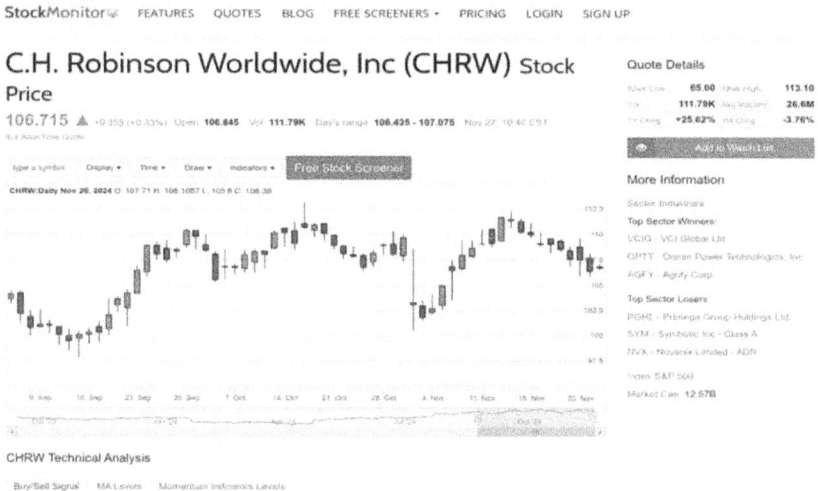

Today, it just had this stock - C.H. Robinson Worldwide, Inc. It looks promising - look at that little indecision doji at the end of November. Which way is it going from here? I don't know, but I think it will make its mind up soon and give me a signal!

It could be any one of the candlestick signals I mentioned above, although there's not really enough room for it to be three white soldiers… they usually signal a much bigger move, so if it showed those, I think the stock would break right out of this range. I'd have to re-think my trade.

The other thing I like about this chart is that I can see my profit target by looking at the previous support and resistance lines. Here, I'm looking for a little bit over $110 for a long trade - so if I get a reversal, I can buy around $107.50, sell over $110, and set a really tight stop-loss at $106 (or because we avoid round numbers, let's say $106.25).

This strategy of finding stocks in a little dip is a nice one because it gets me looking at stocks before they give the signal. I'm focusing on the setup rather than the signal, so I'm filling my watch list with stocks *about* to set up a trade rather than stocks that have already done so. I've found a stock showing temporary weakness, and I will keep looking at it until I get a signal that tells me it's about to break upwards again. That means I will be on the spot right away. If you only screen stocks that have already given the signal, you might be late on the scene - but equally, with some stock screens, you might find everyone else has seen the same signal at the same time, and you end up with a partial fill or even without being able to get your order filled at all.

Chapter 10 Quiz

1. A death cross is
a) Found in a graveyard
b) When the short-term MA crosses below the long-term MA
c) When a golden cross happens on low trading volume
d) A form of doji

2. Buy the dip by
a) Using the guacamole and hummus strategy
b) Buying the share when it bounces off a moving average
c) Buying the share when it bounces off a resistance level
d) Selling a share at the top of the range

3. The Python Squeeze involves which indicator?
a) Bollinger Bands
b) RSI
c) MACD
d) Flake 99

4. Why can't you trade the first couple of touches in 'Swim the Channel'?
a) They happen too fast
b) The share price has to establish the pattern before you can trade it
c) It's bad luck
d) There isn't enough trading volume

5. The trend is
a) Your friend
b) Always up
c) Deceptive
d) Of no interest to a trader

11

Chapter 11: Top Tips for Swing Trading

Why swing trading might not be right for you

1. You are one of nature's nervous wrecks. You're not going to sleep at night because you're worried about what's going to happen to your shares. You worry even when a trade is going *right* because it might suddenly go wrong. You worry even when you've doubled your money because you feel you might lose it all tomorrow. Swing trading - well, trading of any kind - is not a great life if you're a worrier.

2. You have no self-discipline. If you sometimes don't bother reviewing your portfolio, or sometimes 'shoot from the hip' without checking all the relevant indicators, or sometimes hold on to a stock when you really know you should have exercised your stop-loss, you shouldn't be swing trading. The first two issues will just prevent you from fulfilling your potential, but the third - not sticking to your stop losses - is a killer.

3. You're a very emotional person, and you trust your 'gut instinct.' You get drawn into love-hate relationships with certain stocks. You oscillate between being certain that you've picked a winner and you're going to get rich, and being sure your stock is tanking and you're going to lose the lot. Get Prozac, or don't trade.

4. You want to get rich quick. Most successful swing traders regularly take little nibbles out of a stock. Swing trading is certainly a way to make more than the market, but it's not a way to get rich quick. Try reality TV instead.

5. You are a procrastinator. If you keep putting off actually doing anything, swing trading isn't going to lose you any money - but it won't make you money, either. That reminds me of a friend of mine who likes to say: "Never procrastinate today if you can wait to do it till tomorrow."

6. You enjoy gambling. Swing trading is not gambling, and it's not fun. If you want to bet for the adrenalin and the fun of it, bet on the horses. Or go to the casino. Because swing trading is going to either be very boring, very unprofitable, or possibly both.

7. You really enjoy analyzing company reports or doing econometric modeling. You usually spend a good while really combing through the small print before you buy shares in a company. You should probably stick to long-term investing.

8. You worry about how to get through the next month on your salary. Basically, if this is the case, you shouldn't be swing trading; you can't afford the risk, and the amounts you'll be able to trade are probably so small your brokerage fees will probably nibble up most of your profit.

The top rookie mistakes

1. Starting too small. You need to start with a reasonable amount of capital so that you can diversify your trades without betting the bank, without brokerage fees, and without the spread taking the lion's share of your profit.

2. Starting without a strategy or business plan. You need to think hard before you begin swing trading, define the kind of assets you'll trade and how you'll choose them, and determine your position size and at-risk percentage. You need to have a feeling for what would be a reasonable return on your capital and how many trades you need to get there. And you'll need some way of monitoring your progress. Without this, you're just dabbling - it's not a business.

3. Throwing good money after bad. Sometimes, long-term investors 'average down' if a stock price dips to reduce their average in-price. That's okay for them, as they're buying based on their valuation of the shares. But if you're swing trading, and the price hits your stop-loss, that's almost always a sign that the share price movement you expected will not happen because the chart pattern has been broken. Don't hold on to the shares, hoping they'll bounce, or - worse - double up. If you throw good money after bad, you'll likely lose the lot.

4. Betting the bank. Don't ever do this, no matter how certain you are about your trading idea. Every trader loses sometimes, so maintain your position size at a level that if all your current trades go wrong today, you'll still have money to trade with tomorrow.

5. Not having stop-losses or not using them. Stop-losses are there for your protection. If you haven't been able to set a stop-loss, how will you know if the trade is unsuccessful? When you've lost half your money? All your money? Set stop-losses and then use them. Better still, enter your stop-loss order at the same time as your initial order so it will execute automatically.

6. Getting emotionally involved. A trade is not an exam or a performance; you don't have to impress anybody with it. A stock doesn't know that you own it, and Mark Zuckerberg isn't going to know or care whether you made or lost money on Meta stock. A trade is purely and simply an attempt to make money. Emotions are what drive the market machine - and traders are trying to take advantage of them.

7. Chasing a stock. It's easy to feel you've missed out if a stock shoots past your target buy price. Don't let that make you pay more than is sensible for the stock. If the higher price means the risk/reward ratio has fallen below your requirements, sit back. You'll get another chance, or maybe you won't, but you've stayed away from a trade that won't pay off.

8. Lack of focus. You've traded tech, you've traded oil companies, you trade gold ETFs and the Japanese index and the Euro. You trade fifteen different chart patterns and twenty different candlestick patterns, and you look at a hundred stock charts a day. You know what? You're probably missing really profitable trades because you don't focus, and you're spending way too much time doing too little.

9. Converting a failed swing trade into an 'investment.' Swing trading and investment are two different things. If a swing trade has failed, it's failed. Suck it up and move on.

10. Letting trading take over your life.

Top mistakes for experienced traders

1. Overtrading. There's no hard and fast rule for how often you should trade, but you could be overtrading if you're making more than three trades a day or exiting most of your positions within a week. Get a bit more selective and slow down. If you trade too often, you're making brokers and market makers rich - not yourself.

2. Over-confidence. They say you're only as good as your last trade, but in fact, you might not be as good as your last trade. If you're on a roll, it's easy to get over-confident. You might be tempted to double your position size or get sloppy about the risk/reward ratio you're willing to take. Watch out when you feel nothing could go wrong because that's usually exactly when things do go wrong.

3. Taking a chance on earnings dates. No one in the market knows what will happen when a company releases earnings. It's pure randomness. Swing traders trade on probabilities; they don't gamble on coin tosses, so stay away from companies that are about to announce earnings.

4. Being inadequately diversified. Most experienced traders have quite several different positions, but they may end up without a broad enough base of trades if, for example, they end up concentrating on a single sector.

5. Not watching the spread. I learned this the hard way when I traded a stock that I'd traded before but hadn't realized the bid-ask spread had widened considerably. I just scraped out of that trade at break-even - it should have done much better.

6. Tinkering with your strategies and set-ups. It's tempting to tinker with your strategy every time you have a losing trade, but you run the risk of missing profitable trades by setting up increasingly strict rules that don't really increase your probability of winning. Don't tinker. Gradual improvement is not the same as tinkering!

7. Again, letting trading take over your life.

Good internet resources

1. Aswath Damodaran's website at pages.stern.nyu.edu/~adamodar is a marvellous data source. This finance professor provides loads of data on what he admits is a clunky site, but it's well worth getting to know. In particular, I like the details on operating margins, return on equity, and net income per share growth rate by industry, as well as valuations by industry and by country.

2. Magicformulainvesting.com is a stock screener that looks for 'value' stocks with good quality businesses, using the criteria outlined in Joel Greenblatt's The Little Book That Beats the Market. It's a good way to narrow down the stocks you trade. However, you'll need to register to use the screener.

3. Stockcharts.com is one great charting site. There's a certain amount that you can use for free, but if you want additional indicators and the ability to configure charts to your own requirements, you'll need to take up one of the paid options, which is $18.42 a month upwards. There's a one-month free trial if you want to check it out.

4. Reuters.com has one of the best home pages for a quick view of world markets. Price data is delayed 15 minutes, but even so, Reuters is a powerful resource. The Breakingviews section also helps ensure you don't miss major business news items that are often not covered well by mainstream news providers.

5. I like Macrotrends.net because you can easily pull up graphical representations of companies' financial data and ratios, screen stocks, check interest rate charts, and more. In particular, charts of price-earnings ratios and dividend yields are just so much easier to follow than strings of numbers.

6. uk.finance.yahoo.com has all the basic data you need on companies. Just don't bother with the charting function - it's too basic for a swing trader's needs.

7. Zacks.com also has plenty of basic data on companies and a decent enough stock screener. The paid-for service is mainly for those who want to use Zacks' methodology to manage their stock portfolios.

8. Stockmonitor.com operates screeners for different candlestick patterns, moving average configurations, and other technical patterns, which quickly lets you see a large number of stocks in chart form. It's a good place to start, but many of the stocks that come up are penny stocks or illiquid, so be careful - not all the interesting situations will actually be tradable.

9. Finviz.com has another set of screeners, including chart patterns that Stockmonitor doesn't cover. I'm not always convinced by their patterns, but one in ten or a dozen usually sticks out as demanding a little more attention, so I do spend a little time reviewing the site if there is nothing more pressing to do on that day.

Things you really need at your trading station

1. A good LED desk lamp with flexible support. Working in the darkness is good for no one.

2. Plenty of notebooks or yellow legal pads. If you have a thought, write it down - by the time you've finished what you're doing right now, you've probably forgotten it. If you're a visual person, you may find that drawing your ideas out on a piece of paper helps you see what you're doing much more clearly than your broker's trading screen does.

3. Post-it notes. You might want a reminder to check a particular stock, or you might want to jot down a website URL or phone number; don't write your brokerage username and password on a Post-it!

4. A pen holder or mug for your writing implements. If you've ever had to look around your desk to find the pen that's hiding underneath all the other stuff, you'll be grateful for the certainty that a pen mug gives you.

5. A tray for all the bits and pieces - paper clips, erasers, memory sticks, and all the other junk that ends up on your desk.

6. An insulated coffee mug. And - this is very important - an insulated coffee mug with a secure drink-through lid.

7. And finally, a good fast computer and, if you can, two monitor screens.

Things not to swing trade

1. Micro cap shares. Companies worth less than $300m are susceptible to market manipulation.

2. Shares in companies with upcoming results. This exposes you to a completely unknowable risk.

3. Illiquid shares (less than $100,000 traded every day). Swing traders need to get their orders filled - if there's not enough of a market in the shares, it can be difficult to exit your trade at all, let alone at a profit.

4. Companies where a single person or institution holds over 30% of the shares. What that person does could have a big and unpredictable effect on the share price.

5. Leveraged ETFs. Although the leverage means that if your trade goes the right way, you'll double your money, it also means that if things go wrong, you'll make double the loss. Losing money is easy enough without any help!

6. Closed-end funds. Not everybody avoids them, but I find they are difficult to trade. Find an ETF instead.

7. Penny stocks. Stocks worth $5 or less are usually not investment grade and are often illiquid.

8. Tesla. I really don't like trading a stock where the CEO can change the share price with a single Tweet.

The best ways to reduce your risk

1. Automate your entries and exits. If you do this, your trading decisions are all taken in cold blood - not in the heat of the moment - and you'll never be tempted to ignore a stop-loss. You also won't miss a trade or an exit when the market moves too fast for you or when you're not at your trading station (and let's face it, we all have to sometimes visit the bathroom).

2. Use a trailing stop loss so that you never give up your profits if the market turns against you.

3. Skim your profits by scaling out - selling part of your position once you have achieved your initial profit target.

4. Limit the size of every risk to 1% of your capital. (That's the risk - i.e. the loss you make if the stop-loss is exercised - not the actual value of the shares.) This way, even a run of losses won't dent your financial health.

5. Always wait for a confirmation signal before initiating a trade. Don't jump the gun.

6. Always confirm chart patterns against other indicators before entering a position. For instance, check the RSI, moving averages, stochastics, Fibonacci grids, support, and resistance levels.

7. If you are tired or ill, stay out of the market. Let your automatic orders do the work for you, and get yourself back into peak trading conditions for another day.

Basic rules for swing trading

1. Always know your risk / reward ratio. If you don't, don't trade.

2. Never trade on a single signal - always look for confirmation from other indicators.

3. Know which trades work in a *trend* and which trades work in a *range*.

4. Don't jump on too late - don't chase a stock price.

5. Always have a stop-loss and always use it.

6. Look for open space in the direction of your trade.

7. Keep your emotions out of the market. There's enough fear and greed around to move share prices without adding your own ten cents' worth.

8. Never ever bet the bank.

Ten questions to ask about a potential trade

1. Is the market in a strong trend? For instance, is it above both the 50 and 200-day moving averages?

2. If so, which way - is this an uptrend or a downtrend?

3. Are the shares trading in a range or channel?

4. Is the company going to report earnings any time in the next couple of weeks? (If so, avoid it).

5. Have there been any catalysts - recent events to trigger a move in the share price?

6. Have I confirmed the chart or candlestick signal with indicators such as RSI and stochastics?

7. Where are the nearest and next-nearest support and resistance levels?

8. What is my profit target?

9. What is my stop-loss?

10. Has the chart pattern sent me the confirmation signal that I need? Or, at what price will I know that it has given that signal? (That lets me place a conditional order.)

Print this list out and put it on your trading station. Make sure you've answered the questions before you push the trade button.

Chapter 11 Quiz

1. Which of these is not a requirement at your workstation?
a) A good computer
b) A notepad
c) Your trading journal
d) A white Persian cat

2. Which of these is not a good trading rule?
a) Never bet the bank
b) Always know your risk/reward ratio
c) Follow your gut instinct
d) Always have a stop-loss

3. Which of these people will make a good trader?
a) Jack, who always puts things off to another day
b) Jill, who wants to get rich quick
c) Jane, who is self-disciplined but not great at math
d) Jonathan, who is a fantastic securities analyst

4. How can you reduce your risks?
a) Trade only large and liquid stocks
b) Have a stop-loss, and use it
c) Diversify your positions
d) Never trade on Mondays

5. Which of these websites is not useful for a swing trader?
a) Macrotrends.net
b) Tradingview.com
c) Twitter.com
d) Zacks.com

12

Chapter 12: The Routine of a Swing Trader

I already looked at some aspects of the swing trader's day, but let's recap on what your routine needs to be. First of all, let's look at your regular tasks and how often you need to do them. Some are daily, others weekly or monthly, while some are annual.

Daily	Weekly	Monthly	Annual
Check the market	Read your trade journal and learn!	Analyze your returns	Tax filing
			Tax loss harvesting
Check positions		Read at least one trading related book or long-form article	
Scan stocks			
Write down plan for tomorrow / automate trades for tomorrow		Scan sectors to catch upcoming sector surges	

It's important to decide when you are going to fit your tasks in. Most traders, by which I mean 99%, find it's best to have a particular time set aside. You may even enlist the help of the media if, for instance, you watch a particular newscast and then do your daily checks either immediately before or immediately after. It's also important to guard against distractions. If you have a family or live with friends, lock yourself away for the time it takes to get the job done and concentrate single-mindedly.

If you are a full-time trader, this is the time to write down your trading plans for tomorrow. If you have a day job, you'll want to automate your entry trades and stop-loss orders so that they can be executed in your absence. Get the job done quickly and effectively - set yourself a time limit. This isn't your time to stroll around the market or think of new directions you could go in or new strategies you could use; keep concentrated on the job of finding tomorrow's best trading opportunities.

Use your existing scans to find stocks that fit the bill for your favorite strategies. You should ideally have all your scans set up, so it's just a question of clicking on your previously entered 'Top momentum stocks' or 'Golden crosses' and then checking the stocks that show up to see if any of them will make a good trade.

With existing positions, you need to check on them and consider taking action. For instance:

1. Have any stop-losses been missed? You'll need to correct that once the markets open.
2. Are any of your stocks near their profit targets? Take a good look at the chart and assess whether you want to take the profit or leave some money in the market as you think the move has further to run. If you do, add a new stop-loss at the original profit target price.
3. Do you have any stocks that are just not moving at all? Check the charts again. Does your original trade idea still stack up? Or is it time to exit?

I generally check the market as a whole at the end. I don't run an exhaustive check; I just want to know the kind of day it was, how much volume was traded, and any big results or economic or political news. For instance, "The market was up 60 points or just over 1%, it was a pretty average day, the volume was average, there was no really big corporate news, and the oil prices were up." Or perhaps "lots of volumes traded in a very volatile market, Amazon had bad results, tech sector very subdued, and the market ended the day roughly flat." I like to know price rises against declines; that's a figure that you need on your front page, but you really don't need more than that kind of summary just to know where you are. It's like looking out of the window at a subway stop to make sure you get off at the right place; you only need to know where you are, no more than that.

If you have a full-time job and have automated all your trades, you don't need to check in again until tomorrow evening. Let the day play out; you don't need to check your trades as long as your planning and risk management are correct.

On a weekly basis, you'll want to take a more thoughtful look at the week's trades. If you have an automated trading diary, this can make your life a little easier. Otherwise, you'll need to take a little while to calculate some of your stats, such as risk/reward ratios, return on capital, etc.

For each trade, you're not trying to double-think or second guess yourself, but ask:

1. Should you have got in earlier? If so, what was stopping you? Poor execution? Price ran too fast?

2. Should you have got in later? For instance, should you have waited for a confirmation signal?

3. Were you stop-lossed out of a potentially winning trade? Take a good look at the stop-loss and its relation to support/resistance levels and round numbers. If you got stopped out when it tested the support line briefly, maybe you should have just given the stock a little more room – as long as the risk/reward ratio was still good enough for the trade to be worthwhile.

4. Did you exit a trade a long time before it hit the top? You may have been right to do so, but check if there was anything that would show that your original profit target was going to be exceeded. For instance, did the stock move up sharply on very high volumes, showing new buyers coming into the market?

5. Are there particular types of trade that worked better than others for you? For instance, you might have traded better shorts than long positions, or traded support and resistance levels better than other patterns such as head and shoulders.

6. Did life throw you any curve balls? For instance, I once did really well on a trade in Paris-quoted Sanofi… except that when I came to account for the currency, I hadn't done nearly as well as I expected in dollar terms. Whoops, that's something I will give a bit more thought to next time!

7. Just check you are up to date with the major stock and sector news of the week.

As with daily tasks, it really helps to have time set aside for this review of your portfolio. One of my friends does it at six o'clock in the morning on Saturday - then he plays soccer. "It's done," he says, "so if I want to go out after the match, my time is my own." I prefer to do it over brunch on Sunday morning. But whatever time you choose, don't miss your appointment.

Both the daily and weekly reviews are pretty limited in scope. You don't want to change your business plan; maybe you can tweak it. Your monthly review should go deeper. This is when you want to take a long, hard look at your returns and think about how to improve them. You might want to tinker with your scans. For instance, if one of your regular scans is throwing up too many ideas that are not working out, then you may devote some thought to which of the factors you are using in the stock screen that needs to be tightened up. If you do this, it's best to run 'old' and 'new' versions together for a couple of months, so that you can see whether you have excluded good ideas together with the junk, or whether your fine-tuning worked.

You might also want to try out a new strategy. For instance, if you recently read a book on candlestick patterns and have an idea for trying out a new trade, then you could add that to your roster. Make sure that you don't bet the bank on it, though - limit yourself to, say, two trades out of ten, so that your existing strategies are doing the heavy lifting for you.

Don't mess around with your basic business plan, though. Although the changes you're making with the monthly review might go a bit further than with the weekly review, it's best to make relatively small changes. Remember to write them up properly, so you can focus on the success of all those changes at your next monthly review.

Swing trading is a solo business for most practitioners. However, I do know a couple of people who do their monthly reviews with another trader. They head off to a nice cafe for the morning and spend Sunday brunch working through their reviews with each other. That can be really beneficial, as you have someone else to ask questions and make suggestions. It's less boring, too!

I also think you need to make a monthly date with trading education. Read a book on some aspect of swing trading, sit down with a copy of Barron's, or revise areas where you feel your understanding isn't a hundred percent. I personally like to do this with paper copies, so I'm not at my computer - no incoming emails, no Facebook messages, and my mobile's turned off too. You can get a lot more done that way!

Every year, of course, you'll want to do an annual review. It makes sense to plan this around the tax year because a lot of the work you'll need to do for your tax filing will help with the review.

However, be aware that you should actually do two lots of tax work:

1. First, coming up to the end of the tax year, you should look at how to minimize your tax liabilities. Although normally, you'd keep your long-term stock portfolio well away from your trading portfolio, it's worth looking at the two together to see if you have losses on long-term holdings that can offset your trading profits. (Or if you made a loss as a trader, you could use that to offset taking a profit on some of your long-term stocks.) 2. Then, you'll need to complete your tax filing in due course. Naturally, there's a lot more to do for most of us - including income tax on the day job - but you'll want to have all your data ready to file.

For your annual review, you will want, first and foremost, to look at your swing trading business as a business and ask the question: did it repay the hours you spent on it? Did you achieve your targets for the year? What are your targets for the next year?

There are other things you'll want to think about. For instance, if you treat your trading profits as your income, are you earning enough to go full-time? You'll want to benchmark your profits against the market as a whole - and remember, you should be beating the S&P 500 handsomely; otherwise, you are better off just investing in an S&P exchange-traded fund and leaving your money to tick over gently! You might also want to look at eToro's top traders and other prominent traders who publish their returns for the year. Are you keeping up?

Once you have a few years behind you, you'll also want to track the variability of your returns over time. I like to look at monthly returns over my entire career as a trader; that way, I can see if I am coming in with regular profits most of the time. What I don't want to see is one or two months of really good profits in a year but very little profit the rest of the time, which suggests I might just have gotten lucky those two months. I'd rather see most months delivering on target profits and a bit of variation above and below. Obviously, I'd also like to see my monthly profitability improving, as there are two factors in play: first, I hope I'm getting better as a trader, but secondly, as I increase my capital, my position size is bigger so the same percentage return should deliver me a bigger absolute profit. That's the joy of compounding! That's why, as in any business and investment, the long-term counts in swing trading.

Chapter 12 Quiz

1. The data in your tax filing and your trading journal should be

a) Exactly the same

b) More or less the same

c) Completely different

d) Tax? What's that?

2. What do you *not* need to know about the market *every* day?

a) Price rises vs declines

b) The amount it was up or down

c) How each sector performed

d) The volume traded

3. What is a good time to get the weekly review done?

a) Saturday before lunch

b) While watching soccer

c) In a hurry late on Sunday night

d) Any time, as long as it gets done

4. Why is it a good idea to carry out your monthly review with another trader?

a) They may have suggestions or ask pertinent questions that help you evaluate your performance

b) Their math is better than yours

c) It's more fun that way

d) You can show off if you did better than them

5. Why should you make more money the longer you trade?

a) You should get better at swing trading

b) Your profits should increase the amount of capital you can trade with

c) Because the stock market always goes up in the end

d) Because hard work is always rewarded

13

Chapter 13: How to Save on Taxes and Fees

Note: this chapter is written for US-based traders. While the basic principles will be similar in all jurisdictions, the details will differ if you're based in the UK, Canada, Europe, or Asia - and may well differ quite markedly if you're a digital nomad. Ensure you know what rules apply where your swing trading business is located.

Taxes

Taxes are a regrettable fact of life. They are also an act of social solidarity - taxes are what public services run on, and if you don't believe in defunding the police, then you need to work out some way of paying for them - but when the time comes to pay them, none of us are exactly thrilled. One of the biggest issues of life as a swing trader is not paying taxes for which you're not actually liable - and that can take quite a bit of forward planning.

The IRS differentiates between short-term and long-term capital gains (profit from the sale of the investment), defining 'long term' as more than a year. If you're a buy-and-hold investor, you'll pay the *lower*, long-term rate on your profits, but as a swing trader, you'll pay the *higher*, short-term rate on all your trades.

The exact rate that you pay will depend on your total income and the highest marginal rate of tax. Short-term capital gains will be charged at your highest rate of tax, so if you earn more than $518,900 (as a single person), you'll pay 37%. Different thresholds apply for married couples even if filing separately. But on long-term capital gains, you'll only pay 20%. The lowest rate on short-term gains is 10%, but on long-term gains, if your other income is below $47,025, you might not be taxed at all. Fuller information is available on irs.gov/taxtopics/tc409, but it's hard going if you're not a CPA. If you really can't make head or tail out of it, it could be a good idea to get some tax advice!

Some assets have capital gains taxed as a blend of short and long-term rates; this includes regulated futures contracts, non-equity options, and foreign currency futures. However, all equities, ETFs, and options on shares are taxed at a higher rate, so if, like myself, you're swing trading the equities markets, you'll find you want to ensure your trades are profitable enough to pay the tax.

You can avoid a lot of tax by trading in a tax-exempt account such as an IRA. However, there are limits on how much you can put into such accounts, and also when you can take money out (unless you're over 59 1/2 years old, there will be a penalty to pay). For UK investors, ISAs also provide tax-exempt accounts for traders; again, there's a limit on how much you can put in each year.

However, while tax-exempt accounts can shelter your profits from tax, they have one big disadvantage. If you make losses in a tax-exempt account, you can't set them against gains outside the account or against other sources of income. You just have to swallow the loss unfortunately.

The wash-sale rule

Talking as an investor, I suppose I have made plenty of gains this year, but I have one investment that's losing money. I want to keep it because I think it's worth a lot more in the long term. Suppose I simply sold that investment on December 31st (or the nearest trading working day) and bought the shares back in January? Then I'd be able to set that loss against the profit I made that year, right? And if it was big enough, I might not have to pay any tax against my profits, right?

Er, nope. Unfortunately, the IRS knows that this is an appealing tactic for investors who want to pay less tax, so they created the wash-sale rule. This says that if you sell a share and buy it back within 30 days, the IRS will not recognize any loss you made on the sale.

That stops investors from being naughty. Unfortunately, for traders, it's a bit problematic. If you trade Apple, and let's say you are stopped out at a loss on March 13th, then in April, you see another chance and trade at a small profit, the IRS will treat your two trades as one.

That's not so bad, you say. Okay, maybe not - but the problem comes if, instead of March and April, the trades were in December and January. Your original loss won't be there to set against profits for the year because, as far as the IRS is concerned, you bought the shares back, so any overall profit or loss won't appear until next year.

Over time, the effect is the same. But you may need to be a bit careful when you're trading around the end of the tax year.

Similar rules apply in the UK and many other jurisdictions. Though apparently not in France.

Professional trader status

The TLDR of this section is that it won't apply to you yet. That's because the IRS is unlikely to give professional trader status to anyone who doesn't have at least one year's experience of trading and a set of accounts to show for it. And even if you're full-time, you might not get the desired professional status.

It's really difficult to get the IRS to agree that you're a trader. You have to jump through several hoops. You need to:

• Trade regularly and continuously - meaning you are trading most days of the year and devoting a large amount of time to the business. You're going to need to be pretty much full-time to qualify here.
• Trade on a substantial basis - that generally means trading at least 25 times a week, which is on the high side for a swing trader. It almost certainly means you need to be full-time.
• Trade as a business, not a hobby. You're going to want to be able to show that you manage your swing trading business properly, and that means having properly maintained accounts. If you have an investment portfolio as well as a trading book, you're going to need to separate the two. Your long-term investments will be treated one way, and your swing trades another way. It may even be best to use different brokers for the two accounts. You can be less choosy about the trading platform and charting abilities when you're looking for a broker for long-term investments, and you probably won't want a margin account.

So why would you want to be a trader with professional status? Because it brings a number of useful tax advantages to you, that's why. You'll be able to put business costs like subscriptions to trading platforms against your income.

Tax is very complex, so I would strongly suggest that if you think you might benefit from going professional, you should talk to a tax adviser. The best way to find an adviser who understands swing trading is to ask other traders for advice through one of the many trading-related sites on the web. Even if you have an existing accountant, they may not deal regularly with stock trading businesses and are unlikely to be fully up-to-date with all the details of tax regulations that apply.

You won't need a tax attorney unless you have a dispute with the IRS. However, it's not a bad idea to have a couple of names you can phone - or at least know that your accountant does.

Regulation

While day trading is quite highly regulated by the SEC's Pattern Day Trading rules, swing trading is not regulated in the same way. A broker will not care whether you are buying stock to sell in a week, three weeks, or two months or to hold 'forever' as long as your account is solvent.

Swing traders in the UK and some European countries are able to use Contracts for Difference (CFDs) for the purpose of swing trading. A CFD allows you to profit from price movement without actually owning the underlying asset, and it will enable easier access to short trades. CFDs have various advantages; you can get started with less capital, and the costs are generally lower than buying the shares. However, there is a spread that needs to be covered; liquidity may be less than ideal, and regulation of CFDs may be weak. In some jurisdictions, you'll need to be an 'expert investor' to deal with CFDs, which could mean signing away some of your rights as a retail investor.

There's a special tax advantage to CFDs. They are not free from income tax - but in the UK, they are free from stamp duty, a form of transfer tax on shares.

CFDs are not available to US investors.

Saving on fees

Your first and most important time to save fees is when you choose your broker. However, there are a number of things you can continue to do as you progress in swing trading in order to ensure that your trading costs are kept as light as possible.

First, you should always review whether the number and size of your trades would entitle you to get a better deal, either by moving up to a different package with your existing broker or by choosing a new one. It doesn't make sense to review this on a weekly basis, but at least once every few months, you should check where you have gotten to and whether a change might be useful.

Secondly, check whether your trade size is efficient. What percentage of each trade do fees and spread add up to? Would it be more efficient to scale up by a half or a quarter?

If you are using margin, it is worth asking whether that's the most efficient use of resources. For instance, if you rarely have more than 45% of your portfolio invested, you may find that you're paying interest when you don't need to.

Changing your trading or charting platform isn't an easy short-term fix, but if you are paying too much for either, it's worth looking for a better solution. If you've got used to your trading platform and it offers all the functionality you need, ask if any brokers would provide it as part of their package.

However, probably the most important way to ensure your brokerage costs don't reduce your profit is simply not to overtrade. Don't chase returns that are too small and 'churn' your positions. If a stock price movement doesn't look like delivering more than a couple of pennies profit, leave it alone. If you're dealing in small size, don't scale out; either take your profit or simply run your position and increase the stop-loss; one lot of charges is cheaper than two (particularly if your broker charges a flat fee).

Incorporation

Once you've decided to go all-in for swing trading - and that shouldn't be till you have at least a couple of years of experience - you should consider incorporating your swing trading business.

This has several major advantages. First, it provides protection for your personal assets. Your trading book is kept within the company - but your home, family assets, and so on can all be kept outside it. That means if the worst came to worst - and it would really have to be pretty bad like your broker going bust - at least your personal assets are not going to get frozen or, worse, lost.

Secondly, it can improve your tax treatment. While you are a personal trader as a one-man band, the IRS won't let you make deductions for business costs such as computer equipment, subscriptions, education, or bandwidth. Your swing trading income is considered unearned income, like interest on a bank account or any profits you take from your share portfolio.

As a personal trader, you will also be limited in your ability to set trading losses against tax. You can pretty much only set your trading losses against your trading profits. If you make an overall loss on your trading business, you can deduct only $3,000 of losses from ordinary income, and you can only carry forward $3,000 of any losses to a further year. Worse, you can't reduce your liability for tax on trading profits by investing in an IRA or pension fund as you can on earned income.

There is just one benefit: you don't have to pay any self-employed taxes on your trading income, either.

On the other hand, once a trading business has been incorporated, it can carry losses forward without limitation. That means any bad year you might experience can at least shelter your next year's profit against taxes, which in a volatile stock market might be the break you need.

But the problem is that you'll still need to have secured professional trader status for the IRS to let you do this through a company. So, you already need to be full-time before you stand a chance of making tax savings.

Once you have formed an LLC, you have a lot more possibilities open to you. You can pay yourself a salary; this will allow you to make pension and health insurance contributions out of that salary, which you can't do out of unearned income. You can also keep earnings in the company as retained profit, having paid the (lower) rate of corporate tax rather than the personal rate of tax; you'll only pay tax when you take them out, which you can do in a year when you have rather less other personal income, keeping your average rate down.

But of course, there will be a fair amount of paperwork to do; you'll need to do payroll, business tax returns, as well as your personal tax filings, and a certain amount of compliance work. As a rough guide, it may not be worth your while incorporating until you're making past $500,000 a year in trading gains.

There are a lot of very specific issues and different ways to form the trading entity, so whatever you do, your first step will be to talk it through with a qualified certified public accountant (and one who understands the trading business model).

Chapter 13 Quiz

1. What do you need to convince the IRS that you're a professional trader?

a) A supercomputer devoted to your trading business

b) An accountant's opinion

c) A full-time trading business of at least a year

d) A broker's recommendation

2. As a swing trader, you need to pay tax on

a) Your total gains *less* losses

b) Your total gains

c) Only 60% of your gains

d) What is tax? I have to pay tax?

3. How can you reduce your trading costs?

a) Choose a broker with low or zero commissions

b) Choose a broker with good execution

c) Don't 'churn' your positions

d) Periodically reassess your software and platform costs

4. When is it worth incorporating your business?

a) Any time

b) Only when you have over $500,000 of trading profits a year

c) Only when you are profitable

d) When you can afford to pay an accountant

5. What is the disadvantage of trading in a tax-exempt account?

a) It's expensive

b) Your losses can't be offset against other income

c) You can't use a tax-exempt account for short-term trades

d) You won't be able to trade online

Leave a 1-Click Review!

Customer reviews

★★★★★ 5 out of 5

4 global ratings

5 star		100%
4 star		0%
3 star		0%
2 star		0%
1 star		0%

˅ How are ratings calculated?

I would be incredible thankful if you could take just 60 seconds to write a brief review on Amazon, even if it's just a few sentences!

Amazon.com readers

http://www.amazon.com/review/
create-review?&asin=B0FWQB4DZZ

Amazon.co.uk readers

http://www.amazon.co.uk/review/
create-review?&asin=B0FWQB4DZZ

Conclusion

If you made it this far, does that mean you're ready to swing trade?

No! It doesn't!

You need to spend a while paper trading - playing with a virtual portfolio - to learn how everything you've learned works in real life and in real time. Nothing can ever replace hands-on experience, and until you have a feel for the market's rhythms and you've wired the basic routines of swing trading into your brain, you shouldn't be trading real money.

Apart from that, in this book, you should have learned everything you need to get started. You've learned what swing trading is - and what it isn't. It's about taking advantage of the swings in a share's price - whether up or down - in such a way that your risks are always carefully controlled. It's not a way to get rich quick, but it is a way to dramatically increase the returns you can make from your risk capital.

You've learned how financial markets work and how the prices of financial assets reflect the actions of a crowd of market participants. You've seen how fear and greed are the two big emotions that can inject energy into the markets and how the tug-of-war between bulls and bears ends up creating a cyclical pattern. This is the basic understanding you need to be a great swing trader - all you need now is to go and see it in action and get used to the rhythms of the market.

You've also learned plenty of basic stuff about how stocks are valued and traded, how to choose a brokerage and a trading platform, and the kind of costs you'll incur - plus how to minimize them.

You've also seen how you can build a daily routine for assessing the markets and the opportunities they afford, and keeping watch over your trades. It's down to you now to work out how much time you can spend and when and to work out what this means in terms of the number of stocks you can keep on your watch list and how many trades you can run at a time.

All the basic techniques for scanning, finding, and evaluating swing trading situations are now at your fingertips. You've seen the basic chart patterns and the basic candlestick patterns that can lead you to big trading wins. You've also learned some basic fundamental analysis techniques so you understand what might be driving the stock action. There are endless refinements and different ways of looking at these charts, but you have all the basics already in your hands. Who knows, maybe you'll find a new tweak or two for yourself!

And very importantly, you know that trading isn't about luck and energy and talking a good fight; it's about probabilities, and it's about discipline.

Imagine yourself starting a martial art - you go into the dojo, and you have to sweep the floor for a week. You think it's weird, but you're really committed to becoming a great fighter, so okay, you push the rag around the floor energetically, and you do a good job.

Years later, when you have your black belt, you ask the sensei why you had to sweep the floor.

"Simple," the sensei says. "I had to find out if you had the self-discipline to keep doing something even if you didn't yet understand why."

Mike Tyson has a famous quote where he says, "Discipline is doing what you hate to do, but doing it like you love it."

That's the kind of discipline you need to be a good trader. In particular, you need the discipline to walk away from a trade that isn't profitable enough, the discipline to walk away from a trade that has too high a risk, and the discipline to take a small loss right now rather than fudge the issue by hoping things get better.

Do you have that discipline? Maybe you'll need to build that discipline, little by little. It could be hard. But it will make all the difference.

I've shared some of my favorite strategies with you - no doubt you'll develop yours too - and I hope you'll agree they're simple enough to understand easily. But again, you'll want to do some 'pretend' trading with them for a while so that you get into the habit of working out your trading plans and seeing how they pan out. I didn't do it that way, and it cost me a certain amount of money and a lot of pride to find out what I should have.

So you have all the tools that you need, and I've given you plenty of resources you could use to acquire more expertise and experience. All you need now is to go out there, sign up for the free level of one of the swing trading sites, and spend the next month 'pretend' trading. Go and do that right now before you lose momentum!

Good luck with your career as a swing trader!

HOW TO GET THE MOST OUT OF THIS BOOK

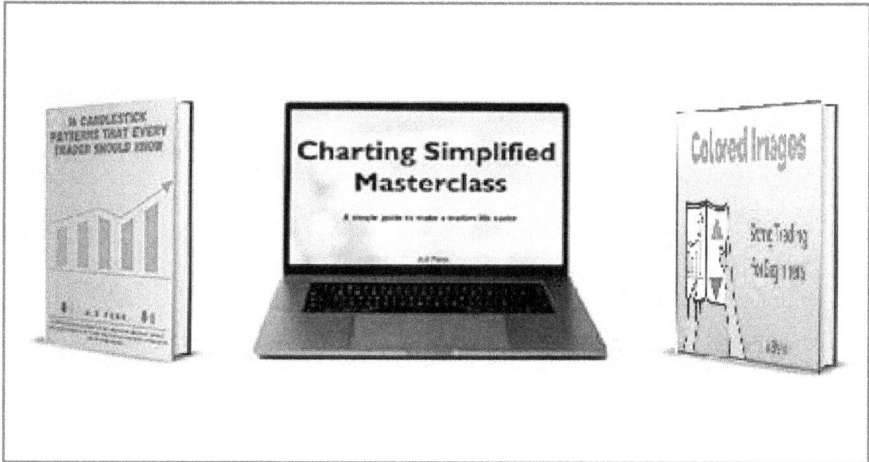

To help you along your trading journey, I've created a free bonus companion masterclass which includes video analysis of real life stock examples to expand on some of the key topics discussed in this book. I also provide additional resources that will help you get the best possible result.

I highly recommend you sign up now to get the most out of this book. You can do that by going to the link or scanning the QR code below:

www.az-penn.com

SCAN ME

Free bonus #1: Charting Simplified Masterclass ($67 value)

In this 5 part video masterclass you'll be discovering various simple and easy to use strategies on making profitable trades. By showing you real life stock examples of a few charting indicators - you will be able to determine whether a stock is worth trading or not.

Free bonus #2: **16 Candlestick Patterns that Every Trader Should Know ($17 value)**

Stay ahead in the trading game with our essential guide on the patterns that are vital for reading market signals, identifying trend reversals, and making profitable trades. Equip yourself with the knowledge to make informed decisions and maximize your trading returns.

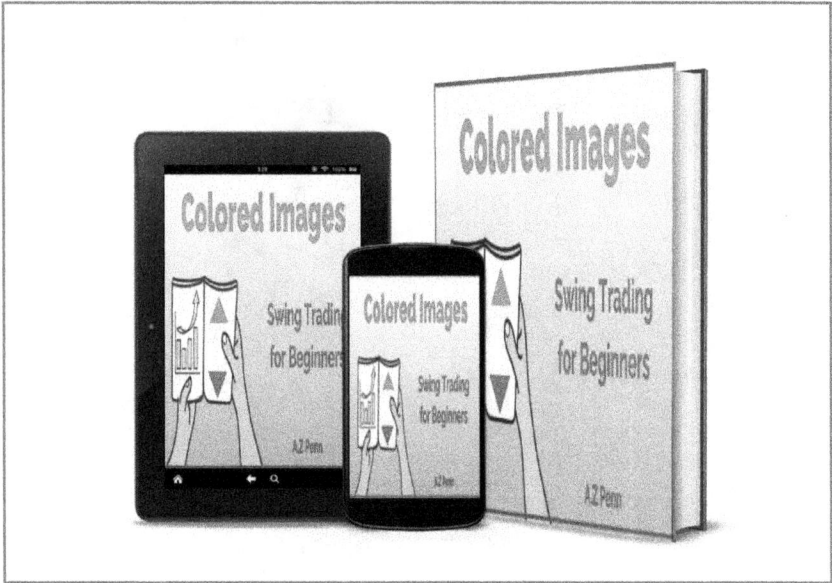

Free bonus #3: Colored Images – Swing Trading for Beginners

To keep our books at a reasonable price for you, we print in black & white. But here are all the images in full color.

All of these bonuses are 100% free, with no strings attached. You don't need to provide any personal details except your email address.

To get your bonuses, go to the link or QR code:

www.az-penn.com

Glossary

Ask - the price at which you can buy shares or other financial assets from a market maker.

Bear - a seller, a market participant who thinks the market will go downwards.

Beta - a way of measuring the volatility of a stock compared to the market as a whole.

Bid - the price at which you can sell shares of other financial assets from a market maker.

Body - the central part of a candlestick, which may be hollow or filled, represents the difference between the opening and closing prices.

Bull - a buyer, a market participant who thinks the market will go upwards.

CAGR - Compound Annual Growth Rate, is the best way of assessing growth of your trading capital over time.

Candlestick - a form of a chart that shows information on the highest and lowest prices touched in a time period as well as the opening and closing prices.

Charting - using charts of security price movements over time to evaluate the probabilities of future price actions.

Close - the last hour of the market trading session. It often sees higher levels of trading or volatility than the rest of the day.

Consolidation - a period during which the market is in balance between bulls and bears, and the share price remains within a fairly narrow range.

Day trading - a style of trading in which positions are never allowed to remain open overnight.

Death cross - when the 50-day moving average crosses the 200-day moving average heading downwards, it can often signal a new downtrend.

Doji - a candlestick with a very small body that represents a moment of indecision in the market.

ETF - Exchange Traded Fund, a low-cost index replicating fund that can be bought and sold on the stock exchange (ETFs replicating other assets can also be found).

Entry - the opening of a trade by buying or shorting a share or other financial asset.

Exit - the closing of a trade by selling a position or covering a short.

Float - the proportion of share capital that is freely traded.

Forex - foreign exchange, usually used to refer to the forex spot market.

Fundamentals - data pertaining to the assets and business of the company in which shares are issued.

Gap - when shares open markedly up or down from the previous closing price so that there is a 'gap' in the chart.

Golden cross - when the 50-day moving average crosses the 200-day moving average to the upside, often signaling a fresh bull run.

Guidance - a company's steer to the markets on its future earnings: this is a highly sensitive figure that is often included as part of quarterly earnings statements.

Illiquid - not easily tradable.

Indicator - a figure derived from the mathematical relationship between price and/or volume data, such as a moving average.

Institutional trader - a trader working for a bank, broker, or other company.

Lagging indicator - an indicator such as a moving average, which emerges after the share price movement has already begun.

Leverage - using debt or margin to minimize the amount of your own capital used in a trade and consequently increase your percentage return on cash.

Limit order - an order specifying the price above which you will not buy or below which you will not sell.

Liquid - easily tradable in size.

Long, going - buying.

Marabozu - a big candle with no shadow/wick at all.

Margin - amount a broker will lend against your trades.

Margin account - an account that enables you to borrow part of the cost of your position from your broker.

Margin call - if the trade has moved against you, your broker may require you to add fresh funds to put your account in order.

Market capitalization - the total value of all the shares issued by a company.

Market maker - a market participant whose job is to provide liquidity by buying and selling shares.

Market order - an order to buy at the market price (whatever that may be).

Moving average - an average of past time periods' prices, which shows the price progression of a share with the 'noise' smoothed out.

Nasdaq - one of the two major US securities exchanges.

NYSE - the other one of the two major US securities exchanges.

Open - the first hour of trading every trading day, which may have high volatility and high volumes traded.

Option - a security giving the option to buy or sell a share at a certain price.

Penny stock - originally a stock trading below $1, now likely below $5 or even $10: usually lacking in liquidity and often in quality.

P/E Ratio - price-earnings ratio, how many years' earnings the share price would pay for.

Position - the total exposure to a given stock in your trading book: can be long or short.

Pre-market trading - trading via electronic market systems (but not through market makers) before the market officially opens: usually has limited liquidity.

Profit target - the price you decide a share should reach before you take profits: should be set by reference to chart data.

Real-time data - prices coming directly from the exchange, as opposed to 15-minute delayed prices.

Resistance - a price level at which shares will find it difficult to break through upwards.

Retail trader - a trader who is dealing on their own account.

Risk/reward ratio - the relationship between the amount at risk in a trade and the amount of profit expected from that trade.

RSI - relative strength index, a way of assessing whether a share is overbought or oversold.

Scaling out - taking part of your profit on a trade but leaving the rest of the position to take advantage of further potential gains.

Scanner - a program that surveys price data to find defined types of situation.

Shadow - the bits of a candlestick that stick out at the ends, showing the highest and lowest prices achieved during the time period: also known as the wick.

Short - a short position is when you have sold the shares in advance of buying them back, expecting the price to fall.

Short interest - all the short positions in the market at a given time.

Short squeeze - when buyers of a stock put pressure on those who are short of it in order to 'shake them out.'

Size - the number of shares in which a market maker is willing to trade at a given price.

Slippage - the difference between the expected price of a trade and the price at which it is executed, for instance, as a result of delay or market volatility.

Spinning top - indecision candlestick with a small body and long shadows.

Spread - the difference between the bid and ask price; a cost of trading.

Standard lot - 100 shares.

Stochastics - an indicator that generates overbought and oversold signals.

Stock in play - a stock that has a catalyst making it keenly traded, e.g. results or a takeover bid.

Stop-loss - a price at which you will share the shares to crystallize a small loss, if necessary.

Support - a level at which shares generally find selling pressure eases up.

Ticker - the three or four-letter abbreviation of a stock or ETF.

Trailing stop - a stop-loss which is raised as the share price increases to avoid losing back profits that have already been made.

Wash sale rule - the IRS rule that shares sold and repurchased within 30 days will be treated as a continuous holding.

Watchlist - your list of stocks that repay particular attention will change almost daily.

Wick - the bits of a candlestick that stick out at the ends, showing the highest and lowest prices achieved during the time period: also known as the shadow.

References

Books:

Bassal, Omar. Swing Trading for Dummies. Wiley, 2019.

Bulkowski, Thomas. Encyclopedia of Candlestick Charts. Wiley, 2008.

Bulkowski, Thomas. Getting Started in Chart Patterns. Wiley, 2006.

Farley, Alan. The Master Swing Trader. McGraw Hill, 2001.

Graham, Benjamin. The Intelligent Investor. Harper, 1949.

Graham, Benjamin and Dodd, David L. Security Analysis. McGraw Hill, 2023.

Milton, George. How to Swing Trade. Self-published, 2022.

Murphy, John J. Study Guide to Technical Analysis of the Financial Markets. Penguin, 1999.

Nison, Steve. Japanese Candlestick Charting Techniques. Prentice Hall Press, 2001.

Pezim, Brian. How to Swing Trade. Bear Bull Traders, n.d.

Rivalland, Marc. Marc Rivalland on Swing Trading: A Guide to Profitable Short-Term Investing. Harriman House, 2003.

Schwager, Jack. Getting Started in Technical Analysis. Wiley, 1999.

Sharpe, Dennis. Swing Trading Strategies That Work in 2023. self-published, 2023.

Websites:

Charts

Chartink - chartink.com

Finwiz - finviz.com

Pocket Option - pocketoption.com

StockCharts - stockcharts.com

Stock Monitor - stockmonitor.com

TradingView - tradingview.com

Fundamental Analysis

Ashwath Damodaran - pages.stern.nyu.edu/~adamodar

FullRatio - fullratio.com

GuruFocus - gurufocus.com

Macrotrends - macrotrends.net

Multpl - multpl.com

Magic Formula Investing - magicformulainvesting.com

Morningstar - morningstar.com

S&P Global - spglobal.com

Rate of Return Expert - rateofreturnexpert.com

Robert Shiller's Data Site - econ.yale.edu/~shiller/data.htm

SEC filings - sec.gov

Yahoo finance - finance.yahoo.com

Zacks - zacks.com

News and Articles

Seeking Alpha - seekingalpha.com

TheStreet - thestreet.com

MarketWatch - marketwatch.com

Investing.com - investing.com

Reuters - reuters.com

Quiz Answers

Chapter 1:
1. D
2. A
3. A, B, D
4. A
5. B, D

Chapter 2:
1. B
2. A, D
3. C
4. D
5. A

Chapter 3:
1. D
2. A
3. B
4. C
5. D

Chapter 4:
1. D
2. B
3. A, B, C, D
4. A
5. B

Chapter 5:
1. B
2. D
3. D
4. B
5. B

Chapter 6:
1. B
2. D
3. B, D
4. C
5. D

Chapter 7:
1. B
2. A, D
3. A, B, C, D
4. C
5. C

Chapter 8:
1. A
2. A, B
3. A, C
4. A, B, C
5. A, B, C, D

Chapter 9:
1. D
2. A
3. C
4. C
5. C

Chapter 10:
1. B
2. B, C
3. A
4. B
5. A

Chapter 11:
1. D
2. C
3. C
4. A, B, C
5. C

Chapter 12:
1. A
2. C
3. A
4. A, C
5. A, B

Chapter 13:
1. C
2. A
3. A, B, C, D
4. B
5. B